Praise for *Framing a Life*

"On days when I despair that nothing much is going right, I look to Roberta and her courage, perseverance, and optimism. Her story could have been the story of a bitter woman, beaten down by life and loss—it is anything but. It is a shining light held aloft for any woman struggling to find that place within that is whole, complete, and at peace."

—Cathleen O'Connor, PhD, author *of High Heels on the Hamster Wheel, The Everything Law of Attraction Dream Dictionary,* and *The Collection: Flash Fiction for Flash Memory*

"*Framing A Life* is about the search for home, family, and love—yet is so much more. This story examines the grief of losing all we human beings long for in this world, but still moving forward with faith, love, and tenacity. You will smile. You will cry. Best of all, you will cheer on Roberta as she learns that home is not necessarily a place; it is embedded in your core, your heart, and your soul."

—Laura L. Engel, author of *You'll Forget This Ever Happened: Secrets, Shame, and Adoption in the 1960s*

"Kuriloff tells her amazing story of resilience. This is the journey of her survival, her intense drive to succeed, and the later death of her partner—a woman she loved. Finding the surprising depths of her spiritual side, she not only relearns how to love, she also relearns how to live. It is an intensely personal yet very relatable work."

—Linda Bergman, screenwriter, producer, and author of *So You Think Your Life's A Movie: The Sequel*

"Roberta's memoir is honest, poignant, and shares with grace how she overcame her life's tragedies. Her courage, optimism, and the ways she found and built her true home—in the deepest sense of the word—will uplift and inspire many readers."

—Rivvy Neshama, author of *Recipes for a Sacred Life: True Stories and a Few Miracles*

"Rarely have I read a memoir that was so captivating. Roberta Kuriloff's resilience and tenacity in the face of adversity is inspiring. Through her work as a lawyer and her interactions with family and friends, she demonstrates what it means to be a compassionate feminist and a joyful, spiritual person."

—Patricia Ould, PhD, coauthor of *Same-Sex Marriage, Context, and Lesbian Identity: Wedded but Not Always a Wife*

"In *Framing a Life*, Roberta S. Kuriloff constructs—from fragments of past scenes, journal entries, night dreams, changing states of being, and reflections—a textual home for herself and the reader to reside in, inside the territory of a culturally evolving America. This narrative is a timely permission to illuminate the manifold pieces of one's own life and reassemble them into a compassionate definition of oneself, alive at a certain moment, in a certain place, in human history."

—Marj Hahne, writer, editor, and teacher

Framing
a Life

Framing
a Life

Building the Space to Be Me

Roberta S. Kuriloff

SHE WRITES PRESS

Published 2023
Printed in the United States of America
Print ISBN: 978-1-64742-495-4
E-ISBN: 978-1-64742-496-1
Library of Congress Control Number: 2022921516

For information, address:
She Writes Press
1569 Solano Ave #546
Berkeley, CA 94707

Interior Design by Kiran Spees
She Writes Press is a division of SparkPoint Studio, LLC.

To Bernice
Without whose love, support, and patience this book
might not have been written.

And to
My mother, Eva, who died too young,
and my father, Abraham, who chose to die.

"Your Book of Life doesn't begin today, on Rosh Hashanah. It began when you were born. Some of the chapters were written by other people: your parents, siblings, and teachers. Parts of your book were crafted out of experiences you had because of other people's decisions: where you lived, what schools you went to, what your homes were like. But the message of Rosh Hashanah, the anniversary of the creation of the world, is that everything can be made new again, that much of your book is written every day—by the choices you make. The book is not written and sealed; you get to edit it, decide what parts you want to emphasize and remember, and maybe even which parts you want to leave behind. *Shanah tovah* means both a good year and a good change. Today you can change the rest of your life. It is never too late."

—Laura Geller, Rabbi Emerita, Temple Emanuel of Beverly Hills
Mishkan Hanefesh: Machzor for the Days of Awe

Chapter 1

Collapse

*Our soul is an abode. And by remembering "houses" and
"rooms," we learn to "abide within ourselves."*

—From the Introduction of *The Poetics of Space*
by Gaston Bachelard

I inherited my mother's engagement and wedding rings after she
died. Well, not right after. A six-year-old couldn't be expected
to take care of such precious objects—such precious memories. My
father saved them for me, symbols of devastating loss, commitment,
and dreams for the future. That is how I had always thought of them.

My fingers slid over the curve of her gold wedding band on my
pinky finger as I walked through the door of my Connecticut home
for the last time. Of all the meanings imbued in a wedding band,
the one I had carried in my heart had been promise. In my mother's
rings, I saw the promise of the life I could create, the love I could have,
and, most importantly, the realization of permanence: the home and
hearth that would bind me to the land, to the earth and soil, sinking
roots strong enough, and deep enough, that they could withstand
life's whirlwind.

What was I thinking? At age thirty-nine, having lived my life mainly
in cities, I chose to move to the woods of Maine—alone. On a blustery

March day in 1984, I stood at the edge of the land in Maine purchased with my former partner, Mary Ann. My hands tingled from the cold as I held a couple of wood stakes marking off exactly where my new house would stand. I was excited. Anxious. My throat spasmed as waves of fear moved through me.

It was no longer *our* land, no longer *our* dream—just mine. Mary Ann and I had been seven years as a couple; it was my first truly meaningful relationship. A year earlier, for my birthday, we'd held a party at our home. Between dancing and talking, I'd noticed Mary Ann and Donna being unusually friendly, sometimes speaking in a whisper. Donna was attractive: tall and thin, with curly black shoulder-length hair, and smartly dressed. For the next few weeks, my communication with Mary Ann was disjointed, words like leaves scattered on a stormy day.

A month later, at a weekend breakfast, Mary Ann rubbed her hands together, her gaze disconnected. She choked out the words, "I'm having an affair with Donna; it just started." She squirmed in her chair, tears falling. I tried to control my tears but failed. She added, confusingly, "I don't want our relationship to end. I don't want to lose all we have together." In a fog, I responded, "Neither do I." We talked through the night, sometimes cuddling, sometimes holding hands, my body exhausted from tears and an empty stomach. I wanted to be angry, to scream, but I couldn't.

A year later, holding the stakes to mark the foundation of my new house, I was still numb, fighting against images of our relationship; we had a life together, now uprooted. Frank, a builder I had hired to clear the land and do the groundwork for my home, explained the land clearing. As we walked, I envisioned the foundation I was cre-ating—my first true home. Even though it was still months until my move, staking the lot marked the beginning of my new life in a new place. I told Frank, as I told my housebuilder, Sue, that I wanted the house to face south so it welcomed the warmth of the sun on chilly winter days.

The foundation of my first home with my parents collapsed before I barely understood the meaning of home. I dreaded that might happen again. When I was six years old, I lived in an apartment in Brooklyn, New York, with my parents and two-year-old brother, Fred. I had a family. I was safe and secure—an innocent child until my mother's death.

I trembled with the memory of my last day with her. Standing on my tiptoes, I barely recognized my mother in bed under a white canopy hanging down from the bedposts, her eyes half closed, her face pale, her long wavy hair now short and thin. I knew she could see me. I asked, "Daddy, can I go on the bed with Mommy?" My mother nodded her head, and my father lifted me. I cuddled into her right arm; smelled her warmth; breathed in the scent of lilac on her neck. My father's face was haggard, his eyes disheartened, as he hovered by the bed concerned I might upset her. He wanted her to return to the hospital. She chose not to. She knew there was no cure. He whispered a word I didn't understand—cancer. They spoke in low voices, my father helpless in managing her pain. I wanted to stay there, tight against her body forever, even though she no longer danced with me in the living room or rubbed me dry after a bath. A few days later, the bed was empty. When I asked my father where she was, he murmured, "In the hospital." I never saw her again.

As Frank finished staking the lot, I set aside the echoes of my past. We reviewed the blueprint I designed and the model of the house an architect friend made for me. Based on the blueprint, Frank sprayed orange paint on the dirt and wild grass to outline the borders of the foundation so I'd have a true feeling of the size, which was wider than the temporary posts in the ground. I struggled to listen, nodding as he spoke.

Plans—so many plans I worked on this past year—alone. Moving to Maine was our dream, mine and Mary Ann's. Instead, I was living alone in the cute, small house we bought together in a friendly neighborhood in Connecticut. Mary Ann was living with her new partner, and I'd soon be moving far away from family and friends, starting over.

While getting ready to meet Frank, I came across my confirmation for a three-week women-only housebuilding workshop. The teacher, Sue, a thin woman, about five feet, three inches, was an experienced builder with a no-nonsense approach to life and grooming, her long hair tied in the back so as not to get in the way when she worked. I met her before registering for the course and asked her how she got into construction.

"Like you, I came here from the city. I built my own house and, in the process, fell in love with construction and working with my hands." Smiling, she reached into her briefcase and pulled out pictures of small, colorful houses. "As a child I was fascinated with building—then it was dollhouses. Now it's dog houses that sell well, *and* homes for people."

I admired her—a woman in a man's world, succeeding at something she loved to do. I hoped some of that Maine *I-can-do-this* attitude would rub off on me.

I strode back with Frank to where we parked, and we made plans to meet again the next morning. As he drove away, I turned to look at my building lot, the wood stakes barely visible. My legs shook as I numbly stared at the ground. Perhaps it was only restlessness, but I suspected it was more.

Chapter 2

Hope

In moments of meditative thought, I asked myself whether *I* defined home or if it was defined for me by childhood circumstances over which I had no control—circumstances that also changed the meaning of family. Did my need for a permanent home control my life choices? These questions challenged me in therapy—a healthy challenge I accepted, though one that didn't allow me to evade memories of my move at age six to my aunt's farm after my mother's death and, a year later, another life-altering move to an orphanage. These were chilling recollections that continued to haunt me in my dreams.

After my mother's death, my father took me and my brother to live with his sister, Nora, and her husband, Morris, on their farm in Flanders, New Jersey. He still worked in the city and came "home" to the farm on weekends. I missed him but loved the farm.

My aunt had a round, warm face, with a smile like the Mona Lisa, making it difficult to know whether she was pleased with me or not. She was much older than my mother and never mentioned her. I was afraid to speak up, frightened I'd cry. Somehow I knew I had to be strong so as not to upset my father.

My uncle was tall and a little hunched over, a serious farmer with wrinkled skin from the sun and hard work. He taught me how to feed the chickens and milk the cows, and he called me "Rivka," my Jewish name. I learned to corral the cows, especially when they wandered into the backyard. Walking them to the pasture, I tolerated more than one poke in my bottom from a bull. I fed the chickens and rode a neighbor's horse. My nose adjusted to the pungent smells of horse and cow manure. After work, there was play on a swing my dad and uncle made, secured to a large tree overlooking the river that flowed through the grazing land.

For school, Aunt Nora washed my short hair and dressed me neatly, not in work pants. The first few days, she walked me the brief distance on the country road, holding my hand as my mother had. Her hand had a farmer's coarseness, different from the softness of my mother's hand when we walked the Brooklyn streets to kindergarten, me trying to match the pace of her feet, two steps for her one. I imagined I heard the sound of our laughter.

We passed other houses with farmland, horses, and cows. Sometimes I'd meet kids along the way, and we'd walk together. I smiled at friendly neighbors working outdoors. My brother was too young for school, so he stayed with my aunt. The schoolyard had swings. One day I stood on one, pushed myself higher and higher, and fell. I cried for my mother, but it was my aunt who came to school. I had a bloody bump on my scalp. It healed, leaving a small notch, a permanent reminder of my time on the farm.

Every morning I looked forward to seeing my aunt comb her long gray hair, which, when taken out of her bun, reached her waist. I watched her in the bathroom, brushing and combing, while next to her sat my uncle's teeth in a bowl of water on the sink. Sometimes she let me comb her hair. I couldn't braid it the way she did. I helped her cook, set the table, and learned how to stack the food and sort and pack the shelves in the large, cold pantry off the kitchen. Like all children, I wanted to help—wanted to be of use—wanted to be loved enough to stay.

My aunt and uncle had three grown children. We spent time with them when they came home for the holidays, especially for the Jewish Passover, when we held the traditional seder, with prayers, wine, and a table full of food. My uncle narrated the Passover story, of the killing of Hebrews by the Pharaoh in Egypt and how Moses led them out of Egypt to find a permanent home in Israel. I listened to his words and stared at my father's face across the table, wondering if the farm would be our new home, especially if he moved here permanently. I naïvely believed that God was watching over us now that my mother was gone.

My cousin Aaron was tall and lean in his Army garb. I had a crush on him, especially when he smiled. I usually babbled a lot with too many questions, but when he spoke to me, I melted into an awkward, shy version of myself, almost forgetting how to talk. His sisters, Effie and Diana, were elegant, even in their garden clothes. I wasn't shy talking with them, their voices being gentle and smooth like my mother's. I pictured myself looking like them when I grew up, without my chubby cheeks.

One day while my aunt and uncle were away, my father and Cousin Diana, whom we called "Nucie," sat me down close to them in the living room. Their faces were somber, unsmiling.

Nucie gently held my hands, leaned close to my face, and in a quiet voice shared, "Roberta, Aunt Nora is not well; she's ill with cancer, like your mother, and will soon die."

My body shook. I screamed, "She can't die! She doesn't look sick. She's not in bed like Mommy was."

Beautiful, calm Nucie held me tighter. "I know how you feel, my sweet. She's my mother, and like you, I don't want to lose her."

My father finally spoke. With blurry eyes, he tried to control his words. "Honey, you and Freddy won't be able to live here anymore. Uncle Morris can't care for you and the farm."

I jumped up from the chair, letting go of Nucie's hands, squealing, "I don't want to leave! This is our home now. I'm in school and have friends. I can help Uncle Morris with the chores. I'm not afraid of the cows anymore. I milk them and collect the eggs. I can also help clean the house, and . . . and I can take care of Freddy. And, Daddy, when you come on the weekends, you can help too."

I barely heard my father speak; my face turned ashen. I screamed inside, *How can God be so mean to us—again!*

"Roberta, Uncle Morris is old and not well. He has to sell the farm."

I ran from the house, not knowing where to hide or what to do. As quickly as we had arrived, our idyllic year was over. For the second time, the word *cancer* destroyed my life.

A few months later, my father moved me and my brother to the Israel Orphan Asylum in Far Rockaway, New York.

I learned only too well at that tender age that a home could collapse as quickly as a child's smile could morph into tears.

Chapter 3

Despair

After my aunt's death, one might have expected support from our extended family. My father had nine living siblings in America. My mother had five. However, most had their own families, their own life dramas. Taking on another family wasn't a workable option for them. One of my mother's brothers and his wife offered to have us live with them, but they had no children and wanted to adopt us. My mother's sister was willing to take us, but she lived in a distant state. My father wouldn't accept those options, especially as the offers were not from his side of the family. No one was going to take away *his* children. So, instead, we moved to an orphanage. In his mind, he was doing the right thing. He maintained control.

My mother's death took a toll on him. An independent but quiet man who loved to sing, he gave up his dreams. He left the business in which he had worked and started driving a cab, and we went on welfare. He struggled and searched for a temporary, safe, and respectable place for us to live, mournfully groveling before government bureaucrats to get us admitted.

On the day we arrived at the orphanage, we stepped out of the car after a long ride. We held his hands, my fidgety four-and-a-half-year-old brother wearing a white shirt, suit jacket, and matching blue shorts, and I, age seven and a half, in a pink fluffy dress.

Confused, I looked up at my father. "Where are we?"

His face was sad, his hand clammy. He didn't answer.

We walked through a tall black wrought-iron gate to buildings on each side of a gigantic play area; it even had a pool. But it wasn't Coney Island. I didn't see Nathan's Hotdogs or the Cyclone. And it surely wasn't my aunt's farm in Flanders.

A strange woman walked toward us. She had a body like a football player. My father let my brother run to play on a small merry-go-round. His thin body pushed off the ground with one foot, gleefully going around and around. I stayed with my father. The woman bent down to my level, her flowery skirt thrust against my pink dress, her hands on my shoulders. I instinctively pulled back from her.

With a rigid smile and wrinkled face, she stared into my eyes, "Hello, I am Miss H. Welcome to the Israel Orphan Asylum."

I looked up at my father and saw his eyes full of tears. Words knotted in my throat as I asked, "Daddy, what's an orphan asylum?"

He didn't answer.

Miss H did. "You and your brother will be living here with us for a while."

I didn't understand what *a while* meant.

My brother threw up on the merry-go-round and ran back to us. My father wiped his face with a handkerchief from his suit pocket, kissed us each on the cheek, and walked away. I turned to watch him leave through the gate, not knowing when I'd see him again. Miss H held my hand; I couldn't run after him.

Miss H turned us over to two different people. My brother was taken to the young boys' building across the play area from me. Another woman, younger than Miss H, with a friendly smile, walked me into an old Victorian mansion with a large covered porch and a central staircase. There were several floors. We walked through a labyrinth of odd-shaped rooms, up some steps, and stopped in an enormous room with lots of beds—like the barracks in the pictures my cousin Aaron showed me from when he was in the Army.

My legs weakened as my body trembled, and I couldn't hold back tears. All I wanted was my father, my aunt, or by that time, any familiar face. But no words came out. The woman sat down on a bed, patted it for me to sit next to her and gave me a tissue to blow my nose. "Roberta, this is where you are going to live for a while."

I still didn't know what *a while* meant.

She smiled. "This is your bed, and see the trunk at the end of the bed? That is yours to hold your belongings. And these pajamas with the birds on them are especially for you." I looked at the pajamas and wanted the birds to come alive and fly me away with them.

The woman put her arm around my shoulders and pulled me close to her. I backed away. "I don't want to be here!" I stubbornly demanded, "Where's my brother?"

"Roberta, I know this is hard for you, but your father can't take care of you right now. He loves you very much and wants you to be in the best place possible until he can arrange to have you live with him again. Your brother is here too, just in another building. You'll see him soon."

As she spoke, I gazed around the room through misty eyes. There were some girls playing together, giggling, and some lying on beds. I noticed them eyeing me, making believe they were just glancing around the room while chatting. The room smelled stuffy, like unwashed laundry.

I was still wearing my pink dress. The woman took my other belongings from my small suitcase and put them in the trunk—underwear, my yellow skirt, two blouses, one of which was my favorite with polka dots, and a few toys my father had included.

"We have a lot of clothes here that are your size, and when you go to bed, we'll hang up your pink dress and keep it safe for you," she said. "I'll show you the closet where you can choose what you want to wear."

I wanted to run, but my legs were like melted candy, sticky and heavy.

"Let's go have some lunch." We walked slow-footed down to the bottom floor of the mansion into a spacious room with long tables, benches, and chairs. The sun flowed through many windows. Some girls were already eating. Others were in line holding trays. The woman sat me in a chair next to her and had someone bring me a tray of food. I drank the milk, ate a small piece of chocolate cake, and pushed the rest away, not hungry. I avoided talking to any of the other kids.

That night, after everyone was asleep, I snuck out of bed and peered through the nearby window, wondering when I'd see my father again. I couldn't see the building in which my brother was living; the window was too small for a wide view. The light from the full moon made the bushes and the gate visible. I didn't move away as I felt safe looking into the dark; I was afraid if I turned to see the other beds, the other girls, the counselors, I would forget my outside world. My body shivered in the cold, forcing me to quietly step back into bed under the itchy wool cover. I spoke to my mother in my head, hoping she'd hear me.

Mommy, I don't want to forget you. Will you be with me while I'm here? Will you take care of Daddy so we can return to him soon? And Freddy—he's a baby. Who will hold him like you did? Will I be able to play with him? Tease him? Miss H is the housemother. But she's not you. I can't cuddle with her. She said she treats us girls equally. I don't want to be equal; I want to be special. Please visit me in my dreams.

The next morning, a counselor lined us up to pick out the clothes we would wear that day. When it was my turn, she helped me choose blue pants and a white blouse. I enjoyed how the pants fitted, freeing, like a part of my body. I had worn dresses and skirts, except on the farm. I followed instructions, moving through the morning like a robot programmed to behave.

The girls showered together in a big open bathroom. There were no curtains. I'd never seen so many naked bodies in varied shapes and sizes. I blushed with curiosity. I didn't want to look but couldn't help it. I saw some girls looking at me. A few girls' breasts were the size of my mother's. Tears flowed down my cheeks, blending with the water on my face. I wanted to scream, "I want to go home! It's not fair!" But I couldn't. I repeated it in my head until the tears dried up with the ending of the shower. I dressed and walked to breakfast with a counselor by my side. I sat at a long table, next to Josie with the big breasts, Frieda with the braided hair, and Ellen with the rolling stomach. I was an orphan. This was my new "home."

Chapter 4

Confidence

Still living in New Haven, I was in Augusta, Maine, for the second week of the three-week housebuilding workshop. We were building an extension on a house for a disabled child who needed an indoor swim lane. It was not easy for my fingers and shoulders to change from typing to banging nails into a roof! I'd rarely used a hammer and had no understanding of construction, especially how to do major work on a house.

There I was, ex-secretary, lawyer, feminist, and political activist with no knowledge of construction, getting ready to build my own home in coastal northern Maine. I was starting over, like the little orphan Roberta, trying to prove herself again. For a few minutes, insecurity whacked me in the face; I was doing something I'd never done, though relieved the class was for women only. I didn't need to deal with men telling me what to do or not do. I'd had enough of that when I was a secretary.

I worked harder and dirtier than I could ever remember. I climbed and participated in roofing and in framing walls. I painted black, mushy, dripping waterproof sealer onto the outside of the basement walls—and all over myself. It came off only with kerosene! I shoveled gravel, cut Styrofoam, and lifted and carried plywood and wall beams.

The sun beat down on my arms, burning my skin. I walked a plank and lost some of my fear of heights. At the end of the day my body was bone-weary but alive—and starving. I hoped I wouldn't gain back the ten pounds I lost. Thinking of Mary Ann, a sinking emptiness filled me. It was inconceivable that I'd be living in Maine without her.

On the weekends, I visited my land, an hour and half away. I needed to feel a part of it, to belong to its beauty, to be confident of my decision. I climbed a tree to get a wide view, recognizing a lake in the distance. I nibbled on early wild blackberries and raspberries. The land smelled sweet and woody from wild ferns. Through friends, I met women who lived alone in Maine, some in secluded woods, and they managed it well. My anxiety lessened some.

I learned new skills as I'd had to do so many times in my life, and this time wasn't the most intimidating. That happened when I decided I needed independence from living with my father and brother in Brooklyn. At age twenty-two, I rented an apartment in Manhattan. My dad wasn't happy but accepted my decision. Fred acted as if he wouldn't miss me, but I knew better. Oh, how my Jewish guilt hit me! The little girl was doing to them what had been done to her—leaving family.

My brother and I had moved back to live with our father when I was twelve. Now it was time to move on. I didn't want to continue being the "mother" in the family and feeling the need to care for Fred, who was old enough to care for himself. Once I moved, there would be no more cleaning up after him or worrying nightly about my father until he returned home from driving his cab in the city. I never slept well when he drove at night, tossing and turning until I heard the key in the door. I abruptly cracked a loud, sad laugh because I knew I'd still worry, even if out-of-sight. Dad was also the cook, something beyond my learning. I would miss his dinners.

I found a small fourth-floor walkup on 81st Street in the city, between First and York Avenues. Fred helped me move and put bars on the fire escape window to prevent break-ins. The apartment had a tiny kitchenette with a half-sized refrigerator and a table allowing only two chairs. The five-foot-long hall to the twelve-by-twelve-foot combination living room/bedroom had a closet on one side and the bathroom on the other. It was claustrophobic, especially as my two windows faced the back of other buildings. The outside world at night was lost to me.

While travel to work was easier, I did miss Dad and Fred. How could I not? We were a family absent from each other for those many years in the orphanage. Shouldn't I have stayed with them? Weekends I worked on my night college courses, but I also looked forward to going back to work in my secretarial job—to being around other people in the medium-sized law firm with others to talk to.

Feeling lonely, I went to an animal shelter and picked out a young beige cat, remembering the pleasure of a cat's company. When living with Dad and Fred, we had found a stray cat in the alleyway and named her Sasha. We'd bring her upstairs during the day and let her out at night. One day while watching TV, we discovered our small, fluffy, white area rug rolling like waves on the beach. We hadn't known about fleas! After that we were afraid to have Sasha come in the house and hesitant to hold her. Fred and I fed and played with her outside. A few weeks later she was gone. I asked Dad if he knew where she was. "Yes," he said, slow to tell me, not looking me in the eye. "I drove her a few streets away and dropped her off on a safe street. Sweetheart, it was so painful for me to see her cry every day and not be able to bring her upstairs." He never considered that we could still feed her and still care for her outside. My brother and I were stunned and then furious that he didn't consider our feelings. Instead, he made yet another orphan, little Sasha.

I named my new cat Lilly. Even with the toys I bought her, she was overly active, jumping constantly. Two weeks after living with me, I returned from work to find my small, neat apartment a mess from her clawing and chewing my clothes and bedding. I couldn't control her. Tears of guilt burned my eyes as I took Lilly back to the shelter in her little box. With every step I relived the confused fear of my seven-year-old self, watching my father release my hand from his and walk away from us in the orphanage, the gate closing after him. I also gained a wiser understanding of his experience when he took Sasha from us—avoid grief. I returned to my empty apartment and dropped on the bed, weeping hysterically, my muddled mind trying to justify my father's actions as well as my own. Tears turned to anger. I jumped up, washed my face, and took a soda from the fridge. I didn't want to deal with grief, only tears. I had to be strong. I had to do what I did in the orphanage—survive on dreams.

After two years, my brother entered the Army, and I moved back with my father. I hated to think of him coming home to an empty house.

I told myself that when my house is built, I would be the one coming home to an empty house, but at least I'd have animals for company.

The building course was almost over. At the end of a hot, muggy Wednesday, back in the Augusta motel where I stayed, every muscle in my body hurt—an honorable, proud hurt. I looked down at my smudged hands and clothes, stained with roofing tar even after several cleanings, and felt exhausted but with an exhilarating mood of accomplishment. This project reminded me of the challenge of winning court cases and feeling the positive vibe of helping others. Here we were giving a disabled child a gift—a pool for her to sense the movement of her legs and hopefully become stronger.

I enjoyed the other hardworking women as we chatted about our histories. Most were from out of state, all doing this for the first time. I wasn't alone with my skittishness. One woman had come from the Midwest to further develop her skills in building a small house on her parents' hundred acres. She was ready to live alone but close to family.

After a warm shower, I stretched out on my motel bed and mused how interesting it was that people could easily share their lives with strangers, knowing we likely wouldn't see each other again. Sometimes, it's easier than opening our hearts to friends.

Maybe moving to Maine and building my own home wasn't such a crazy undertaking. The little girl in the orphanage toughened up to survive. I drew on her strength now and was ready to put what I learned into practice.

Chapter 5

Mary Ann

I met Mary Ann when working for New Haven Legal Assistance Association (NHLAA) in the Family Law Unit—my first job as an attorney. I liked the people working in the office and observed their dedication to their clients' struggles. But like my days as a secretary in New York and later in law school in Boston, I connected more with the non-lawyers, especially an open, unconventional woman named Mary Ann, who worked in another unit as a paralegal. We quickly became friends. She had worked for NHLAA for years and explained to me the ins and outs of the agency, as well as its politics and gossip.

She spoke with her hands in a way that made you think she had grown up in New York City, not suburban Massachusetts. She was excitable and sometimes enraged about the politics in this country, especially as it affected poor people. She was admired in the office for her commitment to her clients as well as her strong vocal opinions, which sometimes got her in trouble.

The most beautiful aspect of Mary Ann was her smile—a big cheesy smile that made you automatically trust her as well as feel welcome without reservation. Her smile was pure and almost innocent, with no manipulation behind it. She was inherently natural. Even her short, curly, deep brown hairstyle was natural—it was what it was when she woke up, uncombed. She dressed casually without caring what others thought. I dressed consciously and was concerned with my appearance. That was the "new lawyer" part of me. I dressed the way people expected me to dress as a legal services attorney, clothes somewhat downplayed.

Mary Ann's eclectic personality enthralled me. Her politics engaged me. I was not yet politically active in the way she was. She was a learning experience for me. When I first arrived in New Haven, before I met her, I immediately got involved in the nascent battered women's and domestic violence movement and helped organize a conference. I was not out on the streets marching as she easily did for various political issues.

We took long walks getting to know each other. She helped build my confidence in being outwardly political. Slowly, our time together increased in intensity.

One Saturday, a few weeks after we became friends, as we walked on the New Haven Commons, I noticed her wearing a wedding band. I was hesitant to ask about it, but of course I did. "Are you married?" She laughed in surprise. "No, I'm not married! This is my grandmother's wedding ring."

She stopped and turned to me. "But I . . . I'm a novice preparing for my first vows to become a nun. I'm not sure it's what I really want now. My politics and the views of my religious order don't mesh anymore. I'm not living in the convent. I live with a group of political nuns. It was a tradition in my town for many of the women to become nuns, especially if you wanted to be independent, get an education, and not be pressured to marry."

I didn't know what to say; my face flushed. This was beyond my understanding, but fascinating. Embarrassed, I asked, "How come you're not wearing a habit? When do you have to make a decision about staying or leaving?" I couldn't picture Mary Ann in a habit, like the old nun on the steamy subway in New York to whom I gave my seat when I was a teenager. I was so proud of my good deed.

We sat down on a bench. "My order responded to the Second Vatican Council in its request for nuns to live a more modern life, so we chose not to wear habits, just a cross. See?" She showed me her cross, worn under her sweater. We continued the discussion, and she answered my many, many questions. I was enthralled with this life that seemed so fanciful to me.

We decided to keep our friendship low-key in the office. I experienced feelings softly rousing, scarily averted. My previous partners had been men. I had never had political discussions with them—never trusted them the way I trusted Mary Ann.

When I moved to New Haven after law school with my two cats and secondhand furniture, I rented a house fifteen minutes from work. This was a new benchmark for me, as I'd never lived in a one-family house. Except for my aunt's farmhouse, my "homes" had been orphanages and apartments. I discovered garage sales to supplement my minimal furnishings.

The rental soon became a place of ardent discovery for Mary Ann and me. Within a year, our relationship had danced into the unknown—my first same-sex relationship and Mary Ann's first meaningful relationship. She decided not to take her final vows as a nun. We experienced the excitement of a new relationship, of love-making both tender and strong, of sharing and delving into deep emotions—so different from how it had been for me with men.

When my lease was up, we rented an apartment together and made a home for ourselves, telling only our closest friends. As a new family, a twosome, we decorated and combined our meager possessions, shopped at yard sales, and shared our tastes, eliciting a sense of belonging I hadn't experienced since leaving my father's apartment in Brooklyn. It was a need fulfilled—a home, family, cats, and community. An added gift was my cousin Ronnie's family living in the next town with her husband and two young sons. She and I had been close as children. Often my brother and I stayed on weekends at her parents' home when my father took us out of the orphanage, depending upon his work schedule.

Mary Ann and I were circumspect around the office and decided to have separate phone lines at home. We avoided telling people in the office of our relationship; it was too new for us to figure out and define it.

New Haven, 1976 through 1984, was a city with a burgeoning feminist and lesbian community. We immersed ourselves in it and made supportive friendships while discovering we weren't alone in our choices. We became more politically active, Mary Ann more outwardly than me. I was still the somewhat "reserved" attorney, not wanting to fall into trouble that could cause me to lose my license. I focused my activism on the developing battered women's movement.

In 1978 we rode in a bus full of noisy and excited women with handmade signs to march in DC, supporting the extension of the seven-year deadline for ratification of the ERA. This was my first participation in a DC march; it was exciting, but I found myself anxious and walked on the outside of the march. I imagined I could be lost in the crowd and reduced to rubble, a feeling I earlier experienced participating in the first women's march in New York City. My orphanage experiences converged in my memories. I rarely had privacy. My daily meals were with a crowd of other girls and boys. I showered with other girls in one big shower room. For most of my years there, we lived in a dorm, with beds only a few feet apart.

In 1979, Mary Ann and I helped organize the first New Haven

Take Back the Night march, which was part of Stop Violence Against Women Week, designated by the mayor. I lectured in the community, educating groups and the police about abuse of women and its effects on relationships and children. At work, I taught women how to do their own divorce when we weren't able to help them.

The paraprofessionals at NHLAA organized to be unionized. Mary Ann was one of the leaders. I got involved in organizing the attorneys to unionize. We then helped launch the National Organization of Legal Services Workers. It was a tumultuous time for our relationship as we argued over organizing methods and how to deal with office tensions.

Over the next few years, our time was filled with politics, work, and activism, at the expense of nurturing our love relationship. Soon we were passing in the night, except when involved on the same committees.

Nightmares invaded my dreams. I had to change—knew *we* had to change—but was it already too late?

Chapter 6

Unraveling

Over the four years I worked at Legal Assistance, I had become friends with another attorney, Barbara, who had her own practice. She and I discovered we shared the same politics and didn't savor going to stuffy Bar gatherings. Recognizing a need for greater independence in the type of work I did, I joined her practice. We asked another woman, Diane (known as "Cookie"), to join us. Cookie had just finished at Yale Law School and was working part-time at NHLAA. Our new law firm, Levine, Kuriloff & Polan, was the first all-women feminist law firm in New Haven.

As my professional life stabilized, my relationship with Mary Ann settled into a calm, comfortable routine.

We took breaks for travel to Cape Cod and other vacation spots, visiting with her family in Massachusetts and mine in New York. It brought us back to our relationship center, our recognition of our love for each other, until once again, we became caught up in our commitments. Predictably, our outside involvements again diverged.

Initially, we didn't talk to our parents about our intimate relationship, not yet having the words to explain something we believed they knew nothing about. We were satisfied for them to see it as a friendship. That changed when Mary Ann decided to tell her mother about our relationship and what it meant to her. She chose to come out to her mother at Thanksgiving, with no advance notice to me.

I cooked the dinner, my first attempt at a stuffed turkey. I baked a nontraditional meal, picking a recipe from a magazine for the turkey, wrapping it in cheesecloth after basting it with orange juice and butter, and making the stuffing with matzo instead of bread. I also made sweet potatoes instead of mashed potatoes. I never had a mother substitute to teach me how to cook, nor did I make time to learn.

It was a delicious meal, but not the traditional meal her mother expected. She was irked and cantankerous, especially after Mary Ann explained to her the meaning of our relationship. They argued, her mother stormed out, and they did not speak to each other for many months. I was upset with Mary Ann as I wanted this adorable woman, who was active in the Gray Panthers movement, in our life. I argued with her. "What a stupid move you made! I loved being a part of your family. I don't want to lose your mother or the time we spend with your other relatives. You could have waited to tell her and not do it when she's upset with my cooking!" I so wanted our lives to stay intertwined. I was willing to keep our relationship hidden for the sake of the family connection; Mary Ann wanted openness and honesty.

Over time, her mother had a turnaround, and before her death, the three of us were once more on loving terms. Our confidence was buoyed when we visited her in the hospital and she told us, "For Christmas, I bought you an electric blanket that has two separate controls. Roberta, since you get cold easily, your side can be heated, and Mary Ann, you can keep your side cool." We were shocked, especially as she stated this in a room with another woman patient listening.

Mary Ann and I decided to buy a house together, the first for each of us. It was a daunting commitment, but we were confident we could handle it. We bought a small two-level with a front porch and small backyard in a diverse area of New Haven, down the street from our previous rental apartment. It became an active home with parties, meetings, and lots of visitors, including my father and Mary Ann's mother.

As my confidence and activism grew, it again stirred difficulties between us. In addition to work, we were constantly going to demonstrations and board and political meetings, and, after intense training, I was visiting hospice patients. Increasingly, we perceived issues differently. We were loving and sharing, yet numerous times argumentative. Our conversations wrapped more around what was happening in politics and less around what was happening in our relationship.

Together our family grew to include five cats and one black-and-white husky dog, Maya—a full house. We discovered huskies have an independent personality, and some of our disagreements revolved around how we trained her. Maya was the first dog for both of us. She was okay with the cats but was otherwise destructive, thinking our books and artifacts were her play toys. She was fine walking on a leash; off leash, she followed but didn't listen. We hired a trainer who successfully worked with Maya, but his skills never transferred to us.

Our relationship with Maya mirrored our relationship with each other. We argued more and listened less. We went on vacations that brought us closer, but once home, our relationship again deteriorated.

On one vacation to visit friends in Maine, we decided to buy property there, with the hope of someday moving out of the city. We aspired to build a feminist retreat center for learning and sharing, with a bookstore and coffee house. We chatted about not having to make a good deal of money, just what we needed to live on and wanted to enjoy. It would be a simple life—an optimistic dream we planned together while lying in bed, the place where we most connected.

I cracked my knuckles and tried to ignore a feeling of apprehension, a subtle awareness that this fantasy was likely not to be attained. Yet, we returned to Maine for the real estate closing on the property.

After the purchase, we drove to our friends' house, and on the way, I stopped the car for Mary Ann to vomit. Both of us were surprised. I became quiet, my legs limp, unable to drive for a few minutes. I flashed back to my brother throwing up on our first day in the orphanage. I held back tears.

Those tears were prescient. Not long afterward, a sledgehammer hit my heart. After seven years, we broke up, like a married couple. I dwelled on the vexing word "wedded": Wedded to a person, a profession, one's dreams. Wedded even if not legally married. Wedded even if you know deep down the relationship is over and it's time to let go.

After she told me about Donna, I had a disturbing dream: *A robin sat outside the bathroom window, and as I looked closer at it, it communicated with me in a flirtatious way and then spoke, saying it was weak and couldn't fly without food. I ran downstairs to get birdseed, chasing the cats out of the bathroom, and returned to feed the bird. But before my fingers removed themselves from the dish, the robin snatched my mother's wedding band from my finger and swallowed it. I was stunned at first and then accepted it: that's life, there's nothing I can do. But on second thought, I decided maybe I could bring the robin to the vet to have it cut open and get my ring back.*

I woke up in a full sweat. It was seven in the morning. In the shower, I pondered the dream's meaning. Was my life falling apart? Was I strong and determined enough to handle these foreboding feelings? Was I exaggerating the dream's meaning?

I avoided talking with Mary Ann for a week.

As a lawyer, I had explained to divorce clients, "An affair isn't necessarily the cause of a breakup. It's a symptom of a relationship that hasn't worked out for various reasons, and rather than face the issues, it's easier to blame the affair." I appreciated that I needed to confront the fears and demons in our relationship and to face this in my own life. For several years, I'd been wearing my mother's wedding ring on my pinky finger, as a symbol of a deeper connection to Mary Ann. The meaning had now lost its connection. I knew it was time to take it off and put it away, yet I couldn't do so. *If I remove it, will I ever have the desire to wear it again?*

I turned to therapy. It had helped me through law school. Hopefully, it would help me through this breakup. I asked myself why I seemed to use the word *breakup*. Perhaps I was succumbing to acceptance. I knew in my heart a separation was coming.

As weeks passed, we lived together, talking and questioning if we could continue our "marriage." We both needed to figure out whether the love we had for each other and for our relationship was still there.

In my despondency, I wrote poetry again, a talent with words and creative vocabulary that often got buried in legalese. I doodled, creating drawings in black and white as I had done at NHLAA staff meetings to help me concentrate.

Feeling rootless, I called our Maine friends, Jen and Emma, with whom we had visited multiple times and shared vacations. Both were in disbelief and decided they would be coming to visit us the following weekend. The house was a mess, with cat and dog hair everywhere, dishes in the sink, clothes and towels waiting to be laundered. I cleaned for their visit as I ached with tangled thoughts, pondering our dream of moving to Maine that now seemed unlikely to happen. I had a strong sense that the push for the move was really mine, not

Mary Ann's. She was a dreamer but in fact a city person. I was tired of the bustle of city life and yearned for an open environment, like my year on my aunt's farm. I avoided telling our friends that Mary Ann was still seeing Donna. I wanted our relationship to continue. I couldn't imagine it ending; our lives were woven together like roots of a tree that had grown together over time. Was it possible to untangle the roots without killing the tree? I didn't know.

Chapter 7

Reflection

I drove back to New Haven after the housebuilding workshop, my mind a tidal wave of embroiled thoughts—the long obsessive list of things I needed to do before I shortly moved to Maine, constantly interrupted by childhood memories. At the same time, memories of my training made me grin with satisfaction. I had survived the workshop!

Some of us exchanged phone numbers, but I wasn't optimistic we'd keep in touch. Our busy lives would get in the way. This new move in my life was like starting over in therapy. The workshop bolstered my belief in my strength and endurance. It helped me appreciate how much I had mastered in the orphanage, becoming a tough, resilient survivor, even when that toughness was a veiled disguise.

I stopped at a highway rest area to eat, gas up, and clear my foggy eyes before continuing my trip to New Haven. I avoided what I should have been processing—the prospect of closing out my client cases, saying goodbyes, packing—that was too much to face. Rather, my mind worked overtime thinking about my mother and how different my life would have been if she hadn't died. I had shared some of my past with close friends and even with some clients when it fit into meaningful conversation to help them through their hurt. Yet the trauma, the childhood distrust, I had shared only with my therapist or in my sweaty dreams.

As I sat at a table alone, away from chatting families, eating a sandwich, I opened my diary, which held a letter I had written to my mother at seventeen. I always addressed my entries "Dear Eva," my mother's name. Now making another major life change, my words haunted me.

Dear Eva, Dear Mother,

I wonder how different my life would be if you were alive. I might have been embarrassed to talk to you about sex and boys, especially during my earlier years, but I know you'd understand because you loved me, even when I felt shame and self-disgust and couldn't talk to Dad about my feelings, let alone my actions. I had a lot of anger, feeling I was being used, playing into the "games" of relationships, when deep down I knew I too had a part in the games.

I remember playing doctor with a little boy in the apartment next to ours before we moved to the orphanage. Of course, the neighbor boy was always the doctor. That ended when Dad walked in and spanked me. That's the only time he ever hit me. Mommy, would that have been different if you were there?

When I was ten, I went into the field with a boy, and we touched each other's bodies. I was a little scared, remembering what the counselor had told us girls about having babies. But we weren't doing anything like that. We were simply curious, and other kids did the same. Another counselor found out and punished me because I was "bad." I couldn't play after school for a week, and she said if I did anything like that again, she'd tell Dad. Mommy, would you have thought I was bad?

At eleven, I joked around with a boy in the hall phone booth. We were each grabbing the phone from the other. My last grab whacked the phone into my middle upper tooth and broke it. The dentist put a yellow cap on the tooth! Yellow! I started smiling with my mouth closed. I know I wouldn't have a yellow tooth if you were there.

Some of my friends started menstruating at age twelve. I was upset I didn't have my period. I was as grown up as the other girls who wore pads and had stomach aches. Now I can't believe I wished that on myself! At thirteen, I saw blood and freaked out, finally getting my period. I remembered what my friends told me about menstruation; their mothers explained it to them. I worried, How will I tell Dad I'm a "young lady"? How will I explain why I need money to buy pads? Would he tell me what it means to be a young lady? What do I do for the stomach pain? I told Mrs. Roach, our daytime caregiver who the social worker sent. She told Dad when I wasn't around. At dinner he gave me a shy smile. I know this would have been different if you were there.

When I was fourteen, Mrs. Roach was gone. In the girls' gym class, we all wore short green jumpsuits with no collar. The teacher told me to go to the bathroom and wash my neck. Humiliation! The girls in the class snickered as I walked with my head lowered as if I were saying a prayer. But my only feelings were ones of embarrassment as the tears ran down my cheeks. I looked in the mirror and saw brown shades of dirt around my neck. Why didn't I notice this before? Dad and Fred didn't tell me—didn't notice. I took showers weekly, sporadically. I had two friends in the gym class. They didn't notice, or if they did, didn't tell me. I'm sure this would have been different if you were here.

At age fifteen, I was necking at parties, making believe I enjoyed it. At seventeen, I started enjoying it but made believe I didn't. I measured myself by the dates I had. I couldn't discuss this with Dad. I'm sure you would've understood.

My aunts have daughters. Friends have mothers. I see them now and then. They didn't take me aside to discuss what mothers and daughters discussed or should discuss. I'm isolated on an island with Dad and Fred. I read books to learn. Sometimes I ask the librarian to explain something I don't understand. She shyly tries.

I mostly learn through painful experience. Dear Mommy, if you were here, I know my life would be different, but also better.

Your daughter

I closed my diary; tears glistened at the corners of my eyes. A few other highway rest-stop diners snuck glances my way, and I quickly dabbed at my teardrops with a paper napkin. The question of whether my life would be different if my mother had been there remained unanswered. This move I was about to make held both the loss of an old life and the anticipation of a new beginning. I was starting over, not just in a new location but with a new identity, an opportunity to again redefine myself, as I did many times growing up in the orphanage. Maine Roberta was yet to be born, but I knew I was ready to meet her.

Chapter 8

Decisions

Back home in New Haven, I saw changes in Maya and the cats. They were restless and quiet. Was that my imagination? Did they feel our pain? When our Maine friends arrived, it was awkward. Even though they had known Mary Ann before they knew me, their lives were now entwined with both of us, like relatives they loved. They needed our relationship to survive and for us to move to Maine—together. I doubted their wish would come true. We chatted intensely without resolution, and I cried while petting the cats and walking around the living room, emotionally lost in my own house. I couldn't sit still.

After they returned home, I looked at Mary Ann's swollen lips and knew it was from copious kissing but not with me.

I'd always tried to protect myself from possible hurt. I talked this through with my therapist. She reminded me I didn't need to be the young orphan kid who dreamed of being Moses's daughter to lead the people to a promised land—a promised land to which I had been denied entry. I couldn't be Superman's daughter, looking down on the world from a safe place, nor Roy Rogers's daughter, galloping away to freedom. I shared with her one of my teenage diary entries.

Dear Eva,

I want an ending I can accept. When I read books, I always read the ending before the beginning. I know that's silly; I'm sixteen and should know better, but if I don't like the ending, then I don't want to read it. The social worker said the reason I do this is because I don't want to be hurt again. I guess that may be true. Sometimes she's right, but not always.

In the orphanage I somehow knew the difference between dreams and reality, what's real and what's not. It was my survival mechanism.

I knew it wasn't real when, in my anger, I imagined Dad gone or a friend in an accident. At first, I feared the wrath of God pushing me through the earth's body to hell. But I got over that soon enough when nothing happened save the guilty thumping of my heart. I think these awful visions are a way for me to cope with loss. I expected I could work it out in my mind, which no one could read, so that when it really happened, I'd be ready. Controlling my hurt and pain. Unafraid.

Unafraid of being alone, of losing Dad and Freddy. Unafraid of friends moving on. Unafraid of being hurt by a boyfriend. I'd have the devil's strength of will. No tears. If I hold back part of myself, I won't be able to be hurt. I'd imagine the different types of possible losses to get ahead of them.

But when I hold back, I feel lonely. And when I don't love, I lose. I don't know what it means to love. And what I try to protect myself from happens anyway, like my breakup with Stanley, my boyfriend in the orphanage.

I have the same scary dream a lot. I'm on the beach, and suddenly the waves get bigger and closer, and I try to run to the boardwalk, but the waves overwhelm me, and I'm caught up in them.

At that point, I wake up. Other times I'm on the boardwalk, and the waves jump over the railing and drag me in. These dreams are terrifying. I think they're connected to my fears. I hope someday they'll go away, and I'll be trusting.

I want to trust people. I can't talk to Dad about this. And I don't want to talk to the social worker. Mommy, I so wish you were here to talk to me. If you were, what I'm writing about wouldn't be an issue. I guess I'll have to learn it all by myself.

Your daughter

With the life lessons I'd since acquired, I knew this soul-searching compelled a full unmasking. With heavy eyelids and a drained psyche, I was untangling, as best I could, this demanding challenge of discovery and learning, viewing myself from afar to figure out the "why" of some of my unhealthy behavior. I pushed myself beyond the old Roberta to the new Roberta—somewhat like a child being reincarnated over and over until she gets it right. Should I have questioned why, in my childhood dreams, I was always someone's daughter—was it internalized sexism? Or was it my hurt and disappointment at my father for abandoning me? *Abandoned*—the word used by my therapist. Was I still the little girl feeling so alone, constantly searching for a family that wouldn't desert me, at whatever cost? Did the need to be loved blind every other need? There were no easy answers, just circles slowly opening.

Mary Ann and I were both in individual therapy and agreed we didn't want to give up these past seven years without first ensuring that we had tried. But that couldn't be discovered in the heat of passion with someone else. We owed ourselves a process of time and struggle, and although it was painful for me to feel the competition of her new passionate relationship, at that point I was willing to accept the pain with support from others and my own internal strength.

I came home from a Saturday night out dancing with friends, where people responded to me the way I needed and enjoyed. I was attractive and animated, feeling the electricity in the room. I didn't have any desire to act on the attention; I mainly enjoyed dancing and, as well, spending time with Mary Ann. But I grudgingly accepted the reality that when one's lover is attracted to someone else, even if still to you, one needed extra assurances to cope.

It was Friday the thirteenth. I was open and vulnerable after a relaxing massage. Mary Ann and I got together and cried and talked and cried some more. She was unsure of what she wanted. I was her first intimate relationship. She was in the honeymoon stage with Donna. Even without Donna in the picture, I didn't think we could again be in a committed relationship. I faced that our connection had become more of a dependency and that as we each struggled to find our own individuality, we found ourselves in competition with one another. I told myself to stop questioning so much and ride the waves of this life change. I dragged myself down by demanding answers where there were none while trying to stay in the present and in the experience. I knew there was much more life ahead of me. I gave myself this pep talk regularly. Sometimes it helped but not always.

I cheered up by organizing a public reading by poet Audre Lorde, held in a church filled with women eager to listen to her read. I had drinks with her before the reading, and we spent time together after the reception. Her voice made me float on waves of erotic air. I'd never heard anyone read so sensually. Her voice could move mountains. I asked her, smiling, if I could take her home and have her read to me every night.

There were other bright moments. My cousin Ronnie granted me a special gift at the bar mitzvah of her oldest son. I was called up to the bimah to carry the Torah around the synagogue during the ceremony. This was unusual for a woman to do, even in a Conservative synagogue. This would never happen in an Orthodox or Hasidic synagogue, which are much less liberal. But I was proud to do so, remembering my bat mitzvah in the orphanage. I didn't realize how heavy the Torah was to hold. It must be all that history it enfolds! I was so grateful I lived close to this family and was able to share in yearly Passover seders and family reunions.

Weeks later, I needed sleep, but it was elusive. I was in a phase of somber restlessness, except when I spoke to clients going through a divorce. I saw myself in them. I became more sympathetic and caring. Mary Ann and I were now "divorcing."

Spring came and buds blossomed. I needed to remember I was a tree with strong roots and robust branches, only a sprinkling of which I'd climbed.

The therapy we'd been going through turned into separation therapy, learning to separate kindly and lovingly. This was so different from my breakups with men.

I had a surprising insight in therapy: I believed in the soul's everlastingness. I lived my life for the experiences and growth of my soul. If that was my truth, then I shouldn't be so hard on myself now for not being perfect in my thus-far short life. I had to learn to forgive myself and not demand unbending perfection. I needed to challenge the dreaded words, *I should.* The question was, would I be able to stick with the challenge?

I wrote in my journal: "Life is a learning experience for the soul, and one can't learn without experiencing pain and suffering, but most importantly, acceptance of oneself." I decided to be positive about how lucky I'd been to have the talent, time, and money to make choices and not be bound to any one road. When I become open to my options, unafraid to ask for what I need and want, I will have made it through this time-warp experience.

I chose not to negate all that I had with Mary Ann. At times it was dispiriting, but also special. I wrote in my journal late one night: "My thoughts are so heavy and overwhelming; I can't imagine this writing can express the depth and fullness of what I'm experiencing. Writing is like the glaze on a sticky bun ready to burst. All the action bubbles inside, yet the glaze makes it deceptively smooth. Gosh, I feel hungry for a warm piece of coffee cake!"

Half a year later, the trees and streets were covered with autumn leaves, a blend of bright colors like a decorated Christmas tree. It lifted me out of an emotional coma. I was more clearheaded and psychologically stronger.

My coworkers and those with whom I had worked at Legal Assistance, where Mary Ann still worked, learned of our separation and were lovingly supportive of both of us. All these years we believed they hadn't known the depth of our relationship. We believed we'd kept it secret. Oh, how naïve we were! We further discovered that many friends in our various communities and organizations were in shock. We didn't know we were considered a perfect couple, a model relationship. It would have been a lot to have lived up to.

I made the weighty decision to move to Maine alone. Mary Ann would keep our New Haven house. I would take Maya and three of the cats.

All these years, I hadn't told my father or brother of the depth of our relationship. To them, Mary Ann and I were just friends and roommates. They'd visited a handful of times and appreciated Mary Ann's openness and interest in their lives. She'd visited my father with me. She loved his noodle kugel, which is a baked mix of flat noodles, tons of onions, oil, and eggs—a thousand delicious calories! I needed to tell them the truth. I called my father. After small-talk, fighting hard not to flood my voice with sobs, I said, "Dad, I need to tell you . . . Mary Ann and I are separating. We won't be living together anymore or sharing our lives together."

He heard the sniffles I couldn't hold back. Quiet. Then he said, "Sweetheart, I'm so sorry. I sensed something was wrong. I know this must be hard for you. Whatever you need, I'm here for you."

Only once before had I heard such supportive words from him. When I was eighteen, extremely sick on New Year's Eve, he took me to the doctor who brought me into this world to remove cysts traveling up my body. He held my hand and cried with me while the cysts were drained. But the hardest thing I needed to tell him about was my move to Maine. It was so far from Brooklyn. I waited a little while longer; I dreaded having that conversation.

Chapter 9

Entangled

My New Haven house filled up with moving boxes marked to show what was in each. Mary Ann now lived with Donna. Maya and the cats maneuvered around like football players through a field of disarray. There was so much to do. I juggled two different lives, one still in New Haven and one on the way to Maine.

As if straddling a life change weren't enough, another ball was added to my chaotic life, disassembling any emotional control I imagined I could sustain. I discovered a painful lump under my armpit that appeared to be swollen. I checked for cuts or bruises or boils near my breast and on my arm. None. I recalled a dream I'd had a number of weeks before that my mother's cancer started under her arm. Iciness ran through me, but I wasn't going to let this take over my life. I made an appointment with my doctor. I asked my cousin Ronnie to come with me, not Mary Ann. I didn't tell my father or brother; why upset them before I knew what was happening? The doctor scheduled a mammogram. I phoned my elderly aunt Jeanette, my mother's sister, asking what kind of cancer my mother had. She said stomach or knee. Another relative said it was melanoma and had spread everywhere. So there were no clear answers. I wouldn't ask my father, and Fred had no idea, no memory of our mother. I teetered on a tightrope across a bridge of wavering information.

Relief washed over me when the doctor declared no cyst or malignancy but had no explanation why my breast was full and tender. I took penicillin four times a day for ten days and waited. I looked at my breasts, the left fuller than the right. They were getting more attention than I'd given them before. I tried to be positive, dissolve the fear, and presume it was an infection. I told myself, *I'm a healthy person; I'll live a long life, dreams notwithstanding.* I couldn't die now. I had so much more to experience in this life.

In therapy I discussed my fear that maybe I had subconsciously willed this illness, but my therapist didn't see in me any self-destructive behavior. That was reassuring.

Feeling physically better, I visited my father for the weekend. We sat drinking tea in his small kitchen. I learned from him to drink tea with jam instead of sugar. He also drank from a glass, something he'd always done. It was his Russian family's tradition. I asked about my mother's cancer, not telling him my personal fear. He stood up on his shaky legs to cut pieces of pound cake for us, which was so far from the active father of my youth. I knew this would be a difficult conversation. I told him what I understood of her illness from what other relatives had shared.

He said, "No, Mommy died of lung cancer, not stomach cancer. It was quick, under a year." He didn't think she knew, although I couldn't believe she didn't. It was hard for him to talk; I noticed him staring into space, retreating into painful memories.

In a measured voice, he shared, "At the end, she was seven weeks home with us before going to the hospital." My mind returned to my childhood memory of waking up one morning and no longer seeing her. I had no memory of how he'd explained to me at six years old why she was gone. I wished I could go back into my child-mind and sense the loss I must have suffered. On second thought, maybe it was best I could not.

He then added hesitantly, "I lost my business. When Aunt Nora got cancer and you and Freddy couldn't live on the farm anymore, I had to fight to get you on welfare—fight to get you into the orphanage ahead of so many other kids, even though you weren't really homeless." Our eyes blurred with tears. Like the crushed man he was when he walked away from us that first day in the orphanage, he lamented, "I didn't want to put you in the orphanage. I could've remarried, but I was afraid . . . afraid you'd get a mean stepmother, and I'd be too weak to confront her." He knew his weaknesses.

Now it was my turn to change the subject. I got more pound cake and tea, and we moved to the living room. He sat in his favorite light-brown cushiony chair, the arms of which were black from newsprint. He always read the news. We easily talked about politics; we were on the same wavelength. Luba, his calico cat, whom I had found on a Boston street and brought to him on a weekend visit from law school, cuddled next to him. We had both since learned how to care for cats. His last cat died, and he was upset when I showed up with a new cat, but it didn't take him long to bond with her and name her Luba.

I sat on the couch across from him and assembled my courage to tell him about my move to Maine. I shared the details of the land and how I would build the house.

He moaned pitifully, "I'll never see you."

I tried to convince him. "Dad, I would never stop seeing you, just like you didn't stop visiting us in the orphanage. Remember, you came almost every weekend, more than other parents." I left the apartment, ignoring the tears trickling down my jacket.

My mind stressed over all I needed to do, as if I had a ticker tape running ahead of me. I planned to visit family and friends in Boston and New York, as well as drive to Maine again to set things in motion, and still make time for socializing with friends in New Haven.

My breast was a swollen question mark. The doctor believed most of the infection was gone, but I had a lump or "ridge" on the side. She directed me to a specialist for a second opinion. In the meantime, I tried to maintain my cool. I spoke with my cousin Ronnie, who held the family history and believed my mother's cancer started with a mole on her leg spreading to the lungs and stomach. So many different stories.

Outpatient biopsy. Pain, swelling, and stitches. Nausea and dizziness after the surgery. Fibrocystic breast disease. The unhealthy tissue taken out. The doctor assured me it wasn't cancer. I was psychically numb. Mary Ann was supportive. Cousin Ronnie remained with me. I hadn't told my father what I was experiencing. It was a worry he didn't need. Home in bed, I slept off the pain and loneliness with a dull headache that Tylenol didn't help. But it wasn't cancer.

I walked through the living room and kitchen full of boxes and unpacked stuff, psychically in two places but actually in none. I belonged nowhere. It was hard for me to cope with feeling unsettled. *How will well-organized, structured me live for a couple of months by the seat of my pants while I build my house and study for the Maine bar exam?* I'd be living in a rental, not on my land, with much of my furniture in storage. The dream I had of Mary Ann and I moving to Maine, not working for a while, leisurely enjoying building the house and playing, was buried in the garbage dump of life.

My questions were like puzzles—would they ever fit together? I sensed that something, more than just land, was pulling me to Maine, something I wouldn't discover in New Haven. Was I a dreamer, like the little "Home kid," the name we gave ourselves in the orphanage, who dreamed of being Superman, flying above it all? This tug to move deeper within, beyond risk, reminded me of my extraordinary traveling dreams in the prior few years, where I experienced going out of my body, flying over land and rivers, sometimes sensing I was in other countries. Early in the dreams, I flew on things like a hard mat, then a surfboard, relaxing in a reclining position until I found the courage to fly without support, feeling safe. Oh, how I wished those dreams would return.

I wanted to be creative again, another loss in my harried New Haven life. I tried to envision living in my new house, lying on my couch on a cold Maine night with a cozy fire in the woodstove, writing poetry or stories, drawing or reading, with Maya and the cats relaxing or playing in their new home. No more projects to do . . . well, maybe just building a woodshed, a deck, a carport, landscaping the property . . . and working as an attorney. Was I the type of person who would always work? I needed to refine the dream.

Mary Ann and I divided tools, books, pictures, glassware, recipes, and odds and ends. The easy stuff. We were amicable with each other—talkative, warm. We both agreed that something special still existed between us, something we would always have but was sadly not enough to keep us together. We transferred deeds. She would move into the New Haven house, and I'd keep the Maine property, an anticlimactic moment.

Chapter 10

Reality

On a cool, spring day, I returned to Maine to help Frank clear the land. We did so for a few days, picking up brush and cutting small bushes and trees so the digging and grading for the foundation could proceed smoothly. I appreciated this productive work, even the sweating—not something I normally enjoyed. I loved the sound of walking on crushed dead brown leaves, and here and there discovering little forest plants budding.

I brought Maya with me. Before Frank arrived, we walked around the property, getting to know it some more. She constantly stopped to sniff the new scents, so different from city streets—so many kinds of trees, softwood and hardwood. On an earlier trip, I'd walked the property with a forester, finding a natural spring, but it was too far from where my house would sit for me to use it for fresh water. I was mentally exhausted from his descriptions of each species of tree. I didn't think I'd ever remember most names. But he did say my land had at least one or more of most every type of Maine tree. My favorites were birch, oak, hemlock, maple, and some of the evergreens, especially the ones that looked like Christmas trees.

I stayed with friends, Jen and Emma, who lived near my land. When Frank arrived, I took Maya back to their home. In Maine, seven miles is considered "near." There are no stoplights. Their home was an old, two-story farmhouse on a hill, overlooking cow pastures and mountains and surrounded by grassy knolls with gardens and shrubs. Scents from the chicken pen greeted me as Maya pulled me to greet the bunnies that lived in the barn. The earthy smells spoke deeply to my soul, reminders of that one short year living on the farm in Flanders. As we approached the back door, their dog barked at our arrival, her wagging tail welcoming Maya for playtime. I was comfortable here. Jen and Emma had created a warm, inviting home. I hoped I would do the same.

Frank stopped work so we could take a lunch break, during which I briefly chatted with my only neighbors, Jim and Rose, a couple with young children. They lived at the beginning of our private dirt road, off another dirt road. Both roads were open to blueberry fields, which were cultivated every other year. The blueberries were raked by hand, unlike the highbush blueberries with which I was familiar. They told me they'd seen bears, foxes, wild turkeys, and, of course, many deer. The kids were happy-go-lucky and friendly, playing freely in the yard with no apparent worries. I watched them with envy, mentally comparing their apparently carefree existence with my childhood experiences.

At ten years old, three years after my father moved us to the orphanage, I was far from being an optimistic kid. I was no longer the innocent girl in a pink dress with chubby cheeks and dark brown hair, cut a la Buster Brown. My hair was wavy, casual, and hung below my shoulders. I enjoyed the texture and freedom of dungarees, a tomboy with a tough facade. But when my father arrived on Sunday, a few days before my tenth birthday, with a big chocolate cake topped with pink icing, this tomboy melted. The cake was large enough to share with my brother and friends, as well as those kids who didn't have family visitors. Even at my young age, I knew I was luckier than most. My father always arrived earlier than most other parents. He wore a brown suit with a white handkerchief jutting from his suit pocket and sported a matching fedora. He was normally courteous and friendly, in a shy sort of way, but not that day. As we exchanged hugs, one of the social workers in the orphanage called him into her office. My brother and I followed and sat on a long dark wooden bench outside the closed office door in the dimly lit building.

We heard his surprisingly loud voice shouting at the social worker. "What are you saying? Do you think I'm not a good father?"

"No, not at all, Mr. Kuriloff. Please. You are a dedicated parent who visits regularly, not like some of the other parents. And I know you sometimes take your children out for the weekends. But don't you think it would be better for them to be in a stable environment rather than in this orphanage?"

We heard our father's strong footsteps pacing back and forth. His voice shook as he shouted, "I certainly want them to be in a stable environment! Do you think I wanted to put them here? After my wife died, they lived with my sister and her husband in New Jersey, but my sister got cancer. Just like my wife. They aren't going to stay here forever. I plan to take them home with me permanently when they are a little older."

Our bodies trembled. We stared at each other and couldn't hold back tears. I was like a leaf ready to fall off a tree. We never experienced his piercing anger. The social worker apologized. We wouldn't be given up for adoption.

After he departed, I returned to the dorm, angry and confused. I wanted to scream at the social worker, maybe even at my father, but he was too dejected. I didn't want to upset him, nor did I want to get in trouble with the social worker. All I knew was that I wanted a real home. I wanted to feel special, like when I lived with my mother, not just one of a bunch of children, rarely seeing my brother. I wanted my clothes in my own closet. In truth, I didn't own any clothes. Rather, I shared the dresses, pants, and blouses from the dormitory closet with the other girls. If some girls fought over what they wanted to wear, the dormitory counselor would make the decision.

I still had the trunk, which held my private stash of candy and cookies, as well as toys and books.

Along with my friends—Josie, Leslie, and Ellen—I felt cheated at not having the money to buy the things our public-school classmates enjoyed. The public-school girls returned home to their families at the end of a school day, to their own bedrooms, their own dressers, their own closets, and their own stuffed animals and dolls sitting on their own beds. Those girls called us Home kids—the kids who lived behind the tall wrought-iron gate that none of our school friends could enter. We sought to fit in with the other kids in school and to prove we belonged. Since we couldn't buy things, we decided to steal them from the 5 & 10 cent store.

We pilfered lipstick, clothes, candy, and jewelry, hiding them under frilly skirts worn over baggy pants or even in our underwear. We didn't wear bras, so we stole some, putting them on and hiding the jewelry in them, except for Josie, who was busty and already wore a bra. We sold a little of our stolen merchandise to other kids in school in exchange for cash so we could eat in the cafeteria with the "normal" kids.

Walking to town one day, we audaciously decided to stop at a number of the manicured homes along the tree-lined streets. We rang doorbells and asked the matronly homemakers if they would like to make donations to the Israel Orphan Asylum. We were very polite so were justifiably surprised that no one gave us any money. When we returned to the Home with our stash, Miss H confronted us. Her cold brown eyes glared down at us in disgust. We called her "chicken legs," as her legs were so thin and seemed to sprout out in different directions. We couldn't read her deadpan face, but we quivered inside.

"I received a call. . . ." she snorted.

Before she could say anything else, I blurted out, "We only stole from Woolworth. No other stores."

Three of us lied, saying that Ellen had stolen most of it. Poor Ellen. She was so honest, and we were so afraid. To our surprise, we learned Miss H had not been aware of our thefts. She was upset that we asked for charity.

I squirmed when I noticed she was wearing the thin white necklace we had given her from a previous foray to the 5 & 10 cent store. None of us mentioned it, and mercifully she didn't connect the dots. The next day she dragged us back to the store. Like sweet and innocent ten-year-old girls, we softly apologized and returned our catch. We were relieved she wasn't wearing our gift around her neck. The manager, a short puffy man, told us never to return; our pictures were on the office wall, and if we came back, we'd be arrested and sent to jail.

If I'd had a tail, it would have been right between my legs. I never stole again.

Weeks later, when my father arrived and took us out for the day to visit relatives, on the return, in a fit of anger, I guiltily but doggedly threw the secondhand clothes an aunt had given me out the window of the car. I was a Home kid once more. The fairy tale of being normal for a few minutes of the day had vanished from my dreams.

My lunch break was over. I rejoined Frank to finish our work for the day. Afterward, I took a long walk with Maya. She ran toward me and kept turning back so I would follow. She led me to a tree stump near a large broken tree and barked at what appeared to be the skull and jaw of an animal, perhaps a deer. She bounded with excitement, reminding me of when Mary Ann and I first adopted her. We had gone for dinner at an outdoor restaurant near the New Haven waterfront, trying to ease our tension from another argument. On the side of the road was a woman with some pups. Maya, black and white, was small enough for the woman to hold in her hand. At the time, we had five cats, most of whom were strays, but had never had a dog. Neither of us knew how to care for a dog, but it seemed an exciting adventure, maybe to bring back the excitement we had once experienced in our life together.

I sat on the stump, holding the skull and jaw in my hands. Tears flowed as I thought of the good old days, seven years before, when Mary Ann and I became family. The word *family* seemed meaningless now, a word I had to shed with the setting of the sun.

"C'mon, girl," I told Maya. "Let's get back." I almost said "back home" but caught myself.

Chapter 11

Endings

On a cold day in March, the board of the New Haven Women's Center held a pizza and champagne goodbye party for me, my last board meeting. There were so many loving hugs from talented and committed women. Laughs and sadness mixed like an ambrosial drink. It was odd to turn over my files, my memories of history—"herstory"—made.

I met with my business partners, Barbara and Cookie, to close out my side of the law practice, handing over my office caseload. I tried to be stoic while saying goodbye to them and the office staff and to the legal practice I'd helped build. Stoic wasn't me! I melted into their arms, and we cried together and separately. I packed my personal stuff—taking down posters and pictures from the walls, knick-knacks, and memorabilia—things that represented my growth and life in New Haven. I took a last look out our eighth-floor windows, glanced down on Church Street to the tops of Yale's buildings and then across a large parking lot to the building where I had previously worked with Mary Ann at NHLAA.

Barbara gave me a fun-loving goodbye party at her house. Seventy-plus people from all parts of my New Haven life attended. There were gifts, hugs, dancing, and Polaroid memories, plus a six-foot-long goodbye card signed by everyone. Returning home around midnight, I fell in bed feeling as if parts of my body had withered away, each slice of skin peeling off an essence of who I was.

During my last day in the courtroom, I noticed more lawyers than usual hanging around for calendar call. The judge entered, and we all stood. The first thing he did was to call me up to the bench. *What did I do now?*—a refrain I'd echoed countless times in this courtroom. I hesitantly looked around trying to understand what was happening. To my shock, the judge made a speech commending me and my practice of law before the bench and wished me well. The clerk handed me a framed picture of the page I signed when I was admitted to the bar. When the crowd applauded, my face turned red as when I have a hot flash. As usual, I couldn't hold back tears, especially getting hugs and well wishes from lawyers with whom I had battled on opposing sides of a divorce or custody case. Later I was given the transcript of the judge's speech.

In early April, I visited my father, and together we drove to my cousin Aaron's house. Aaron had grown up on the farm where Fred and I lived for a year when he was in the Army. He was still the handsome man who had left me tongue-tied when I talked to him as a child, but now he also was a talented, well-known artist. We reminisced about my brother's and my short childhood on the farm. Clearly, my love of Maine came from my Flanders life—Aunt Nora and Uncle Morris, the mill, cows, chickens, and the family Passover dinner. My dad was quiet during our conversation.

When we returned to his Brooklyn apartment, I sensed a weighty sadness in him, a slowness in his walk. Still in his suit jacket, white handkerchief in his pocket, he sat in his favorite chair. With his eyes fixed on his glass of tea, and without a question from me, he defended his choice. "Sweetheart, I also loved Flanders, especially when I visited you and Freddy on the weekends. I wanted to keep you home with me when Nora died, but I didn't know how to care for you both." He blew his nose and continued. "I wouldn't allow Uncle Sidney to adopt you . . . and Aunt Jeanette lived in New Hampshire where I'd barely get to see you. At least the Far Rockaway orphanage wasn't far away so we could spend time together on the weekends. I knew I would take you home as soon as I could."

My emotions knotted with childhood anger and adult understanding. I didn't know how to respond. I finally said, "I know," and kissed him on his forehead.

I made time to have brunch with New York friends I hadn't seen for a long time. It was a needed emotional change of pace.

The next day I had Passover dinner with my brother and father. We weren't religious, nor did we keep kosher (the practice of eating in accordance with Jewish dietary law), although my father tried. We didn't switch our set of dishes for the holiday as is traditional for Passover, like my relatives did. We also didn't embrace the full seder ceremony. My dad cooked a simple but delicious meal of chicken with potatoes and carrots in light gravy. He was a better cook than me. We followed the tradition of eating matzo (unleavened bread), which I loved, instead of regular bread. Our dessert was from the local Jewish bakery.

In the morning, he cooked my favorite breakfast, *matzo brei*, a mix of matzo blended with water, scrambled eggs, and salt, fried in butter just like fried eggs, sometimes topped with applesauce or jam. When I moved to Maine, I would miss those bakeries and traditional Jewish foods, which were far from common in the area of my new home.

I returned to New Haven in a rainstorm, my mind unclear. The word *home* haunted me—it had and still has so many meanings in my life. It was a major step, albeit exciting but unknown, to leave my life of almost eight years in Connecticut, to leave friends and a positive reputation in the community. I was proud of what I had made for myself, and now I was giving it up. I knew I wanted and needed to do so. I'd dealt so much with the practical aspects of leaving; I hadn't the time or the inclination to deal with the emotional aspects.

I remained melancholy until I attended a traditional Passover ceremony at my cousin Ronnie's house, with talkative relatives and friends, prattle from kids, and laughing conversation. This was likely my last Passover with them, once I moved farther away from family.

A young woman visited me at home to take my history on tape for her oral history project on the New Haven Women's Center. We sat in the living room, now full of boxes. It was a poignant interview and reminded me how I had grown into my activism and how much I had learned and experienced through it—how I had released my need to follow societal conventions to be a formal and refined attorney. After she left, I sat at the kitchen table looking out at "our" small fenced-in backyard and wrote a goodbye letter to the women's community for its newsletter.

I rented a U-Haul truck. Mary Ann helped me pack. Three friends planned to travel with me: one to drive their car and two to drive the U-Haul. Maya and the cats were with me in my car. The caravan readied for departure.

Mary Ann was outside the house, tears streaming from her eyes, blending with mine. We hugged for four minutes, struggling to let go. So much was still unresolved. She wanted to join me for the trip to Maine, but I said no. I needed to move forward without her.

I stared at her round face, with her open honest smile that had captivated me when we first met, and any leftover anger melted. I accepted the reality that we had done the best we could with what we knew about ourselves and our relationship at the time. She would always be a part of my heart.

Chapter 12
Vulnerability

I landed in Maine, the beginning of my dream of a new life. I moved into a mobile home with my three cats, Shadow, Maja, and Ming, and dog, Maya—a temporary residence in the town of Penobscot while my house was built. On the drive to Maine, my anticipation overflowed and offset the melancholy of leaving friends and memories—and Mary Ann. I told myself I must look forward, into a new beginning, like a cowgirl riding into the sunrise instead of the sunset.

The yellow rental faced the beauty of rolling hills and Blue Hill Mountain. I'd be living there until moving into my new home, my hopeful corner of heaven, even though it would be bare-bones finished for many years. The friends who drove with me relaxed on the deck, choosing to enjoy the view, and were excited about seeing a fox. I didn't see the fox. I was inside, obsessively unpacking and putting things in order, even though my pictures, artifacts, and other odds and ends would stay boxed until I moved again, permanently. Maya was confused and the cats fearful of their new environment. I searched for a suitable spot for their litter boxes. Jen and Emma cooked dinner at their house for me and my traveling companions. The following day, I played tour guide, cheerfully showing my friends around Cadillac Mountain, the place of the earliest sunrise and sunset in the United States.

Before they left, I showed them my new land and described how my home would be built as a passive solar house. I had read extensively on this new technology and looked at examples of these homes. Passive solar was the wave of the future, so I decided it would be the way I'd build. My house lot and surrounding land was in a place where, if other homes were built nearby, I would still maintain my privacy. An architect friend from New Haven created a model for me of the design I chose. Within the design I planned *not* to have outdoor lights placed near the doors to avoid as much as possible sharing of my home with flies, luna moths, spiders, and wasps. I made sure to include large windows and a sliding glass door that faced south so the house would harvest the most sun and warmth in the dead of winter.

After my friends left, I called my dad, brother, and dear cousin Ronnie, needing to talk and share. Loneliness brought tears to the surface. I didn't want to cry, so I tamped down those feelings. I needed to be strong and look only forward. My past life was gone.

I outfitted the long, thin rental as comfortably as I could, considering most of my stuff was still packed. I opened a bank account, obtained my new temporary checks, and picked up my mail at the post office, as I wouldn't use my new mailbox until I moved to my actual home. My town was Orland, but my mailing address was in Penobscot. I used the rental phone until I moved into my new home.

In addition to building, I also had to study for the Maine bar exam and had picked up the books I needed. Until I could work as an attorney, I was unemployed. Luckily, I was hired to be the director of the Student Legal Services (SLS) program at the University of Maine, a job I had applied for two months earlier.

I wasn't yet adjusted to the total darkness of a Maine night. There were no outdoor lights, just car lights now and then. It was hard to fight my fear of the unknown, even though as a kid living on my aunt's farm, I hadn't been afraid of the dark. Now I was a city person. It amazed me how at times I could still feel helpless, even when my brain knew I was in control.

A week after moving in, while getting dressed to go out at eight in the morning, I received an obscene phone call. After that call, every man I looked at became a suspect. An obscene caller can so easily invade a woman's space and impel fear. I immediately thought about keeping a knife by my bed but decided I wasn't going to live that way. I hadn't done so in Brooklyn, Boston, or New Haven, even after my Manhattan apartment was robbed on the day I moved back with my father. I wasn't going to start here—here where I hoped for some peace after the hustle of city life.

Fortunately, Maya began to bark at sounds, which eased my insecurity as she rested innocently next to me. This new life was such a dramatic change from living in my New Haven house with a fenced-in backyard and front picket fence next to many other similar houses and streetlights.

It was a rainy, windy night, and I was relieved, feeling protected as if the "bad" people in the world don't go out in storms. Crazy thoughts barreled through me as I looked around my small space. Should I block the back door with a dresser? Put scissors on the night table, closer to my reach? What if I stabbed myself while trying to use them? Maya licked my face, and I laughed out loud at my wild imagination.

Work at the house site was paused. My solitary state in the rental spawned further vulnerability, as if I were still the frightened little kid camouflaged in windy bluster. But then I caught myself. I wasn't going to sulk—not on this cool, sunny spring morning. I took Maya for a walk along the tree line of Alamoosook Lake and then returned for breakfast, acknowledging my capacity to change moods as easily as I changed clothing.

I again visited with my friendly neighbors, Jim and Rose, and their two young children, a girl and boy. Jim was a "true Mainer," meaning he'd been born here. Rose was from Maryland, "from away," so not a true Mainer. Some Mainers seemed to be awfully specific about location of birth. Even before I moved here, I heard the joke by Tim Sample, a well-known Maine comedian, expounding on whether one is or is not a true Mainer. "If I had a cat had kittens in the oven, I wouldn't call 'em biscuits." In his laconic Maine accent, he continued his yarn that transplants aren't true Mainers, even if they'd moved here at six months old. Now a substantial number of non-Mainers live in this captivating land. I wasn't alone in that respect.

I became cautious and reticent when meeting new people even though I made friends, having visited over the years my "from away" buddies, Jen and Emma. Through them I became friends with a number of other women and men, mostly transplants, who had moved here to live a more peaceful life.

I was used to the busy, hectic, fast-moving world of city life— talkative, quick to curse, honest, sometimes saying too much too soon, or being too open, shocking those who didn't know me. I didn't have the circumspect Maine personality. While Maine is full of transplants, the culture I had moved into was far from the ethnic, racial, and religious diversity of my past.

My neighbor Jim and I shared something in common. He had also built his house himself, with help from family members. It was similar to mine—open concept with a second floor. However, at the time he built, awareness of passive solar wasn't commonplace. He understandably chose to enjoy the view of open fields, causing his big wall of windows to face north, a view that didn't receive the necessary sun in the winter. My windows would face south.

When my house is built, it won't have a view of theirs, as I wanted to ensure privacy. Theirs was in the open, near the main dirt road; mine would be hidden in the woods, a short distance down our shared private road. I would pass their house regularly when I walked Maya, which I hoped would keep a budding friendship growing.

I sat with them at their dining room table, facing the blueberry fields with trees in the distance. Jim asked good-naturedly, "I know you moved here from Connecticut. Where's your family from?" My mouth tightened like I'd just bitten into a particularly sour lemon. How do I explain my background to strangers? How do I tell them a history that may be foreign to them, and the sharing of which would likely make me cry? I gave them the uncomplicated version. "My dad lives in Brooklyn and is a retired cab driver with health problems. My brother lives in Manhattan and is an electronics engineer. My mother died from cancer when I was young." They blanched at my last few words, lowering their eyes, and Rose said, "I'm so sorry." I thanked them and broke the mood by asking for water and one of the tasty-looking cookies on the table.

We chatted for about two hours. I got to know their background and the history of our land. I played with their two young kids, stimulated by having children in my new "neighborhood." They reminded me of my little cousins in Connecticut; when I took them out for hikes and shared in family dinners, I experienced some of the fun parts of being a kid. We laughed over their story of the woman who first owned their land. Jim sat back in his chair and chuckled as he told me, "She once threatened me outside my house holding a shotgun, stating that she still owned the dirt road because she had once owned this property and the property across from our house."

I responded, "I'm grateful and lucky her family sold me my land *after* she died."

I left my neighbors to return to care for my "family," Maya and the cats. In my early teen years writing to Eva in my diary, I had wondered how my life would be when I married and had kids. I'd envisioned wearing my mother's rings on my finger. I smiled with a sense of sadness and acceptance. My life had taken a different road.

Chapter 13

Roots

Dusk—a quiet time to reflect, like the hazy state of mind upon waking from a dream partially captured, not wanting to open one's eyes for fear of losing the memories or the learning. It was a time for reflection after having been with my neighbors. I sat on the small living room floor of my rental, surrounded by family albums and loose pictures, intent on braving memories that have rolled over me with an urgency to unearth answers to imponderable questions. I wanted to be reminded, to feel the memories of my history—questions that haunted me, particularly in therapy.

Who or what defined my essence, my identity, my nature? Me? Family? Society? Was I my mother's daughter, even though I barely knew her? I pulled images from childhood pictures as well as black-and-white wedding pictures of my parents. March 14, 1943. Eva and Abraham looked out at me from a frame I couldn't enter. My eyes misted, recalling my father's joy and smiles when he took pictures.

I stared at the image of my mother seated in a chair as my father stood behind her. Her wedding dress flowed in a curved wave over the floor in front of her. She wore a long veil with a headpiece around her light-brown hair. I saw her thin eyebrows, brown eyes, and lips pursed almost in a smile, holding an elegant bouquet of flowers. Apparently it was a very formal wedding. I could see her engagement and wedding rings on her hand, the same rings I now cherish that are a lifeline for me to her—her dreams and mine silently entwined. I gazed at myself in the mirror. I had the shape of her chin. I also possessed her brown eyes and brown hair, but my hair was deeper in color, like my father's.

In the photo, my father was distinguished, a cross between Cesar Romero and Clark Gable: dark hair, thick eyebrows, and a thin mustache; black suit, white shirt with bow tie, and a white handkerchief in his breast pocket. I inherited his eyebrows, which were darker and thicker than my mother's, and the shape of his lips. He was the same dapper father who visited us in the orphanage on weekends, stylishly dressed in fedora and suit. I also saw the older father, body worn by age and hard work, mind tired. Tears blurred my vision, and I gulped back a sob that caught me by surprise.

I was lost in memories. Another picture showed my father's mother, hair pulled back in a tight bun, sitting in a chair next to my mother. It was a soulfully serious face on a small, jaded woman. My grandparents were strangers to me. My father's mother died when I was three. I never met my other grandparents, as all had died before I was born.

My mother's recorded name was Evelyn. Family always called her Eva. She had five brothers and one sister. My father's name was Abraham on his citizenship paper. Friends called him Abe or Al. Family called him Abrasha, his Russian name, my favorite of his names. He had twelve brothers and sisters.

The photos didn't reveal the lives they lived before or after marriage. My father shared the short version of their meeting. My mother's sister told me the long version. He worked in a clothing store in Brooklyn. My aunt and mother walked in to look at hats. After browsing and chatting for a while, my mother asked about a job opening. They fell into a teasing match, which became a flirtatious encounter, and my father offered her a job but with the intent of firing her. Instead, as the story goes, they fell in love.

I pored through the pictures of my mother. She held me with a gentle smile on her face, my legs wrapped around her waist. Picnics in the park, visits with relatives, enjoying animals at the zoo. I didn't see deep laughing smiles in these pictures. Perhaps she was already ill but not yet aware. I became momentarily angry that I couldn't unearth the depth of memory I so wanted. My spirit was heavy, like an important part of my body had suddenly evaporated.

My father saved my mother's pin with green stones, a simple and inexpensive treasure. It was stolen when I lived in my first apartment in the city. So many meaningless things taken; why couldn't the thieves leave me the memory I wore on my coat? Thankfully, I still had the rings, then protected in my father's apartment, and a large seashell my mother found, in colors of brown, pearl and beige.

I looked at the seashell sitting on the dresser by my bed. I couldn't leave it in a box. I stood and smiled as I lifted it to my ear. A gentle sound still resonated through the waves of life and death.

I remembered my mother walking me to kindergarten. I was frightened, but she was calm, softly talking to me as we walked. I rubbed against the softness of her skin standing beside me at my brother's crib, changing his diaper, when he suddenly peed, spraying both of us. First surprise; then a shared belly laugh.

When young, I used the pictures to make up stories to share with friends. As I aged, I called her "Dear Eva" in my diary. The diary was my savior when I learned to write. I had private conversations with my mother, having her all to myself. She didn't answer back. She allowed me to rattle along, just listening and watching me build my survival skills, supporting me quietly.

My aunt told me that my mother loved to dance. When I was sixteen, half the age of my mother when she died, I pondered whether she sensed that half of her life was over. Did it really matter to my Polish, Jewish mother, a southern belle, born in Charleston, South Carolina? Well, "belle" may be stretching it. My aunt said my mother very briefly lived in South Carolina. And, anyway, Jewish immigrant families didn't produce belles. But I hoped that in her sixteen-year-old mind she was a belle, at least on the dance floor, gyrating to her own music with other young women, eager to be free, not waiting for some pimply boy to ask her to dance.

Did she know she would give me her dance genes? Did she live full of life because she sensed she would be the first of six to die? I imagined a photo of her at age sixteen, hair flowing to her mid-back, like mine did at the same age. Was she unafraid to speak her mind? Had I imagined this picture from the limited stories I'd heard of her life or from the strong-looking woman in the family albums?

She answered my questions within my dreams. I often dreamt of her guiding me, soothing my tears, and teaching me how to dance. I waltzed around the dance floor with her, like Ginger Rogers. I jump-stepped to Irish music, and Eva's legs moved me faster when my body wanted to fall. She was my muse.

I explored again my father's pictures, reminding me that my DNA flowed through the Jewish survivors of Tsarist Russia. One cold winter Saturday when I was eighteen, my father and I shared tea and rugelach sitting at the kitchen table in our Brooklyn apartment. As soft music played in the background, I asked him about his childhood in Ukraine.

He took me into his memories, sharing how as a small child he saw his sister, Leah, taken away by soldiers during the pogroms. She was never seen again. He witnessed soldiers laughingly drag a rabbi by his long beard tied to a horse's tail. He described his fright at seeing a gun pointed at his mother, my grandmother, ill in bed. In his gentle voice, he added, "The soldiers were searching for whiskey or wine. If they'd found any, our whole family would have been killed." He continued with tearful eyes. "Fortunately, they missed the wine bottle in a basket hanging above the kitchen door." My nose and eyes flooded. I held his hands, a oneness of historical sadness.

He adjusted himself in his chair restlessly and shared that his parents had a tobacco business with beautiful gardens. The government would change about every six months, and each new regime would invade the homes of Jews, stealing whatever they chose. When his parents would hear soldiers say, "Kill the Jews and save Russia," the family would hide in the woods, away from the house, sleeping on the ground until it sounded calm again. I studied his face as he spoke and saw a little boy who had witnessed too much torture and experienced too much pain.

He became quiet drinking his tea, eyes staring into the past, recalling his painful childhood. In our silence I wondered whether he had put my brother and me in the orphanage to ensure he didn't lose us, like the little boy seeing his sister taken away by soldiers. Maybe he was afraid if we lived with my mother's relatives, we wouldn't be returned to him. Like looking at a framed picture, I remembered him leaving us at the orphanage gate. At that thought I took his hand in mine, both of us broken with our memories.

I again stared at my grandmother's serious, unsmiling face. My forehead pounded as I thought of the trauma she must have endured, the painful memories she carried to America. How can I complain about my life? The family left Russia and traveled around

Europe until they were welcomed into America, crossing the ocean in packed ships. His parents came first. My father and some other siblings came about five years later, living with strangers during the years in between. He was fifteen when he arrived. While he traveled in Europe, he played small parts in Yiddish shows, mainly singing.

Later in life, we saw the play, *Fiddler on the Roof.* Through my tears, I noticed his tears. I asked him what he thought of the play. He shrugged his shoulders. "I've seen more."

As I gazed at another picture of my father holding me in front of the tiger cage in the zoo, it struck me that in some way he had also lived an orphan's life in his childhood, just like me and my brother. That was a connection I'd never made. I sobbed, my heart heavy with grief for both of us, releasing some of our mutual pain.

My glazed-over eyes saw the marriage of a dancer and a singer so full of love and life, unaware they would share only eight years together. I came from survivors as they did. I had some answers. I was confident I had inherited the parts of my parents that gave them strength and belief. Without that, I was *not* my parents' child. Drained of emotion, I gently moved the pictures back in their protective boxes and drifted into a dreamy sleep cuddled in soft blankets like a mother's embrace.

Chapter 14

Grounding

The groundwork for my new home happened swiftly. I met with the mason, well-digger, and septic system workers, and with Sue and Niki, my housebuilders, who would begin work after Frank finished the foundation. That's when I'd be all-hands-on-deck.

I contacted the lumber company and the power company, among many other phone calls. I got my first firewood delivery dumped in the parking area, to be stacked after moving in. Exhilaration flowed as I pictured sitting in front of my first woodstove fire.

I met with the electrician and showed him where the temporary power lines should go. I spoke to my neighbor Jim about placing my mailbox on his land off the main road. I called the electric and phone companies. I reserved a private phone line; I couldn't believe they were planning to give me a party line! I advised them I was a lawyer and explained I needed privacy speaking to clients, so they abandoned the party line idea. I also changed my driver's license to Maine and obtained new car insurance.

The foundation was ready for Frank to fill with gravel and dirt to build the floor of my home. The chimney footing was also ready to begin. I decided to cut back on the size of the chimney and happily saved $2,000. My design had called for a twelve-foot-wide red brick chimney; it now would be six feet wide. The solar purpose for a large chimney was to have the south sun hit the chimney during the day, holding the warmth from the sun until the night, when the heat would bounce off the brick, warming the open room. While extra warmth would be comforting, I'd had second thoughts, realizing it would take away precious wall space for artwork and pictures.

At night I couldn't sleep, with a to-do bulletin board percolating in my head. I jumped out of bed at five o'clock, cooked scrambled eggs and hot chocolate, and burned my tongue. I fed the cats and then walked Maya on the road, viewing a rising sun over Blue Hill Mountain. There was no traffic and no noise, except the wind gently touching my neck and the enchanting conversations of various birds. Learning bird sounds was an aspiration for the future. I was adjusting to living without streetlights, which especially allowed viewing a multitude of stars in the sky, so dissimilar from the city.

Yet during the day, anxiety and edginess mounted, causing my chest to constrict. I had sudden fears about how much money I needed to build this house. Was I over my head? Would it all fall into place? I found myself even fruitlessly questioning whether I'd find love again.

I'd generally been confident in my decisions around this move, yet I began second-guessing myself. Doing so much alone was getting the best of me. I lost the confident lawyer I had been, the take-charge person. Workers took over my life, reminding me of difficult early encounters with various male lawyers with whom I had worked. I missed my father's supportive words but didn't call, not wanting to worry him.

Friends thought I was so brave and courageous; maybe I was just nuts! Everything became a question—even whether this piece of land was the right choice.

In a little over a week, the ground of my new home had become a reality. It would be a mess of parts coming together over that spring and summer, but soon enough I'd be moving in, even if the inside wouldn't be finished. I again looked at my to-do list, albeit less anxiously, and acknowledged I really was my own contractor. My plan was no longer a dream.

Chapter 15

Ernie

At four in the morning, I abruptly awoke from a dream of my father and my first serious boyfriend, Ernie, talking and singing together. The cats and Maya popped their heads up, surely wondering why I was up so early, but fell back to sleep. *Why was I dreaming of them now?* The past week, surrounded by men at the house site, I had missed them. I missed being closer, able to just call if I needed their support. Maybe drastic life changes haunt the mind, seeking stability, although my life was never stable, especially in my late teens and early twenties. My father and Ernie were both singers but never together, and not once had they communicated.

Ernie kept in touch with me after we parted ways. I enjoyed hearing his voice. He knew about my relationship with Mary Ann and wasn't turned away. Like my father, he was supportive when she and I broke up. Ernie and I had a strong, deep connection, a connection that had been there from the very beginning. Yet my lies to my father about Ernie, including that he was not married as my father had believed, still disturbed me.

As a teenager, I read romance comic books and was drawn to the women on the cover who had silver-gray hair that was short and curly. They looked so sophisticated. My hair then was long and wavy and brown. I wanted the life in the comic books and the love stories on television.

Every day after work as a secretary in a law firm on Wall Street, I looked forward to meeting my boyfriend, Ernie. This was my first meaningful relationship. Ernie lived in Queens and worked on the docks, not far from my office. He was nine years older than me. I had dated only one other guy who was so much older. I was mesmerized by Ernie's smile, deep voice, blue eyes, and sexy Italian looks, like Brando in *On the Waterfront*. Our bodies moved so well together. He sang and wrote songs. He called me Sherry, my middle name, and penned a song for me:

Sherry, you're the girl for me. You make me so happy and free.
I love you so and I'll never let you go. Sherry, you're the girl for me. . . .

We met in a bar one night that my friends and I rarely frequented. I noticed him from a distance, and suddenly he walked toward me. I hated barhopping, so I sometimes drank a little too many whiskey sours to survive the night. That night I'd had one too many. I later learned that Ernie had the bartender dilute my drinks with water; by that time, I couldn't tell the difference. To my disappointment, he couldn't drive me home.

Ernie was so different from the guys I had previously dated who were more my age and sexually and emotionally immature. We'd go dancing in clubs and to motels to make love. He was gentle in our lovemaking, wanting to make sure I was satisfied. I trusted him more than I'd ever trusted any man—or boy—before.

I wish I could say he was the one to whom I gave my virginity, but I couldn't. That was lost two years before to a suave, older guy I met on the subway, who enthralled me with his way with words as a writer. We would fool around in his apartment. I told him I wanted to save myself for my future husband, but he didn't care. I didn't realize what was happening until, in pain, I went to the bathroom and saw blood running down my legs. That was the end of my short, intriguing affair. I was no longer "pure," as I wrote in my diary, and my dream wedding faded from my expectations.

For a long time, I didn't introduce Ernie to my father, as he wasn't Jewish and was much older than me. My father worked nights, so a few times I snuck Ernie into my bedroom when my brother was asleep but couldn't deal with the guilty feelings that followed.

Almost a year into our relationship, my heart and dreams were filled only with him. We were sitting in an expensive hotel restaurant after he had won $50 at the races. I was excited as that was the first time I'd been to a horse race as well as my first filet mignon. I felt sophisticated like the women in the comic books.

I smiled lovingly when I glanced at my handsome boyfriend. Oddly, he seemed nervous, playing with his fork and knife as if he weren't hungry. His blue eyes welled up as he spoke.

"Sherry, I need to tell you something . . . I'm sorry, but . . . I'm married." He spoke so fast I didn't catch all the words. "I wanted to tell you right away, but we hit it off so well . . . and then I fell in love with you. I didn't dare tell you. I want to divorce my wife, but we have two sons."

Acid filled my stomach, and anger rose. I was no longer feeling sweet, and I didn't care what I said in this fancy restaurant.

"What . . . are you fucking serious? A wife . . . and kids too! How could you do this to me?" I ran out of the restaurant with no place to go. Ernie drove me home without speaking.

Yet I kept seeing him on and off for five years, keeping my guilty secret about Ernie from my father.

One frigid New Year's Eve in the city, I was bundled in a thick coat and boots, my hands warmed in Ernie's pockets, waiting in line to get into a movie. I turned to warm myself from the steam rising out of the subway grate and saw my father across the street, also bundled up, walking from his half-hour subway ride from Brooklyn to the cab company for which he worked. His six-foot-tall body was bent toward the wind as if he were carrying a bale of life's burdens and disappointments. I had a stinging pain in my stomach as I stared at him. Guilt settled in like sour milk.

I didn't tell Ernie my father was across the street; I'm not sure why. As if I were my father's twin, I breathed in his tired eyes, his arthritic feet, his daily boredom of not being the man he expected to be when he left Ukraine at age eleven and traveled around Europe until he was fifteen.

Before he arrived here, he lived with a family in Holland for a few years. The man of the house told him not to go to America as he'd end up working on pushcarts. In Holland, he could "do anything and become rich." But my father said no. He was excited to go to America and be with his family.

He landed on Ellis Island in a white suit, with confidence and hope, expecting maybe to attend college or to sing and act, as he had prior to arriving in America. He was worldly enough to sightsee on his own the day of his arrival. His family had to call the police to locate him. Lamentably, the man in Holland had been right; his first job was working in Brooklyn selling dry goods from a pushcart.

Standing with Ernie in the movie line, I didn't have the courage to run across the street to say hello or hug him. I was embarrassed, perhaps guilty, knowing I was having the enjoyment he had missed in his life.

During his years driving his cab, he once met Cesar Romero. Cesar signed a dollar bill for him to give to me and admitted he and my father looked alike. I had many signed bills from famous people who graced the bumpy yellow cabs driven by him. Stupidly, during my teen years, I cashed in the famous people for treats and other indulgences.

My father had girlfriends, two of whom I met on our weekends outside the orphanage. But he wouldn't wed again. As he later shared with me, he was afraid he might not be able to protect us if his new wife were mean. After my mother's death, he slowly lost his confidence and hope, mostly living a worrisome life, especially as he aged.

There I stood in the cold New Year's night, looking at the two most important men in my life, keeping secrets from both.

I dated other guys occasionally, but none of them could keep me from Ernie. By the time Ernie divorced his wife, I knew I wouldn't marry him, even though I loved him to the extent that I understood what love was. By then we were in different worlds. I had been going to college at night with the hope of becoming an attorney. I'd also discovered the blossoming feminist movement. Ernie's life was stationary. We didn't have fights or even strong arguments.

Eventually I became that working woman from the comic books—the somewhat sophisticated looking one with short, wavy, silvery-gray hair. Like my father's, my hair started turning gray early.

When I moved to Boston for law school, Ernie kept in touch, remaining a precious part of who I was. Somehow he seemed to know when to call—when I was down, upset, feeling insecure at school. He always sent me birthday cards and a few letters. When I moved to Connecticut for my first legal job, he called now and then, and we met once over lunch. He loved me enough to stay in my life, even when I couldn't return his love. And later in Maine, after I moved into my new home and experienced a shocking tragedy, Ernie suffered that pain with me in a way I would never have expected.

The first rays of dawn lit the sky. I took Maya to my land, a little groggy after a sleepless night of ruminating. In the quiet, with the workers not yet there, we walked around the building site, along our private dirt road, and then down the traveled dirt road that had only one house on it, hidden in the woods. Very few cars drove this road. I stroked Maya's neck, telling her this was her place too. I wanted her to know this was her home as much as mine. She licked my hand, and I took a deep breath. Tomorrow the foundation would be laid. Tomorrow my dreams for a permanent home would pour themselves into concrete posts, just as my heart poured itself into hopes of a new beginning.

Chapter 16

Commitment

On a warm, early May morning, I watched Frank and his helper begin the foundation of my new home. The reality of my move was coming alive with each swing of the sledgehammer. This part of the construction I couldn't directly work on, except for now and then handing them a tool and asking some probably annoying questions.

The ground was in chaos, broken up with huge piles of dirt and rocks sitting on the sides of the deep trenches, which reminded me of a burial site. I was riveted watching them dig holes deep beyond the frost line—three rows of five holes, each to hold an eight-inch-wide concrete post. Later they would add pressure-treated wood, crisscrossing alongside each row to support the house, which would not sit on the typical cement basement like my New Haven house. I decided not to have a traditional basement, having read about the problems with leaks, and I had been advised it wasn't necessary with passive solar construction. Down the road, such advice was a detriment. I had to fight to obtain a mortgage without having a basement or cement floor. I paid an appraiser to find similar houses where a mortgage was granted. Luckily, he found two.

My body was alive with anticipation to get my hands into the actual work, but that had to wait until Sue and Niki started the housebuilding in another two weeks. Yet, like a kite drifting through the clouds, I found my excitement tinged with mental turmoil as I acknowledged the permanent reality of this move. I couldn't turn back.

Frank had another week or more of hard measuring and pounding work. The days were tiring, mainly standing around watching the goings-on and not yet able to be productive. I tried to be patient; I was not a patient person. I reminded myself to use these two weeks to study for the bar exam and prepare for my new job at the university, which would start in a few months. I also had to adjust to the times Mainers seemed to start and end work. Frank and his helper, John, arrived at six o'clock and ended about three. These were not my normal hours, but I needed to be there. While I couldn't participate, I still desired to be a part of every aspect of the construction, to experience the building from the ground up, even accepting the upheaval that propelled me into a new adventure at this stage of my life.

I'd been in Maine for a month. With unpredictable weather, soon a white-and-gray world of rain slowed the foundation work for four days. I used the time to study for the bar exam, reading material spread over my queen-size bed. Maya slept on her back at the end of the bed, legs up in the air, so trusting. The cats rested closer to me between the books. Shadow, deep gray in color, had one paw over an open page of a book as if she were studying with me. Long-haired, gray Ming and Shadow had been my company during my last two years of law school. Maja, a calico, had been pregnant on the streets when Mary Ann and I found her. She gave birth in a box in our house to five littles. We found homes for them, and Maja became another lovable house cat living with us. I smiled, surrounded by my small family. And then I cried because it was no longer *our* family.

The week of rain turned into sun and warmth, allowing Frank

and John to continue the meticulous footing work. After having dug the three parallel trenches for the footings and placed a gravel base, they set fifteen twelve-inch diameter cylindrical tubes, called Sonotubes, five in each trench, which they filled with concrete. They then placed a four-by-four-inch metal bracket into the top of each. They took a break for two days to ensure the concrete fully dried before placing the pressure-treated wood posts into the brackets.

I was amazed at this technical and mathematically exacting work, in contrast to the chaos of human relationships that kept ensnaring me into a mind-challenging quest to unravel and release the questions that gave me sleepless nights. Dreams challenged my sanity.

I was exhausted from too much contemplation, as well as too many blackfly bites on my body. No one had warned me about black-flies! You don't feel the bites, but when you look in the mirror, you see bloody bumps. Toward the middle of watching the foundation go up, I bought a khaki-colored hat, shirt, and netting to wear over my head and upper body when necessary.

After the concrete was cured, Frank and John secured the pressure-treated wood foundation posts into the metal brackets. They then placed the three rows of wood beams across the posts to support the first-floor framing. The foundation was completed.

My New Haven life was now over, even though the gut emotions hung on. I knew if I had chosen to stay in New Haven, I would have survived and likely blossomed. I was a survivor. I recalled a profound question my Home kid friend Leslie asked me a long time ago: "Are you surviving or thriving?" *Yes*, I told myself. With all the changes I was tackling, *I am thriving. I will thrive.* Before Mary Ann and I broke up, I wanted to move to Maine. I wasn't running away. Even as I anticipated there would be more chaos in my life, I had reconciled the past enough to move into the future. Now it was time to look forward. I was committed.

A few days later I strolled around the smooth ground surrounding my new foundation, waiting for Sue and Niki to arrive to start the next stage of my housebuilding—the floor, the fundamental stability of my home. *The beginning of a new security blanket!*

Akin to the deep-rooted oak, maple, and pine trees surrounding the foundation on the north and west sides of the house to protect from winter winds and storms, I was establishing new roots, hopefully to be as deep-seated and secure as these trees. I walked over to an old tree stump and noted the rings of old age growth in its base.

Staring at the circles of life on the stump, my body tensed as I breathed, lungs expanding to take in a heavy flow of air. As I breathed out, I knew that not all trees weather a storm, even if deep-rooted. I took a second aching breath. I wanted to feel positive and optimistic, but dread wavered through me. I had a young girl's memories of other deep-rooted trees surrounding both the Far Rockaway and Yonkers orphanages, and then the trees in Brooklyn, when my brother and I moved back with my father. Each time I was a stranger in a strange land, like now.

Sue and Niki arrived at seven thirty. I was relieved to see them, drained from indulging my childhood insecurities, but also tense. Like me, Sue and Niki were women with strong personalities. I'm usually in control of my work circumstances. Here I was a novice, out of my element. We chatted for a few minutes and then got down to business, laying and nailing wood joists in a parallel series to support the eventual subfloor, connecting them to the three rows of wood beams installed by Frank.

I helped lift the joists from the parking area to the foundation, then held them in place for nailing. I also assisted with some nailing, learning all over again how to nail. The housebuilding workshop hadn't taught me as much as I'd expected. Even the building information in the books I read didn't stick in my brain when it came to the actual work; it was a lot harder for me than reading law books.

The daytime sun and heat tired me out. Clouds and wind made me happy, especially when the winds kept the blackflies at bay. Sue and Niki were serious workers, so there was not much casual conversation. They were about my height, around five feet, three inches. Sue was thin, and Niki and I a little heavier. Their arms were muscular; they lifted joists as easily as I lifted a law book.

We broke for lunch at eleven thirty, leaning against the foundation to eat our sandwiches. Sue smiled and said, "Roberta, don't be so hard on yourself. It'll get easier."

I laughed and replied, "I hope so. I don't think I'm cut out for this work, but I want to learn. I need to be a part of the intricate building of my house." I asked them, "How do you survive these damn blackflies? Do you realize you have some blood spots on your face and arms? Some on my arms have swollen."

Both laughed. Niki stood and wiped her face, ready to get back to work. Weeks later, when the blackflies were gone, I discovered Niki's face was a lot thinner when it was no longer swollen from the bites.

I drove back to my rental—no stoplights, three miles away—to give Maya a quick walk and then returned to the house site. There was still not much small-talk until the end of the workday at three. Most of the joists were in place. We arranged to meet the following morning at seven thirty to finish the joists and start the subfloor. I was exhausted but confident that Sue and Niki were stable forces in my life and that my house would be well-built.

My sweaty body returned to my temporary "home" after an invigorating but draining workday. After feeding the cats, I drove to the lake with Maya, ran into the cool water for a swim, then floated on my back, visioning faces and designs in the moving clouds. Maya walked along the waterline, not being a swimmer. She tried catching tiny fish and frogs. I sat on the grass, wet, the sun warming me. As I waited to dry, my mind retreated back to my yearning for stability and security. I remembered my childhood fear that had been focused on the day when most of the kids were uprooted from the Queens orphanage and moved to another orphanage in Yonkers. I had been nervous that Fred and I would be separated and questioning whether we'd still see our father.

Chapter 17

Focus

My tough, eleven-year-old body trembled, trying not to let others see. So many disturbing questions churned in my head. I was finally settled in place, in the ways of doing and being, and then there was another move—another orphanage, another "Home." I worried if my father would be able to visit us on weekends as before, if all of us girls were moving to the same place, if we'd have the same counselors, and if my brother would be going with us.

The counselors helped us pack our finite amount of personal stuff. We asked questions but received limited answers. "Don't worry. You'll like where you're moving."

I found out Miss H wouldn't be going with us. I'd miss her. She was no longer scary—more a security blanket of stability.

Some friends and I were on one bus, surrounded by numerous yellow school buses. I kept looking to confirm that we were going to the same place.

I didn't talk to my brother during the move; we spoke so little except when we spent outings with our father. Finally I saw him from a distance on another bus. I wept thinking about him. He was my lifeline, my only real family.

After we arrived, I called my father. He assured me the drive from

Brooklyn to Yonkers was roughly the same as from Far Rockaway. I was reassured he didn't have a longer drive.

We learned from one of our counselors that the Yonkers orphanage had been a boys' home. Girls of all ages were now moving in, as well as the boys from our old Home.

In Far Rockaway, the girls had lived in a separate building from the boys. In Yonkers, we all were in one long brick building of four floors, with a front entrance about ten feet long with wide front steps, like the steps of the New York Public Library. In the front of the building and around the sides was a substantial grass courtyard with hedges and some trees, enclosed by a tall gate, as in Far Rockaway. Most of the wide, school-like windows faced the front grounds and outside play area, which was set in a grassy field surrounded by trees, with swings, seesaws, slides, and monkey bars. We were overwhelmed walking around outside, as well as excited discovering so many new places to explore.

An outsider could easily presume the building was a school, a hospital, or an asylum.

The building had several playrooms, a library, a theater hall with a stage, and a synagogue. It also had a piano room with couches and soft chairs. The piano room soon became the spin-the-bottle room when the counselors weren't around. Some of the boys kissed like fishes. I wanted only Stanley, my first boyfriend, to kiss me. No one knew we'd been practicing kissing behind the piano.

Stanley had lived in the Yonkers Home before we moved there. We had met almost immediately. He was a year older than me, around my height, with brown curly hair. He liked to look into my eyes and play with my wavy shoulder-length hair, making my stomach flutter and my face flush. We kissed when no one was around or during spin-the-bottle, if by chance we picked each other. We rode a bike together and took walks around the field, behind the play area. I was less guarded with him than with my girlfriends.

However, the boundless excitement for the girls were our bedrooms. No longer were we in a dormitory. Four of us shared a room. We each had our own night table with drawers and a lamp. I jumped and bounced on my choice of bed, spreading my full body on it. It was so different from the hard dormitory bed. In between the night tables on each side of the room were vanity tables with chairs and mirrors. In the middle of the room stood a wooden circular table with four padded chairs, likely for doing homework. The floral trim on the bedspreads and curtains were the same as the trim on the bulletin boards and mirrors.

Over each bed was a bulletin board. I excitedly put on *my* board cards of Elvis in all his gyrating moves. Startlingly, I began sweating; I didn't have any pictures of my parents or my brother. Despite all the photos my father took, I never had any with me! I asked my father to bring pictures when he next visited, especially of me and my mother and Aunt Nora.

Initial fears changed to feeling slightly special! While I didn't have my own room, the room I shared looked a little like the rooms of my friends in Far Rockaway who lived with their families—but without closets. Our clothes were not yet all our own. Disappointingly, we still showered in a big room with lots of sinks and ate in a large dining hall. I concluded I could live with that.

Harder to live with was that we no longer attended public school, as school was taught inside the Home. My body constricted, like a penned dog. In Far Rockaway we enjoyed walking to school and having friends outside the Home. This new home was "exclusive."

My brother and I were again separated. He was on the floor above the girls' floor, and we saw each other mainly when our dad visited.

Every five weeks or so, I met with a social worker, Mrs. T, in her office on the first floor. I sat in her stuffy chair that made me feel smaller than I was. She was tall and always wore a jacket and skirt, with her blouse or sweater tight against her neck. When she spoke, her words had the same boring tone as a teacher reciting a homework assignment.

She didn't always sit when asking prying questions. She walked around the room; I assumed she did so to force me to look up at her.

Every time I visited, she asked what I had done during the past weeks. I looked down at my hands and responded like an idiot, "I don't know; I can't remember."

"Spent time with friends? Who are your friends here?"

I wrestled in the chair with my words, trying not to curse. "Why's that important? Why do you need their names?"

She forced a smile, lips tight together. "It just makes our conversation easier if I can place a name with an event. I remember it better."

"Why do you have to remember it? Do you put their names in your notes?"

"Roberta, I am the counselor. I ask the questions."

"Well, you're making me uncomfortable again." I pulled my feet up to my body on the chair, wrapping my hands around them. I knew my shoes weren't dirty. "I watched movies with Sharon, Stanley, Josie. Also played stoop ball and double Dutch, which I'm really good at."

In a softer voice, she said, "Do you feel you are settling in well? I can imagine the adjustment wasn't easy, moving from Far Rockaway to the Yonkers orphanage. I know you enjoyed public school. Now the school's inside, not outside. How are your present classes?"

"Okay."

"And your room?"

I responded with slight enthusiasm, "I love that I have a private room with three other girls. It's better than living in the dorm."

"I'm glad to hear that. How are your visits with your father?"

"Okay."

"Can you share more?"

"He comes almost every weekend and takes us out. He's always here early on Saturdays. We have fun."

"Roberta, can you tell me more of how you are feeling?"

I tried not to scream, but my words raced, holding back tears. "I don't know how I'm feeling. I just want to go home and live with Daddy and Freddy. Do you talk to my brother too?"

No answer.

"I know you talk to the counselors about me. You know everything."

"Dear, I do get reports from the counselors. But I want to hear it from you, too. I'm interested in your well-being. I want to understand the full picture."

I responded more loudly, with tears cascading down my flushed cheeks and runny nose. "You're not my father—not my mother. I don't want to talk to you. I just want to go home!"

I ran out of the room and sat on the hall steps, not knowing what to do next.

I was compelled to meet with Mrs. T regularly. I couldn't constantly avoid her questions. I could have told her lies: that I was happy-go-lucky; that I had great friends; that I saw my brother and we hung out together. All lies.

I did have some friends, but we were always on guard—fighting over the same clothes, hiding our candy stash so it wouldn't be stolen. I stole candy once, always afraid I wouldn't have enough. That caused too much guilt.

Besides Stanley, another boy liked me—tall, thin George, a loner, who was much older than me. He'd stand back from the play area, sad faced, not talking much to others. Even though I was outgoing on the outside, I suspected there was a part of me similar to him—detached and protective. He bought me records and pictures of Elvis. I ignored him a lot and hated myself that I hurt him, harboring feelings of guilt that lasted for many years after I moved back with my father.

I barely spent time with my brother, except when our father visited. I hated seeing Fred cry when we said goodbye. In Far Rockaway, I sometimes walked Fred to his building. In Yonkers, he was in the same building. He was still so small and lost. I tried to help him through his tears, but I needed to be strong.

I had outgrown my frilly pink dress as I became interested in boys but maintained my tough veneer. I didn't let anyone bully me. All I wished was for our father to take us back with him, but I knew he couldn't. I hated feeling sorry for myself and hated that I had to adapt to yet another orphanage.

Chapter 18

Insecurity

I thought I was losing the feeling of being a stranger in a strange land, but it seemed to never go away. It just buried itself in some hidden cells of my body, even though the adult in me knew our cells die and constantly renew themselves. I wondered if accepting the little "stranger" in me was maybe a positive quality. However, instability was harder to accept. That one needed work.

I came from a family with deep roots from across the world. My tree trunk was expanding, albeit slowly, but the branches were thickening like an oak, extending strongly upward, with the lighter extensions flowing like willow branches in the wind. I was a work in progress.

One early morning, I had an urge to again find my childhood diary, remembering a letter I had written to my mother after returning to live with our father about facing the insecurities still in me.

Dear Eva,

I'm thirteen, and we're home with Daddy in Brooklyn! I have my own room! Well, almost. It doesn't have a door, as it's connected to the living room. It was once a porch. My bed is kind of hidden in the corner, so I have some privacy, not like the dormitory

*in Far Rockaway or the shared room in Yonkers. I even have my
own closet for my own clothes.*

*We're on the street level, and my windows, the length of the
room, face the street. It's a little scary hearing voices of people
walking by at night. The nighttime in the orphanage was so quiet,
except for the muffled sounds of crying. Freddy's sharing a room
with Dad, on the other side of our small living room and kitchen.
Wow, "our," a word I don't remember using before!*

*Three other families live in this house. Next door is a tall brick
building with lots of families. It reminds me of the building we
lived in before you died and where Daddy still lived when we visited him from the Home on weekends. I still picture the big bed
you slept in; I picture you in the bed. When we moved here, it was
gone, like you. Now Daddy sleeps in a small bed, like mine and
Freddy's.*

*There's also a small yard in the back. Daddy loves to lay on a
lawn chair and enjoy the sun when he's not working. In the warm
weather, neighbors sit outside in front of the house and along the
street by the tall bushy trees keeping them cool from the sun. Some
of the mothers sit by my bedroom windows, gossiping and talking
so loudly that I can't concentrate on reading—or writing to you.*

*Aunt Fay and Uncle Sol live at the other end of our block. My
aunt cooks delicious dinners for us on the weekends, and sometimes we eat in their apartment with my two cousins. I like feeling
part of their family—my family—like when we lived on the farm
with Aunt Nora and Uncle Morris.*

*When we left the orphanage, Mrs. T, the social worker, hired
a woman to take care of us while Daddy works driving a cab. Mrs.
Roach is very caring and already took us to the Brooklyn Museum,
Botanical Gardens, Prospect Park, and Coney Island.*

I'm in high school, but my first day was scary walking into the building. It was like the Yonkers building. I relaxed when I met two of my new neighborhood friends.

One of the hardest things for me is to walk into the high school cafeteria by myself. It reminds me of the Home's big dining hall, but unlike then, I don't know everyone here, and if my new friends aren't with me, I don't know where to sit. I'm awkward sitting with strangers, anxious, and I want to run, but there's no place to hide in this big school. I'm no longer the confident, tough girl I was in the Home.

I wish you were here to help me with another problem. I'm ashamed—I sometimes miss my life in the Home. We lived together and shared everything. I had friends whose lives were like mine. We became family.

I wonder if you ever read the book The Endless Steppe by Esther Hautzig? Esther was a ten-year-old Jewish girl living with her family in Poland until the Russians came, and the people were herded into cattle cars and taken to Siberia to be slave laborers. It was an incredibly harsh life, but Esther was eventually able to make friends and came to love the steppe. When the war was over and they could go home, she asked her parents if they could stay in Siberia because she had friends and liked the school. She said, "I told Mother that I was afraid to go back, afraid to meet new people, afraid to live in a big city again."

Mommy, I love being with Dad and Freddy, and I've made some friends, but it's not like before. I feel like Esther. My new friends have their own families. In the Home, I was popular. I had friends who understood me as I understood them, even when we argued and fought. I don't have that now. I'm less outgoing. I feel lost in a sea of students in my first year of high school. Confused.

What's wrong with me? Even though there were good times in the Home, there were bad times too. I remember many times crying my heart out because I wanted to leave. And when I saw Freddy cry, I cried.

I shared a little of this with my aunt. She then told Daddy that I wanted to go back to the Home! I didn't say that. She misunderstood. Dad looked so sad and asked me if I liked it better in the Home. Through tears I tried to explain that I was adjusting to a different world. His eyes were also teary. He didn't understand. Mommy, I push myself to be friendly, but I don't feel comfortable talking to strangers. When I left the Home, I became a stranger in my new world.

Your daughter

Chapter 19

Expectations

I was like a kid playing with blocks for the first time! I carried the joists, dropped the joists, hammered my fingers instead of nails. Fortunately, the day was windy, so there were fewer blackflies. I understood they'd be around well into June or later. We finished nailing down the remaining wood joists and would next lay the subfloor for my new home, progressing faster than expected.

The tough lawyer in me had gone to sleep as I doggedly hammered away. In my role as general contractor, I was sent by Sue to the building supply store to order more materials. I walked in with a smile on my face, dusty dungarees, short work boots, a long-sleeved shirt, and a cap, and recognized one of the two men behind the counter. Joe's round friendly face smiled in a flirtatious way as his tattooed hand took my shopping list and leaned on his portly belly to review it.

When Joe showed it to the other worker, the guy looked at me inquisitively: *Why is she here for this stuff? Where's the contractor?* Then, in fact, he asked those exact questions! I responded with a sharp tongue. "I'm my own contractor. I designed my house. My builder, *Sue*, is requesting these additional items. I can take some in my car, and you can deliver the larger ones."

I turned and stared at awkward Joe, who responded, "No problem, I'll take care of this; I'm familiar with the building project."

I smiled sweetly at Joe, then walked out upset that I had smiled sweetly while seething inside. How many times have men questioned my abilities just because I'm female? Waiting in my car, I thought about my conversation with Rabbi K, my Hebrew teacher in the Yonkers orphanage, where I made my initial "legal argument." It was my first experience with chauvinism—an experience more meaningful than the typical ones that followed throughout my life.

Before I had a chance to stand up at the release of class one day, Rabbi K declared, "Rivka, you stay seated." I liked it when he called me by my Jewish name, just like Uncle Morris had. I never heard it otherwise. My body trembled.

I watched my classmates leave. They looked grateful they weren't being held hostage by the rabbi. I was seated in the front row of the class, near his desk. He had recently put me there as I always asked questions.

I looked up at him, tall with a small potbelly, wearing round black-rimmed glasses and with a shaved face, unlike most rabbis with long beards. He stood in front of his desk, looking down at me, clearly not pleased, his usually friendly face stern.

"Rivka, do you know why I'm upset?"

"Well, maybe. I'm sorry, Rabbi. I know I lied and blamed Fran for leaving all the peanut shells on the floor. I shouldn't have blamed her. But I also shared them with the other kids, so I'm not all to blame."

He walked back and forth along the length of his desk, probably contemplating my punishment. I was now sure this talk was not *just* about peanut shells.

"Rivka, you are twelve, shortly to have your bat mitzvah. This is an especially important responsibility requiring discipline. Just like boys when they have their bar mitzvah at age thirteen. You'll be standing on the bimah reading from the Torah in Hebrew. You must learn enough Jewish history and law to understand what you are reading."

My face turned red, as I recognized I was in serious trouble. "Yes, Rabbi, I studied hard to learn the history and prayers. I know it's important. My father's coming to hear me read the Torah."

"So, my dear girl, why did you scare the younger children with your story about Moses?"

I sank in my chair, my feet almost touching the rabbi's when he walked by. "Rabbi, I can explain. I was trying to help them understand the story of Passover and Moses. You taught that we are descendants of Moses. So I sort of told them I was Moses's descendant and I'd help take them out of the orphanage like Moses took the Children of Israel out of Egypt . . . but instead of going to Israel, they'd go home to their parents. I wanted them to have hope they'd go home someday, just like the early Hebrew people. You know, my father's going to take me home someday soon."

He frowned while I spoke, but I noticed a turn in his upper lip moving into a smile—even though he tried to fight it.

I sat up in my chair, remembering my dreams of walking the kids out the gates like the Pied Piper or like Roy Rogers, galloping into the sunset on Trigger to see the world or at least to get me home to my father in Brooklyn.

I stood up and started reciting the Torah prayers I had memorized.

"Rivka, that's enough! I know you studied a lot for your bat mitzvah. But you can't tell wild stories to the young children. They're new to the Home. Remember how scared you were when you first came. They're asking me why they can't go home like the other Jewish people you told them about. Remember, many of them are not as lucky as you. They don't have homes to return to."

He sat back down in his chair, and I knew I was going to be okay. "Rabbi, I apologize. Instead, I'll tell the kids the other parts of the Passover story, how God told Moses to tell the Pharaoh that if he didn't let the Hebrews go, then there'd be ten plagues on his people, including killing the firstborn children, even the Pharaoh's son, because God was upset that the Pharaoh ordered all Hebrew baby boys be killed."

The rabbi gave me an odd look I couldn't read.

"Rabbi, do you think the Bible stories are too scary for the young kids? Shouldn't we tell them hopeful stories?" Before he spoke, I thought maybe it was better to tell the kids about Superman and Roy Rogers. I didn't understand all I would be reading at my bat mitzvah. In Hebrew, the translation is different from English.

"Rivka, the Torah is God's words. The stories have a deeper meaning beyond the words on paper. That is why the rabbis study so much and pray so much. We look deep into God's words. I know this is difficult for you to understand now. Wait until you are older and study the Bible and appreciate God's reasoning in telling Moses what to do."

"Can't we find nice stories in the Torah? Less scary stories to share?"

"Rivka, all the stories in the Torah are important. When I share the stories in class, I explain the history of the story and its meaning. As you know, life is not always nice or easy. Sometimes it is scary."

Before he had a chance to continue, I stood up and told him, "Rabbi, I want to understand God's stories, so when I grow up, I will be a rabbi."

The rabbi looked at me and spoke slowly and carefully. "Rivka, women cannot be rabbis."

As I sat in my car outside the supply company, my anger flashed back to other sexist encounters when I was a secretary and later a lawyer. I breathed deeply, calmed down, and let go of those bitter memories, and then I drove back to Sue and Niki with the supplies. I continued sweating with them as we lifted and nailed, feeling emotionally lighter inside. I accepted that I couldn't be adept at everything I did, even though the little girl in me would like to be—would like to have total control, would like never to be hurt or disappointed, would like to know it all. For right now, it was okay being a kid playing with blocks.

At five in the evening, the sun still bright in the west and the joists and subfloor done, Sue and Niki built some steps to walk up onto the "deck." After they left, I walked the circumference of the house. The ground under the house was uneven, so the west side of the house was four feet higher than the front. I sat in the middle of the deck, being one with the wild and open woods surrounding me. Soon this open space would be closed in, protected from the west winds, the north storms, the hot south sun, and the east rains. In the next stage, the walls go up.

Chapter 20

Purpose

The rain was intense for two days. I used the time to study for the bar exam, yet one evening, tired of studying and lost in the patter of rain on the metal roof of my rental, my psyche chose to indulge in memories of my early activism and legal practice in my first job in New Haven; this was less stressful and more self-supportive than studying for the bar. At that time I wanted to protect children from being taken away from parents and put in the foster care system, the fear that I had lived with as a child.

A handful of people in the community had uncovered the problems of women who were battered—women abused by their boyfriends or husbands. I joined the group, and we organized and educated the public about this hidden issue. Many of my female clients who were battered had children removed by the Department of Social Services (DSS). Due to fear, women didn't talk about being abused, thinking they could lose custody if they disclosed their situation.

As I became more versed in the intricacies of these issues, I recognized a major lack of understanding by DSS workers, as well as judges, as to the adverse effects on women who were battered. I spoke passionately with my clients about abuse by their boyfriend or husband. Lamentably, some took the violence in stride, not considering it an important issue in their custody battle or divorce. It required years of education and arguments to enlighten the community on the ramifications of abuse and what protections were needed.

Numerous abused clients had difficulty concentrating. They lived in fear. The man was calm; he excised his demons by releasing them with his punches or kicks. Generally, he had a paid job; she worked caring for the kids and sometimes also worked outside the home, especially if the father/boyfriend wasn't working. The world closed in on her. She was less and less in contact with other family members and friends, especially if her skin showed bruises. Ultimately, the children were harmed emotionally and sometimes physically. I struggled to explain these circumstances in depth to DSS workers, to help them understand the services women needed to keep their children from being taken away. In court, I argued their issues, hoping the judge would comprehend why the man seemed so calm in contrast to his wife or girlfriend.

In one of my first cases at NHLAA, I was appointed to represent Charlotte in a DSS hearing. The department wanted to take away her children and to grant temporary custody to her husband's parents, even though they were not fit to care for the kids.

When I first met her, she was twenty-six, a little taller than me, with disheveled brown hair and a distant stare reminiscent of an elderly person with early dementia. I quickly discovered she was drinking too much to release the body pain from her thirty-year-old husband's regular punches and smacks. They had a five-year-old daughter and a two-year-old son. Her husband, Jed, worked at odd jobs, not earning much. Their income was supplemented by the state.

In our first meeting, I learned she had married him to escape her family. Her parents argued all the time. Older siblings had flown the coop early. She became pregnant, and her parents forced her to marry Jed.

We discussed her possible options. In tears, she softly said, "I'm out of options. I can't live with my parents again. I deeply love my kids, but it's so hard to care for them by myself. I don't want Jed's parents to have them. They're as crazy as mine. I know I'm messed up. I want to stop drinking and not live with Jed; I don't love him. He doesn't love me. And he's really not interested in the kids."

I listened to her distressing words and recognized she was smart with potential to stand up for herself. In some ways, I saw myself in her. I didn't have choices in my childhood. I escaped in my late teens and early twenties by drinking and sexing, blocking my fears. I could easily have ended up in her situation.

The staunch advocate in me pushed hard against the hearing officer's efforts. Initially the children were put in foster care, not with Jed's parents, while the case moved through the court system. That gave Charlotte time to get counseling, stop drinking, and spend more quality time with her children.

I obtained a restraining order against her husband and represented her in the divorce, arguing he should not have unsupervised visits with the children as he made no attempt to get help for himself. I educated both the DSS worker and the judge about the ramifications of the cycle of domestic violence abused women experienced.

Ultimately, Charlotte obtained custody of her children. But to my naïve surprise, after a year she returned to Jed. The cycle of her dysfunctional life continued. She again lost custody. I chastised myself. *I failed in my work! Maybe I should have done more, continued following her life, supporting her.* But I finally acknowledged there were too many lives like Charlotte needing representation. I was their advocate, not their mother. I never learned what happened to Charlotte, but I hoped she turned her life around.

Instead of continually berating myself, over time friends and I educated the community and the police on domestic violence, especially explaining why women stay or return. We achieved changes in the law so the abused could obtain restraining orders and abusers could be arrested. We negotiated the first domestic violence guidelines with the New Haven Police Department and later negotiated the same with the Connecticut Chiefs of Police Association.

A group of us established the first battered women's shelter in New Haven. In the beginning, we didn't want even the police to know the location. We warned the women to keep the shelter secret for the safety of themselves and other residents; otherwise, such action could cause the shelter to close. Over the years, the community grew more enlightened, and we were funded by grants and the government.

Early on when the shelter first opened, our biggest fear for the women was the nighttime hours when we usually had only one staff person on duty. The board members made a plan that if one of us were called by staff, we would call the others, and all would immediately drive to the shelter. Mary Ann and I lived about four miles from the shelter. One Sunday at two in the morning, we received a call and began the call tree to other board members. We grabbed pots, frypans, and a baseball bat for protection and sped through stoplights to get there. By the time we arrived, the irate husband was gone. Yet, too many irate men kept us busy.

One evening Mary Ann and I tried to help a thirty-five-year-old sex worker we met on the street who had been beaten by her pimp. With a disillusioned gaze, she told us, "My family no longer wants anything to do with me. They think they know what's best for me because they're rich, and they want to put me in some kind of institution." We suggested she stay in our shelter. She said no. We succumbed to letting her stay with us for a few days to heal. She slept in our extra bedroom. At night we heard her body turning and banging against the wall together with eerie cries. As she became stronger, she called her family. They agreed to help her and let her live at home, but shortly thereafter we met her back on the streets. It was another harsh way to learn we couldn't help everyone; we could only be there if we were needed.

I didn't have choices in my own childhood. Yet, thankfully, I had aspirations, even though at the time I didn't know what that word meant. As my Home kid friends later reminded me, even in the orphanage I was always acting like a social worker, giving advice and being an advocate when I believed the actions of the counselors were unfair or unnecessary. The dream of being Superman—well, Superwoman—supported my loneliness and gave me purpose. I survived by seeking purpose.

Now in this new stage of my life, I struggled again to find purpose, to find meaning—to thrive, not just survive.

Chapter 21

Choices

Walls and space seemed to determine my interior needs. Finally, my dream of a home was coming true. I was proactively making my own choices—allowing light or dark, my privacy, the size of the rooms. Home! It was a new sense of the word that had controlled my life thus far. I had more awareness of my choices. *Am I yet my own person, undefined by the outside world?* I was far from such rose-colored idealism. But each step was forward moving.

I named my property Crumblesweat. People often asked what the name meant. I joked, "I'm crumbling under the sweat of designing and building my home." A little true. But really, the name came to me in a dream months before, when my mind was in the processing stage. The dream confirmed my daunting decision. I had drawn out the placement of the rooms while in New Haven, after an architect friend designed the model.

One early morning, a cool breeze against my face, no bug protection necessary, I stood on the deck prior to Sue and Niki's arrival, walking around my empty structure, pragmatically foreseeing the rooms of my dream home. My downstairs bedroom would be in the northwest corner of the house with two windows, one on the north and the other on the west, both facing the wooded area to protect from the winter cold.

I walked a few steps to what would be the adjoining small bathroom. Even though I'd lived in apartments and houses with a private bathroom, my chest tightened, awakening the memory of shared bathrooms and showers in the orphanage.

On the other side of the bathroom would be the area of my potential small laundry room, next to my future kitchen.

The rest of the downstairs would be open concept with an L-shaped kitchen, dining room, and living room. Large windows and a sliding glass door would face south, ensuring direct sun in the winter and less in the summer, when the sun is higher in the sky. Later, after moving in, I discovered the two windows became mirrors at night when the outside lights were on, and I danced and exercised as if I were in a dance studio, with my only audience the tall pine and oak trees. I had no shades or blinds on the windows. I hoped to eventually add a grassy yard with flowers and bushes and a large dog pen for Maya, the extent of the length of the house and wide enough to play catch.

Two windows were planned for the kitchen, on the north and east sides. The dining room would face east, with two tall windows. I envisioned sitting at my dining room table, looking through the sliding glass door on the south and feeling the warmth of the morning sun through the east windows.

The upstairs was designed to be half the width of the downstairs, allowing for a high ceiling with skylights facing south. I envisioned the sun shining through the skylights lighting the house on a cool summer day, with the wood floors reflecting the movement of trees—a meditation.

A windy gust unexpectedly embraced me, and for a few moments

I stood still, numb with both belief and disbelief; my dream home was vividly becoming a reality.

I looked up, envisioning my second-floor area. The upstairs would include an office on the northwest corner with three windows. It would be a place to do office work I likely will take home since I never get all my work done in the office. The second floor would also hold my guest bedroom. Between the two would be a bathroom.

A walkway would run outside the upstairs rooms, along the six-foot chimney, with bookcases on either side of the chimney, adding more privacy to the rooms instead of closing them off with walls. I looked forward to being upstairs looking down to the open floor plan.

The downstairs part of the chimney would be in the living room for the wood stove, with the backside warming the bathroom and laundry room, as well as the heat rising upstairs.

To my delight, the housebuilding glided like a strong breeze. We had finished framing the first-floor north and west side walls a week earlier and commenced working on the south and east sides of the house. The early June weather was mostly mellow. My clothes and body were sprayed with protection from the blackflies, although one day when my guard was down, they had a tasty meal, giving me two big bites on my ears and a few on my neck. Many Mainers swore by Avon's Skin-So-Soft bath oil as a cure to keep the blackflies away. Since it was difficult nailing while wearing my hat and insect netting, I used the bath oil, even though it was slippery and I smelled like a mix of potent perfumes from the makeup counter in Macy's.

In a few days, I stood facing south and looked through the frames of what would be the two large windows and sliding glass door to eyeball my view—an open area of rough ground, eventually to be grass, with woods about six hundred feet away. I was framing a new life—not the frame of the fields past the wrought-iron gate of the orphanage or the cow pasture on my aunt's farm or the streets and small trees outside our Brooklyn apartment. My new optimistic frame would be sitting on my wood deck reading a book, Maya chasing squirrels in her pen, and the chickadees and cardinals eating from a bird feeder.

While living in the rental, the cats stayed inside gazing out the windows, even though they itched to romp outdoors. They'd played outside in New Haven during the daytime, surviving cars, dogs, active kids, and even raccoons, skunks, and opossum. They were streetwise. Hopefully, they wouldn't encounter any worse here. That would be a decision for later.

At the house site, music played on the radio, loud and energetic, like the intense physical work we were doing. It kept us upbeat. Sometimes I would rather have been dancing to it! Surprisingly, I had become physically stronger. I lifted and carried the heavy wall studs and helped with nailing, while adjusting to the hot weather.

We fell into a routine. Each day started about seven and ended around four, with a lunch break where the three of us sat cross-legged in a circle on the house deck, music lowered, to chat and eat, surrounded by tools and sawhorses. Every morning I walked Maya before work, and then at day's end, I took her for an extra-long walk or played ball, depending upon whether I was running on empty.

The days tumbled into each other, and I lost track. It was odd, not having client appointments or looking at a calendar. My to-do list was also shorter—sleep, build, walk Maya, try to study for the bar, and eat. In the dark of night, I sat on the deck of my rental, looking up and viewing a full moon, the stars bright and Blue Hill Mountain sharply visible in my view. I was a happy camper.

We finished building the first-floor walls, framed the windows, and began working on the upstairs floor. I helped carry three twelve-foot, four-by-ten-inch bulky, dense crossbeams to run along the length of the upstairs from east to west, to which the knotted-wood floorboards would be attached. These floorboards had a dual purpose; they were also the downstairs ceiling. The work was physically challenging and draining, even though I was working much less hard than my builders. As I turned to pick up some nails, I took a deep, slow breath and smiled in wonderment. *How did this Jewish girl from the streets of Brooklyn who never lifted a hammer find herself living in rural Maine?!* At times it was surreal, dreamlike.

We finally built steps off the west wall to the second floor. Workdays continued quickly with friendly weather, meaning enough wind to hamper the blackfly attacks. I could now walk up to the second level instead of needing to climb a ladder.

Relief. Three New Haven friends visited and cheerfully helped with the lifting and nailing for two days. My rental filled with pajama party energy, all of us sharing stories and laughing out loud. Jeanie did a pantomime of me from a Halloween party at which I had dressed as a nun. "You looked so great . . . a white bandanna on your forehead, a black slip hanging from the bandanna behind you, and a white slip wrapped around the top of a long black dress, topped with a white rope around your waist!" They knew me and Mary Ann and found it especially funny that I had worn a nun's costume when Mary Ann, who had been a nun, never wore a habit.

Laughter. So good. So needed. There were more shared memories, laughs, photos, and meals—lobster, clams, and corn on the cob. For a number of hours, I was back in my New Haven life. Their visit rejuvenated me and left me relaxed, trusting that as my past life converged with my new life, it would bring a welcome sense of wholeness.

Chapter 22

Skyward

The walls of the second floor not yet standing, I looked skyward, open to the world around me. The tops of the trees made visible the distant mountain and lake, not the roofs of city houses almost touching each other. My knees weakened, not from the height, but from the realization that little Roberta's persistent dream of an enduring home was coming true. This was so different from living in places over which I had no control. I recalled living with my father in Brooklyn, how he loved to sit in the backyard of our four-family apartment house or go to the beach and swim in the ocean. He needed space, just as I did. Maybe his need for space was triggered by spending so much of his life driving a cab.

I returned to my rental and called him, picturing him sitting at the edge of his bed or in the living room in his big lounge chair. He answered from the living room where, having had dinner, he was drinking tea with a tablespoon of strawberry jam in his favorite wide glass, probably his fifth glass of the day.

We talked casually. He then reminded me, "It's the beginning of Shavuot. I'm going to try to go to synagogue."

"I know, that's why I called you."

Shavuot is the Festival of Weeks, a major religious holiday but not as significant as Passover or Sukkot to those Jewish people not particularly religious, like me. Shavuot commemorated the time when the first fruits were harvested, celebrating the giving of the Torah at Mount Sinai.

My father and I chatted, as we generally did on the various holidays. He asked me how the construction was going, and, as usual, before I could fully share my excitement, he jumped elsewhere, telling me, "I've been sitting outside with the neighbors. Mrs. Steiner, you know, the lady in the gray house, made me a plate of chicken and potatoes with gravy. Too much gravy! Not as good as mine. I gave most of the chicken to Luba, instead of her cat treats."

We also discussed his and Fred's upcoming visit in August. He was looking forward to seeing my partially built home but was nervous about flying from a combination of his age and health. He traveled around Europe as a child waiting to come to America but since then had not traveled outside the East Coast—and never on a plane.

We hung up, and I relaxed in bed dwelling on my religious heritage. I suddenly laughed out loud; the cats' ears perked up as I recollected how often in the orphanage I had bombarded the rabbi by questioning the stories in the Bible.

These days I was far from religious, although deep down I grappled with my Jewishness or maybe my life's experiences as a Jewish woman. I'd always been torn about religion, mine and others, especially as religion in our world seemed mostly to cause hostilities between people. My feminist sensibility rankled when I considered how unequally women were treated in religion. While dedicated believers had surely decoded the religious justifications more devotedly or loyally, I couldn't.

I recalled the rabbi telling me women could not be rabbis. Times had changed; in more progressive branches, there were a few women rabbis.

When I entered the world of full-time work after high school, still living at home with my dad and brother, reality and religion blended. I yearned to attend college, but in my second year of high school, an uncle told me, "Roberta, your dad can't afford college for both you and your brother, and of course Fred has to go to college." I didn't have the courage to rage at my uncle, and I couldn't show anger at my father; it would invoke his unbroken remorse for leaving us in the orphanage. Reluctantly, I changed my plan and prepared myself to be a secretary, learning stenography for dictation.

I grudgingly accepted my uncle's opinion; I didn't question it. But not for long. I had the urge to learn more than what high school had taught me, even though I hadn't been the best of students. Trying to fit in had taken priority. While working, I took college courses when I could. Entering the workforce was an additional push for more education as I quickly became disillusioned, especially having to circumvent the sexual demands of my male bosses, like a football player running with the ball deflecting his attackers. Sometimes I used my sexuality, thinking a pay raise was more important than my self-respect, but I soon discovered that, emotionally at least, it really wasn't.

My world of family and friends were mainly Jewish. In my teen years, we talked about everything but religion, except with the rabbi in the orphanage. I wasn't familiar with other religions except from reading books that included religion as part of the story. I studied Hebrew in high school, thinking that would be the easiest language to learn as I already knew a little.

My father's synagogue was Orthodox, the strictest denomination regarding religious customs, although he wasn't devoted to following them. It was the closest synagogue within walking distance. Religious Jews didn't drive on certain holidays or on the Sabbath between sunset Friday and dusk on Saturday. Later, when we moved, he attended a Conservative synagogue. In his synagogue, congregants prayed separately, women upstairs and men downstairs. I didn't appreciate or understand that separation. My father tried to explain the purpose, but it was beyond my understanding, especially when my brother had his bar mitzvah at age thirteen and I had to be upstairs with my women relatives.

We didn't attend synagogue regularly—mostly on holidays and sometimes for Friday services. On Yom Kippur, the Day of Atonement, we'd fast for twenty-four hours. I'd go to synagogue with my father during the fast, but then when it got close to the twenty-fourth hour, I guiltily ate potato chips with friends. I trusted God wouldn't punish me because I was hungry. But the real guilt I carried was that I no longer had a desire to be a rabbi, as I had when I was young.

One of my first secretarial jobs was working in a law office for Mrs. P, who was Jewish and regularly attended synagogue. She was also the first woman lawyer I ever met. I had worked for other women in different types of businesses, many of whom had short tempers and cold demeanors. She was not significantly different; she was a stickler for detail with an eye on my trash to make sure I wasn't wasting paper.

One slow day when we were alone in the office, I hesitantly asked her, "How come Jews don't have to confess to a rabbi like Catholics do with a priest?" This question arose when I learned the other secretary in the office had to ask for a priest's forgiveness because she had hickeys on her neck.

That question led to a back-and-forth discussion. "Roberta, Jews don't require a mediator between us and God. The rabbi educates us on the Bible and leads us in prayer."

"I know. I had a bat mitzvah."

In her businesslike voice, she continued, "Jews can talk to God directly and trust he will give us direction. The more we learn the lessons of the Bible, the more we understand what is important, as well as the subtleties of figuring out what is right or wrong. We have the responsibility to make our own decisions and decide if we need forgiveness. We have a big burden through life. Our sins can't be expelled with nine Hail Marys."

I stupidly uttered, "But that sure makes life a lot harder for us."

To my surprise, she didn't get upset; instead, she relaxed in her chair and grinned. "Yes, we can question our religious beliefs and traditions. I don't believe Catholics are able to do that. Unfortunately, that's why some Jews educate themselves out of their religion!"

I sat up in my chair, eyes widened with surprise. I didn't understand what she meant about educating ourselves out of our religion. So I smiled, thanked her for answering my questions, and quickly left her office.

Looking back, I can see Mrs. P was right—I had in many ways questioned myself out of my religion. I enjoyed many of the traditions and cried easily during the service when I was in the synagogue on holidays, the tears connected to the tragic history into which I was born and my father's bloodcurdling memories of his young life in Russia. Yet I considered myself a spiritual person, always searching, hungering, for primal understanding and meaning.

I was also a lawyer with a different consciousness than Mrs. P; I finally understood her history. She had to be formidable and forceful; so much was against her as a woman lawyer. Regardless, I followed in her footsteps, always trying to be forceful as an attorney and as a woman, many times repressing my emotions and passion.

As I stood on the second floor of my unfinished house, I

challenged my unfinished self. I stretched skyward with a smile, hands in the air, looking forward to the open world around me, and thought of the words from Helen Reddy's song, "I am strong / I am invincible / I am woman!" Well, I was surely not invincible, but I had confidence that I could—women could—be who we chose to be, with all our imperfections, strengths, and sensitivity, without shame. Well . . . at least in some countries.

Chapter 23
Whirlwind

Sizzling July days arrived. Finally, the blackflies were gone as we positioned the upstairs two-by-four wall studs as well as nailed plywood on each corner to strengthen them, similar to the first floor. Sue was in a no-nonsense mode, framing the spaces for the windows, which allowed me vivid views of the outside from upstairs. The north side was mainly hardwood and pine trees interspersed with small bushes. When we relaxed, I spotted cardinals and other birds dancing through the trees. My plan was to open the area around the house. Even though the trees would protect the house from the winter winds, as on the west side, I didn't want to live in a cocoon. I preferred being able to catch sight of deer and other wild animals through the trees, especially when the snow was on the ground and particularly at night under a full moon.

Lifting and nailing had become *almost* second nature to me. *Wow, I can't believe I thought that!* My body was stronger, sweatier, but ached like when I fell off a bike accelerating downhill. I made a new friend, a chiropractor, who helped with the pain in my neck, shoulders, and back. In my hectic life in New Haven, neck pain from reading and typing had been healed regularly with massage. Life here was also hectic, just different, working on building and studying for the bar. In New Haven when I daydreamed that Maine life would slow me down, it was obviously vacation thinking. Now I couldn't imagine I'd ever have a non-hectic life. It seemed to be in my nature. My mind was always working, making mental as well as written to-do lists.

Building the walls was completed within a week, and we next framed the roof rafters. I made a surprisingly joyful discovery—mosquitos weren't particularly active during sunny daylight hours. But at night, as I sat on the deck of the rental and watched the fireflies whirl like ballet dancers on a stage, the mosquito buzzing tested my perseverance. I laughed at myself; I was still such a city person!

The air was pungent with the scent of scraps of new wood mixed with wildflowers. I lifted the rafters for the roof with Sue and Niki but wasn't up there setting them in place. It was too high up for me! I carried the sheets of plywood over to the house for nailing, with Niki cutting out spaces for the two skylights, one larger than the other. I took pictures of these two strong Wonder Women sitting up there, so free and unafraid, par for the course in their lives.

While they did their Atlantean work, the red brick chimney emerged from earth to sky above the house. This detail work was slow for a couple of weeks. On the first level, the mason laid some of the bricks in layers below the mantel, giving a feel of dimension to the bricks that were intermittently mixed with blended dark and light colors.

As the house grew, so did my activism in the community. With two friends, I attended the Take Back the Night rally in Bangor, its first, enjoying participating without having to organize it (as I had in New Haven). Almost one hundred people of all ages, mainly women, carried colorful signs, sang, and chanted. As the music intensified, we also stomped to the beat. It was so nice to hear speeches with more substance than rhetoric. Women had come a long way with this issue but had much further yet to go, reminding me of my early experiences in New Haven when I was a newbie activist, unsure of myself, wanting to fit in, trying to hide my apprehension.

July Fourth celebrations were planned in my new town. Orland had about two thousand residents and a total area of around fifty-three square miles. A river ran through it where the festival was held, against the backdrop of a white church and houses on both sides of the banks. I walked the short road along the river, stopped at booths of food and handmade items for sale, and chatted with strangers as I bought cookies and potholders. Dogs barked at each other and their owners, begging for morsels. Attending my first festival was to experience one of those charming small towns seen in many television movies. It was a good feeling—like I belonged in this tranquil, homey place, which unexpectedly reminded me of walking with my aunt in Flanders on Halloween, collecting goodies from homeowners on the country road. My afternoon ended standing on a homemade wooden raft with three friends, waving colorful flags, and fervently holding on to a corner post trying not to fall into the cold water as we struggled, laughing, to balance the raft. It was a welcome break from building and studying.

I also attended my first political meeting of the Bucksport Area Peace Action Committee, which supported being a Sister City to a town in Nicaragua. We were ten dedicated people of different ages and different styles of dress, including two old hippies. I was enthused that my new home had a world interest, like my New Haven activism. Bucksport, the town next door to Orland, had more traditional town amenities—a supermarket, various stores, a waterfront, a paper mill, and a police department.

I was slowly finding my way. I felt safe in these picture-perfect communities, until disbelief and fear struck with the murder of a young gay man, Charlie Howard, in Bangor. Three underage boys threw him off a bridge into the Kenduskeag Stream, where he drowned. I doubled over in pain when I heard the news and, later, cried with friends attending the memorial service at the bridge. This horror, coming so unexpected in my new home, briefly made me question my move, while at the same time reminding me that hate knows no borders. Unsettled, my whirlwind of busyness and less sleep continued.

The mixed smells of old books, musty file cabinets, and chairs hit me as I walked into the student legal services office when I visited the University of Maine campus. I'd be working there at the end of August. Several desks and tables overspread the huge room with a few small private areas without doors in the back. Work signs and odds and ends covered the walls. I presumed I'd be sitting in the private area. Large windows spanned one side of the room with the hall and doors on the other sides. I took a deep breath, a hint of a smile playing about my lips as I thought about how different my new world would be from my office and life as a lawyer in New Haven.

Paige and Gene, the two long-term paralegals with whom I'd be working, greeted me. We met when I was interviewed for the job by the attorney I was to replace and some students from the student board. In fact, the student board was my employer, to my disappointment. I would have preferred the university as my employer, feeling that would have been more financially secure.

Both Paige and Gene, in their late twenties, worked full-time. When I settled in, we'd be hiring five students to train and work with us. I loved teaching and looked forward to that part of the job. We sat around a table, and they shared the ins and outs and customs of the office as well as university protocols, exciting me about this new challenge in my professional life.

Paige, casually but professionally dressed, with blond hair surrounding a sweet Irish face, reminded me, "The student body is quite diverse. Besides the normal-age students, many are married and some have children. We represent graduate students as well as undergrads." Gene, bearded, married, with an effusive smile, added, "We handle interesting cases—landlord-tenant issues, drinking and driving and loss of license, consumer rip-offs, even divorces."

We reviewed a few pending matters that the current attorney was managing until I arrived. It was clear the two were both quite competent with easygoing personalities. My body relaxed, and I looked forward to this new venture. After two hours, I said goodbye and took a leisurely walk around the campus with its wide central quadrangle, currently quiet before the storm of students blew into their dorms.

Arriving back to Maya and the cats, the reality of my new life engulfed me. Evening plans wrapped around studying for the bar. Reading material had taken over the kitchen table, my alternate desk. I recalled taking the exam in Connecticut, where I'd had most of the summer to study, even while working at the NHLAA office and beginning my friendship with Mary Ann. Juggling now wasn't so simple, especially when I spoke to my father and learned he'd been hospitalized for a biopsy and removal of a bump in his groin area. Guilt flooded me because I couldn't be there for him. I knew it was a minor operation, but it intensified the reality of my distance from New York. We talked daily, and boundless relief spilled over me like a waterfall when the biopsy was negative.

I burrowed into my small couch in my rental, striving to hide, overcome by life at the moment, recognizing that as much as I had need for my new home, land, space and animals, I also needed to be active in the world. I thought I wanted an easygoing life in Maine, but I couldn't seem to take much time to relax and play. Instead I filled my time with more projects. *Aren't building the house and studying for the bar enough?* It became a struggle balancing my desire to be engaged in the beauty of this place and my need for purposeful work that helped others. I didn't want to become overinvolved and burn out again, but I needed to make time as well for what was important to me politically and personally. I seemed to have forgotten the lessons of my hectic life in New Haven.

At the same time, all the tasks of building my home carried additional fears. I was confronted with extra expenses requiring a mortgage as well as the knowledge that the house wouldn't be finished by the time I had to start my new job. The salary from my job wasn't going to cover my expenses. I'd need to develop a private practice on the side, something I hadn't considered in my planning. More importantly, I needed to find a way to center and find balance—maybe return to therapy. It had helped me in law school and in New Haven.

My need to learn and understand competed with so many goals and desires, creating a constant inner clash brought on by all I wanted to do and be in this lifetime.

Living in my rental should have been a beneficial time for contemplation, making choices, and getting to know myself better, but it was bittersweet. I was no longer with a partner. Seven years of sharing was gone. The dream Mary Ann and I had of moving here together was gone. I still suffered the loss of our relationship, experiencing flashbacks of our evolution together and tenderness shared. We talked on the phone, and I cried when we hung up, especially when she said she missed me. I got upset hearing how well she was doing back in the house, *our house*, with Donna and her cats, while I was swamped, sometimes sinking in self-pity.

The last week before the bar exam was my alone time to study. Despite that, I took a break on Saturday night and had dinner with three new friends: Holly, Kelly, and Nancy. The comforting scents of apple cinnamon pie, sweet potatoes, and turkey greeted me as I arrived at Holly and Kelly's house. Their friendly black lab jumped on me as I sighted a piano in the corner and a chimney and woodstove in the middle of the living room. I loved the hominess they had created together as long-term partners; they lived about three miles from me.

Sharing in the evening was Nancy, who was active in the Bucksport Area Peace Action Committee that I had recently joined. I immediately sensed a connection to her and her humor, big smile, and naturalness. She reminded me of myself with her commitment to activism while at the same time being absorbed in a difficult long-term relationship. She had helped create the battered women's movement in Maine, particularly in Bangor, before I helped jumpstart it in New Haven. We shared our experiences, and she tried to convince me to get involved with Spruce Run, Bangor's battered women's organization. I said I'd think about it—but not right away or soon. Too much was on my plate.

My studying was over. Cool breezes gently tempered a warm day as I drove back from city to country after the long bar exam taken in Portland, two and a half hours south. I stayed overnight in a motel and didn't fall asleep until eleven thirty. But it was over! No more studying.

Back with Maya and the cats, I hit the bed with a tired smile of emancipation—also, tears of relief and a gist of unsparing loneliness that I had no intimate partner with whom to share my joy.

Now to wait. In early September, I'd learn if I passed.

A whirlwind month I hope not to undergo again. As I thought those words, I tapped myself on the head. I had choices. I made my own bed. *I am the whirlwind*—or not.

Chapter 24

Blending

At seven thirty on a Monday morning, I sat alone on the first floor of my unfinished home, the outside encased in Tyvek and insulation board. The wind glided around my neck, the temperature a pleasant sixty-five degrees, yet I sat rooted in the spot, kneading my fingers into my thighs like my cats do, maybe to lighten both my tense muscles and my uncertain mind. Sue and Niki had finished their work, having completed the shingling of the roof and installation of the glass for the skylights. The next stages included the siding and adding the interior walls, as well as the electricity and plumbing.

Again I questioned myself. *Can I really do this? Will others follow my lead?* Maybe I relied too much on Sue's directions because of my limitations, especially as she had been my teacher in the housebuilding course. I depended on her, like a child following her mother's directions or demands, even when at times that part of our relationship frustrated me.

At the suggestion of some friends, I hired Ron, a tall, thin, quiet man in his forties. He was experienced doing siding work. I'd have to learn from him, too, or anyone I hired—a challenging admission for this woman who still fantasized about being Superwoman.

Ron drove up in his blue truck. My thoughts weighed on me as I

stood to greet him. After small-talk about the weather and the hours
of work, we began. Over the next days and weeks, my flesh worked
up a healthy sweat using the electric saw, nailing, cutting, carrying,
and setting up scaffolding as we moved from area to area putting
up siding. Ron was quiet and shy—not macho. The tightness in my
body loosened, my bones became stronger, and my mind's to-do list
decreased for a while.

I became less inhibited about trying. Maybe it was easier to try
when working with a man because I expected and demanded more
of myself and he probably expected less of me, a woman. I wanted
to feel like the competent lawyer I was. With Sue and Niki I bore a
competitive edge, an easy thing to do since I'm naturally averse to
hard physical labor in the hot beating sun. Now I was more effort-
lessly adjusting to my new life. When Ron wasn't around, I worked
by myself, albeit slowly. Standing alone, I stepped back in awe. *Wow,
I'm really building my house!* I'd had so many dreams and plans about
the move to Maine, this building project, and so many fears, but I
was doing it. Every now and then I pinched myself. This was my new
reality.

While the house was slowly becoming a home, my life in
Maine was slowly *feeling* like home. With the bar exam over and
not yet having started my job, I relaxed into life and attended a
Shabbat dinner with two friends from Connecticut who now lived
a fifteen-minute drive from me. The house was warm from summer
breezes. The blended aroma of chicken, fresh mixed vegetables, and
salad dressing floated through me. Before we ate, Hannah stood by
the table and lit the candles. She covered her eyes to say the blessing
before eating.

In New York and New Haven, I rarely participated in a traditional Shabbat dinner or attended synagogue services on Friday

nights, except sometimes on holidays. Now such an evening gave me contentment and a few hours of belonging. For religious Jews, Shabbos is the time each week, from sunset Friday until darkness on Saturday, when one stops working, traveling, and doing, and instead shares with family, community, synagogue. It's a time for reflection. For me, it was a time to just be. It was two serene hours with Hannah and Fran and three other women who joined us, sharing in meaningful conversation, away from housebuilding and politics. Driving home, I decided I'd try to make room for this peaceful, reflective time more often, but just as I thought those words, I somehow knew I likely wouldn't; maybe it would happen sometime in the future.

While Ron and I worked on the siding, I also juggled meeting with the electrician and the plumber and getting a bank loan. I chose to spend a little more than I'd planned for the electric and plumbing to ensure everything was properly done. I also made the weighty decision to move into the house while the interior was incomplete— another challenge for this organized, overwhelmed woman. This move was definitely a spiritual journey of sorts!

Sue and Niki returned for a few days to finish some odds and ends needing completion. At the same time I discovered the gable end vents were too small, and I needed a roof vent. Another unexpected cost.

Just when I was irritated from working long, hot days, I garnered a timely surprise. Five friends visited from New Haven. They helped with nailing the siding, plus cleaning around the house, piling kindling, and picking up nails lying everywhere. Again, two worlds blended into one.

I was like a host, even though my friends were independent and learned easily. Some had already worked on their own homes in Connecticut. Still, it was hard for me to be dependent and accept what was generously offered. Maybe the fallacy was thinking that to welcome help meant I was dependent. Someone truly self-assured and independent could graciously accept help without guilt. In between working, my friends and I took a needed break. We canoed and swam in the lake, walked in the fog under a semitransparent full moon, and ate like tourists.

A new friend, Allan, much older than me and retired, whom I met through local friends, offered to help with the siding at a reasonable hourly rate. This tall, bearded man in overalls was a talented worker with a strong sense of his abilities. He had built his own home. At the same time, Sue stayed to help with the siding. I was grateful, as even with this extra help, siding was a slow process. Not surprisingly, Sue and Allan clashed, requiring me to mediate egos. I tried to be calm and accept it all with grace, but I wasn't too successful. Instead I took a day off to shop for appliances and fixtures. A week of fog and dampness didn't diminish egos, but work got done.

Sometimes I considered whether I was crazy not to hire a contractor. The idea of doing it myself seemed so exciting when I was in Connecticut dreaming I could do it all. Now, in my doldrums, I thought that if I should ever write a housebuilding book, I would name it "Never Again," for those people who read all those idealistic building books that make it sound so easy. Maybe that would be for others; at this moment, too late for me.

Sunshine dropped in my lap when an orphanage friend Leslie and her boyfriend suddenly showed up, having been camping through Maine. She lived on the East Coast, and we kept in touch, visiting every now and then. Leslie and I also remained in touch with Josie, who had moved to California. These were my two closest Home friends. Now contact with Josie was by phone and mail. The Yonkers orphanage closed shortly after my brother and I returned to live with our father. The remaining kids moved to Queens. Josie and Leslie lived in group homes until age eighteen, while I lived in Brooklyn.

Leslie looked the same as when I had seen her about six years before. She was the opposite of me in dress and personality: a poet who worked as a counselor and lived her great love of traveling the world, a female alone experiencing dangerous countries. She still wore her hippie clothes wherever she went. She carried a backpack, stayed in hostels or camps, trusted and learned from people she met, and sent me cards and small gifts from around the world. She never seemed to fit in, so she made *that* her attribute, her character. I was the opposite of her—organized, obsessive—except when I let loose dancing.

We sat in the small living room of my rental and shared our memories of life in the orphanage, a habitual conversation, both of us releasing pain and laughs. As we sipped wine, I asked her if she kept in touch with her mother. She confessed, "Me and my mother are on different planets. I barely knew her growing up. When we got together, which was rarely, it was like a battle between two strangers. She had no empathy or ability to connect with me or my sister. Remember when she tried to beat you up in the orphanage after I told her we fought a lot?"

I belly laughed. "How could I forget? I hid until the counselors got her out of the building! I was scared shitless."

Now that we were older, Leslie revealed she never knew who her father was; her mother had so many "boyfriends." She shrugged her shoulders and sat up straight. "I've accepted our lack of relationship. I'm better without her in my life."

As I listened to her words, I pictured her young, thin, sad, lost face. Her eyes were crossed, and kids had made fun of her. Both of us had always been tough because that was the only way to be.

We shared a day of walks, swimming, and catching up, and then she and her boyfriend moved on in their travels. As I sat on the couch, with Maya cuddled next to me and the cats sleeping, I thought about Josie, Leslie, and me—the three musketeers, all of us without mothers. Josie's mother died in childbirth. Her father was quite elderly and couldn't care for her, an only child.

Three days later in a salon I frequented to get my hair cut, the young owner of the shop had pictures on the wall of two smiling older women: her mother and grandmother. She looked up at the pictures with adoration and raved, "They were so much fun and supported me in everything I wanted to do. They could be tough, too, especially when I was young, but I always sensed their love. I'm so happy my daughter had time with them." The name of her shop was a combination of the first name of each.

I smiled and walked out mumbling that I unhappily didn't have those experiences. Sitting in my car, I couldn't control my tears. I had never met either of my grandmothers, and my memories of my mother were a six-year-old's dream. Back at the rental, I looked at my parents' wedding picture, pulled out my mother's wedding band from its special wooden box, swirled it around my finger, and for thirty minutes tortured myself with dream memories we didn't share.

Leslie and me: motherless but blending into the world; always attempting to take charge; building our dreams—for Leslie, one country, one poem at a time; for me now, one nail, one board of siding at a time.

Chapter 25
Recognition

A full moon veiled itself in hazy orange clouds. I went to bed early to have the energy to clean the rental for my father and brother's first visit. At four thirty, Maya's bark woke me. Peering out the window, I spotted a black bear in the front yard. I was now truly initiated into Maine life!

The bear stood within a few feet of me, on all fours, exploring the grass and moving in a leisurely way back into the woods at the side of my rental. His fur appeared glossy, soft, and huggable, like a child's stuffed animal. Maya barked, but I didn't dare let her out. I excitedly woke up friends with my impassioned news. Later when I spoke with the game warden, he reassured me that bears stay away from humans and dogs. This one likely wouldn't return, but I recalled a story about a cub in Baxter State Park that attacked a hiker.

The house siding wasn't yet completed and I soon would be starting my new job, so I hired Frank, who had done the foundation, to finish it up. I relaxed after getting the news that my new mortgage had been approved, so Frank could also install the wall insulation and sheetrock. I decided to extend my stay in the rental for another two weeks, allowing me to breathe more easily and not be so rushed.

Trusting Frank's work, on a sunny late Monday morning, I

picked up my father and brother at the Portland airport for their first short visit to Maine. My father enjoyed the ride, commenting on the hills and valleys: "The fields remind me of the Flanders farm." Arriving from Russia as a teenager, he had lived his life in cities. He only left when we traveled by car on vacations to upstate New York after my brother and I left the orphanage.

While driving, I looked at him through the rearview mirror, his window partially opened, as I eagerly described the different sights. I sensed his nostalgia, his remembrances for what maybe could have been. Fred, sitting up front, was quiet, his normal way of being unless he is doing or explaining something.

I first took them to my building site. My father's initial hesitant question was, "It's beautiful here, but will you be lonely?"

I declared, "No. I have nice neighbors, and friends are nearby. Dad, I told you I chose to live here as I didn't want to live in the city anymore. Shopping's not too close, but driving's easy. Very few stop lights."

Both were enthused about how the house looked, my father smiling more than Fred. I could see Fred's analytical mind working. They walked through the two floors, looking out the window openings. Fred remarked, "There sure are a lot of trees around the house." I smiled. Living in Manhattan, he had forgotten the trees on our Brooklyn street and lacked any memories of the farm in Flanders.

I asked, "Dad, wouldn't you like to be sunning yourself here on a chaise lounge like you did in the backyard of our Brooklyn apartment?" He beamed a smile.

I proudly walked them through every room, explaining how the inside would eventually look. Fred, almost six feet tall, still walking somewhat like the soldier he had once been, took pictures as he asked a lot of questions about the electricity, plumbing, and the underpart of the house, many of which were not easy to answer. Annoyed, I finally said, "I'm not a technical expert; you are. I learned a lot to understand things generally and then hired specialists to do the work."

I grinned at his seriousness but couldn't avoid remembering the scared little boy in the orphanage and his lost dejected face; he had been only two years old when we moved there. When he signed up for the Army at age twenty, I was afraid he might go AWOL not wanting to be confined again, but instead he ended that career as a Specialist E5, the same rank as a sergeant. He attended Brooklyn College and Polytechnic Institute, obtained a bachelor of science degree in electrical engineering and biology, and became an electrical engineer.

Walking through the house with them, I was aware of an inner sense of loneliness, emptiness, like when I moved into my first apartment in Manhattan and was missing them both. The last time the three of us shared an important event in my life was my law school graduation. Even with his shyness, my father's pride had showed on his face; his daughter would be a lawyer. My brother had been pleasant, taking pictures and chatting with my friends.

Fred and I had such divergent life experiences: isolated in early childhood, living in separate buildings in the orphanage, seeing each other only on weekends. We didn't bond until we moved back with our father. That's when we started making memories; we were so opposite in personality and life views but always connected by the experience of shared loss.

After the walk through the house and around the property, I took them to the rental. I had shopped in Bangor earlier in the week, in the one store selling bagels, salami, pickles, and other Jewish treats. I'd stocked up on what I knew they'd appreciate.

They stayed with me on this short trip. We crowded together, family cozy. My father slept in my bed, Fred took the bed left by the owner in another room, and I slept on the couch. Tuesday was sunny and clear with a light breeze and no humidity. I took them to Acadia National Park to experience the awe that originally caused me lightheadedness driving the three and a half miles to the summit of Cadillac Mountain, stopping along the way to sightsee. The road to the top of Cadillac curved and circled, with 360-degree views of the town of Bar Harbor, the ocean, and distant mountains. The side of the road bloomed with rose and blueberry bushes. As I looked down, shaky legs hit me again. Fred had his fancy camera and shot videos and pictures. It was a treat to share it with them, as I'd done with friends.

When we reached the top of Cadillac, I showed them the side of the mountain where the sun first rises in the country and then the side where the sun first sets. I walked with my arm through my father's, making sure he didn't fall. He was no longer the strong man I had known as a young girl. He wore a heavy brown-and-white sweater and, as always, a fedora—this one brown to match his sweater. I made sure he brought sneakers with him, which, as he'd aged, he wore more often even though they were not to his liking.

At one point I scrutinized his ripened and mellow face, misty-eyed with a smidgen of tears on his cheeks, and acknowledged to myself how alike I am to him, not a daughter like her mother. My traits were so reflective of his—sentimental, sensitive, protective when it came to emotional risk-taking, reticent in expressing anger. I witnessed him afraid to live, to remarry, to suffer the pain of the world. Sometimes I asked myself, *Why can't I give and feel for myself all I give and feel for my clients, political work, friends, others?*

There were no answers to these difficult questions on a beautiful day spent with family, seeing my father smile in awe of his surroundings and Fred take pictures as he enjoyed walking around. On the way home, we stopped in Ellsworth, and Fred helped me choose lighting fixtures. I wished I had some of his skills. He was always the technician, even as a kid. In his teens, he built a pendulum clock from scratch, using a set of LED lights in rows and columns that resembled a pendulum swinging back and forth. It brightened our living room wall. I told him to try to sell it to Macy's. It was the type of unique gift wealthy people would buy. He grinned and shrugged his young shoulders, not believing me.

Wednesday arrived too fast, and I took them to the airport. Dad and I hugged fully and Fred and I awkwardly. Driving back, I pondered how different my life would have been if my mother had lived longer, especially during my teen years. In one therapy session in Connecticut, a burst of pain shot through me as I encountered head-on the little girl in me, wrenched from her mother, then her father, put in a strange place, and feeling like a hostage, jailed. I couldn't leave; there were no parents to protect me; I was separated from my brother. I was controlled by adults I didn't know. I recalled my brother's frightened face, but not my own.

I desired to be my mother's daughter. But in this life, I was my father's daughter. He had lived a hostage life in his childhood, even while in a loving family. The hateful anti-Semitism of Tsarist Russia had scattered his family, forcing him to live with strangers in other countries until he came to America at age fifteen to reconnect with his parents and siblings. He and I weren't much different, but unlike him, I wouldn't settle. Even with my insecurities, I was prepared to begin my new law practice, to complete my new home, to begin a new life.

Notification date arrived. Eager to find out if the bar exam results had been posted, I opened my computer and looked up the website.

The list of who passed the Maine bar was posted. My hands trembled even though I was confident that I passed. *Where's my name?* My legs weakened, my mind fearful. I had failed!

Chapter 26

Chutzpah

Chutzpah—a word a friend once suggested for the name of my new home. She reminded me, "Chutzpah represents the guts it took you, all alone, to move to Maine without initially knowing whether you had a job. And . . . with *no* previous experience, you designed and built your home." I didn't use that name for the house but soon assuredly needed chutzpah! Guts. Courage. Belief in myself.

Is this actually happening? Did I really fail the Maine bar? This was a daytime nightmare, one from which I couldn't awaken. My chutzpah sat in a mental cave of paralysis. Disbelief clouded my thinking as an intense hot flash flooded my body, reddening my skin with embarrassment and shame. I sat on the floor of my rental alone and cried.

Just as I had settled into my Maine life, I was once again uprooted, like a bowed tree. Remembrances of so many losses surged through me like the turns of a kaleidoscope. And now, I had finally obtained my bank loan, the house was almost ready to move into, I'd seen sun over the horizon . . . and then this news. *This can't be my reality. It just can't!* In moments of clarity, I told myself I'd not let it pull me down. I knew I was a good lawyer. Maybe I was a lousy test taker, yet I had passed the Connecticut bar the first time. Buried under the covers in bed, I dismally acknowledged I had lacked the energy to devote to serious study while managing and building my home and adjusting to this new life.

So there I was, little orphan Roberta feeling sorry for herself and coming unglued. I was a Connecticut lawyer of eight years, still able to practice in Connecticut and federal courts but not in Maine courts. My body shivered as if an icy gust of wind had thrust me down, recognizing I had to take the Maine bar exam again in February. How would I manage my role as director of SLS without being able to practice? Would I lose the job? Would I be able to finish my housebuilding? Was I a failure?

As I moaned on the phone to Barbara, my ex-business partner in New Haven, she tried to nourish me with words *I* would share with someone in trouble: "It's only a setback; in the scheme of things it's not major. It will only slow you down for another couple of months."

I lamented, "Still, it's painful and humiliating and disrupts my life." No words eased my mind. The thought of telling my father and friends exhausted me.

I had accepted the SLS job anticipating it would be calm compared to my bustling New Haven law practice. I didn't want my life in Maine to revolve around work. I was excited at the thought of training students and paralegals and being a teacher as well as a lawyer. It gave me meaning to touch another's core and excite them to learn and struggle, to not give up—a lesson I needed to now relearn.

I'd only been working at SLS for a few weeks with Paige and Gene, the two paralegals. I was mortified when I told them. My face reddened and my shoulders bent like dead weight as we attempted to figure out how we could get by financially until I passed the bar. They were clearly unnerved, finding it difficult to look directly at me. In shame, I understood. They questioned, "How will cases go forward?" I had no immediate answer. *Think, woman!*

I quickly speculated, "Maybe I could find a local attorney who would help me out pro bono. Then I'd be considered a visiting lawyer and could practice in court as I did when I was waiting to be admitted to the Connecticut bar." I added hesitantly, "I see we have very few cases necessitating court involvement in the next few months." Their faces lit up a little. Oh, I hoped I was right.

I wondered if I'd have to take a cut in pay, even though the pay was so minimal. Already I was earning less than half my income in New Haven. I avoided discussing this issue with them.

Taking a break from wallowing in self-pity, I drove back to my unsettled home life, contemplating my double bind—being a lawyer and *not* able to practice as one, thrown out of the role that had shaped my identity for so long.

It was a consuming challenge to remember there was more that defined me than being a lawyer, more than how *I* allowed society to define me. In the orphanage, I convinced myself I was better than the social workers in helping the younger kids survive. In high school, I saw myself as Little Orphan Annie, not fitting into my new outside world. In my teens and twenties, I used sex to define me as a woman and, later, allowed the law school experience to initially pull down the self-esteem I had built up as a budding feminist.

Roles, definitions—for my sanity I had to outmaneuver my insecurities and shed self-pity about failing the bar. After meeting with some lawyers in Bangor, I became friends with an attorney who agreed to help me without being paid. SLS would keep the same routine, and she would function as the lawyer of record, initially with some help from the previous SLS attorney. I wouldn't have to take a pay cut. It was both a reprieve and a lesson in humility, as asking for help wasn't my forte.

Friends thought I was strong and not falling apart. I didn't feel strong, and at times I did fall apart inside, hidden, so others wouldn't see. *What does it mean to be strong?* I just moved on as necessary, trying to stop overanalyzing or feeling sorry for myself. I always believed that everything had a purpose for our ultimate growth. Now I needed to figure out the purpose of my failing the bar, somewhat avoiding the fact that I hadn't put much effort into studying, or maybe not enough earnest concentration.

I missed reading books that encouraged me in times of stress, like M. Scott Peck's *The Road Less Traveled.* They helped me get through hardships and to eye life with an expanded perspective. But my books were still unpacked, and anyway, I was compelled once again to concentrate on studying for the bar.

Amid my work drama, my house project continued while I lived in the rental. Surprisingly, it was a necessary stay of execution from my nonstop restive mind. Workers arrived on a cloudy weekend with rigging equipment to drill the well. This was noisy and slow. If I had been a kid, I would have thought they might soon hit China! However, in 150 feet, we hit water. Being a city person, I hadn't thought much about where water comes from; I just knew it was there from the faucets and later learned about reservoirs.

While watching the men work, I closed my eyes, and the rush of water transported me back to the river running through the cow fields, along the chicken barn of my aunt's farm in Flanders. I vividly recollected the black-and-white picture in my album of six-year-old me in my skirted bathing suit, standing barefoot on rocks on the side of the river, holding tightly onto the wooden barn wall. I was smiling at my father taking my picture. It was a fond memory of a hopeful time that was short-lived and without the picture possibly not even remembered. That brave young girl was surely still in me.

As the digging and cleaning wrapped up, I stood by, not

participating and instead staring ahead, distracted. Thoughts of office work, housebuilding, and childhood meshed in my head, garbled, like talk radio sounds when you keep switching channels.

I found relief from my incessant internal chatter when I concentrated on the inside of the house. The plumbing and electrical were finally done. Frank and his helper put up the inside insulation and drywall. I had decided having the wall insulation be six inches thick, rather than the traditional four, and the roof insulation twelve inches thick, purposely planned to be warmer than my inefficiently insulated New Haven house.

Walking into my unfinished house over the weekend, I dropped to the floor in astonishment. Tears erupted as I looked at a nauseating mess and wanted to hide, run, dream away life. Instead I spent five hours sweeping and vacuuming a snowfall of sheetrock dust and sawdust, regularly blowing my nose. It was sixty degrees and sunny, with a light breeze. I took breaks for the breeze to wash over me as I relaxed in a deckchair. When my nose cleared, I returned to cleaning. I naïvely thought Frank would have cleaned up after himself!

Traveling back and forth to SLS was a weary forty-five-minute drive each way, but at least I was not battling back-to-back city traffic. My spine and legs stiffened, unused to the daily long trip. In New Haven, my one-way commute had been fifteen minutes. I partially listened to music or news when not fretting over my work predicament, as well as adjusting to leaving my pet family for a full day. This was not emotionally easy, especially since I missed Maya during long workdays. When I returned, we took walks along the lake in the slanting sunlight, stepping on crumbled brown, yellow, and red autumn leaves tumbling from the trees with the cool weather. Sometimes I took her to the house to check on the status of the cleaning work I expected to do on the following weekends until Frank's work was done. *Where is the simple life I anticipated?*

Frank twice returned to finish the inside work, and the snowfall repeated itself. I was told I'd have to live with the dust and a bloody nose from inhaling the construction residue until the walls were painted. Frank graciously gifted me his time to build shelves in the kitchen, bedroom closets, utility room, and downstairs bathroom. I bought a Vermont Castings woodstove and got the chimney pipe installed, a step closer to moving in. My ordered appliances arrived— an electric stove and a secondhand refrigerator.

Finally the work at SLS settled in. My legal cases were meager compared to my New Haven caseload, which had been a perpetual juggling act. Even with the frenzied atmosphere of students coming and going, appointments made on the fly, and chatter like in high school, my mind had more time to process—and it was a relief that no major court cases popped up. I mainly negotiated landlord-tenant matters and drunk driving charges while also training the student assistants.

A treat, almost like ice cream, was to leave the office at the end of my workday not carrying files home to work on. What a difference from my previous work life. In the evenings, I studied for the bar. Life was still busy, but my concentration was rekindled. I had five months until the next exam and relaxed into studying as diligently as I had in Connecticut.

Fascinating dreams, albeit somewhat confusing, supported me. In one I traveled alone in a large boat, following the shoreline as if I were driving a car. A black cloud suddenly hovered over the boat, immediately turning into a rugged silken bear with a broad paw stretched out to me, reminding me of my bewildering childhood dreams in which my mother's hand attempted to touch me. I reached back, and my fingers gently touched the paw, comfortably. I wanted to go with it, but it vanished as fast as it had appeared. I woke with a smile on my face, feeling it was a positive omen for the future. That was the little Pollyanna in me, hoping she'd always endure.

Financial support arrived in the form of a check from my New Haven practice as some of my cases settled. The money paid for the septic system and other minor expenses. Relaxed, I watched TV, ate popcorn, and took a few hours off from planning and worrying.

While wandering around the university campus, I discovered the Nautilus and exercise gym, a good place to release and unwind, even with the odor of sweat. While exercising, I met Janet, tall and thin with friendly brown eyes and an earnest face. She was an older student who lived near campus during the week, returning on weekends to her home forty-five minutes from mine. To my surprise, I soon found myself in a budding relationship.

We didn't see each other regularly, but one weekend we shared a romantic night in her mountain cabin beneath a multitude of bright stars and cold breezes. My senses were fully alive; I wasn't holding back. I allowed my vulnerability and desire to emerge while being upfront that I wasn't looking to be part of a couple. I treasured my personal time, especially while prioritizing my life around studying and soon moving into my new home. I was learning to acknowledge my needs and not walk through this romance without accountability, having absorbed stark lessons from the pain of my breakup with Mary Ann. Janet understood and felt the same way. My sense of self was slowly returning.

I'd never attended an AA meeting. One day Janet took me to her eight-year anniversary meeting in a women-only group. I was allowed to share in a thought-provoking discussion. I found myself jealous, missing such personal sharing. We discussed powerlessness, the recognition and acceptance of it, as well as the positive nature of such recognition. I found the twelve steps of AA impressive in their summation of the human condition, especially now after failing the bar.

I wasn't an alcoholic, but I had various levels of addiction to other things: control, food, laziness. We discussed the role of power, the ego, and letting go. So much applied to me, reflecting such human issues. I delighted in being a part of a group again, remembering I was part of a whole and was not alone; I could share experiences as well as being intellectually challenged. I left with added perspective, which was so needed at this tumultuous time in my life. Like therapy, this meeting gave me the needed reminder to accept what I couldn't now control and move on with a smile and thankfulness for all I did have.

After the meeting, we danced away excess energy at a large dancehall jamboree for all ages and types. It was constant, freeing, physically exhausting dancing—two hours, almost nonstop. I was oblivious to everything but the music and my carefree body.

During the fall and early winter, Janet and I shared more warm days together but soon decided we were in opposite places in our lives. Our romance ended affectionately, settling into a friendship.

My chutzpah returned. I no longer punished myself for failing the bar. I just studied more. I took one day at a time, sometimes one hour at a time. I accepted that my home might not be fully finished for many years, but it was now livable enough to move into. I walked through my vacant house, looking out through the windows not yet fully framed in, and breathed out a summer's worth of relief, accepting the remaining sheetrock dust as I blew my nose.

Chapter 27

Optimism

I was finally in my new home—Crumblesweat. My body crumbled from the effort and sweat of moving, but my hard work paid off. I was walking on air. Friends helped me move, driving two trucks and my car back and forth, and unloaded everything in the living room. Janet kept me company my first night. Without heat, we cuddled and chatted in the chill of my new barren bedroom, unpainted, its only contents the queen-size bed and an empty dresser. I didn't sleep much with my hyper mind creating a new to-do list. It was odd to sleep without shades or curtains, but there was no need, as the view was only of the woods.

The cats were bewildered, exploring to find places to hide. I was concerned for them, having had two moves in such a short period. At least they found the litter boxes in the laundry room and upstairs bathroom. Maya was familiar with the surroundings so was not perturbed, except for the last ride to the house when her husky stubbornness again set in. She wouldn't jump into the car. Instead, she followed me along the side of the road, three miles to the house, traffic passing around me as I constantly stopped to coax her until, finally, too exhausted to challenge my ceaseless pleas, she jumped in.

After Janet left in the morning, I sat alone in my worn work clothes at the table sipping tea. The rough skin on my hands circled the hot cup on a crisp fall morning, and I inhaled the scent of new pinewood mixed with the musty smell of old furniture. The dining room was warmed by the sun through the east windows, just as I had planned and hoped for.

There was much to be completed in my little corner of heaven. The plywood subfloor needed to be covered with flooring. The walls required painting. The windows and doors lacked trim. The stark ceiling revealed insulation wrapped in plastic, like an arid desert, eventually to be finished in tongue-and-groove pine. The upstairs walkway along the chimney needed a banister, as did the steps. The kitchen cabinets required doors . . . and more. I was filled with gratitude to be in my dream home, but I couldn't stop kvetching about all that wasn't finished.

My first call was to my father and brother, who were together at my dad's apartment eating potato knishes and salami on rye, a frequent weekend meal. I breathed in the remembered aroma of the warm crusty softness of the knishes. It was so bolstering to hear their voices, especially my dad's aged gentle tone calling me "sweetheart." The conversation was short and simple. They recognized the thrill in my voice. When tired, I usually masked my emotions and acted cheery; it was easier, but for this call I didn't have to try. My exuberance was genuine. After hanging up, I drove to the rental, cheerfully cleaned it, and returned the keys to the owner.

In between the busyness of day-to-day office work, I slowly unpacked and put my new home in order. Friends invited me for dinner. I wasn't ready to cook a real meal. Instead, I mainly ate sandwiches, spaghetti, or pizza. On the weekends, I made my easy favorite, tuna casserole, and persevered in studying for the bar.

Mary Ann called to cheer me on, but I cut off the conversation when she shared the changes in *her* house. To me, it was still "our" house, and it rankled me that she no longer saw it that way. My life in New Haven seemed simple compared to my life now, even though I'd been living in Maine for less than a year. I missed her and much of our life together. It was still an adjustment not to be part of a couple, and I encountered unspoken societal pressure as a woman on my own to pair up, especially in this rural state. I missed having someone to share the burdens and joys. As well, I still loved her and always would. She'd been a major part of my life, a part I didn't want to lose. In the past, my reaction to this pain and anger would have been to turn to another lover and lose myself in a new relationship. Now I could no longer use that naïve escape. Therapy had lighted my way, yet I still had to work through my feelings of loneliness and resentment. I needed to center myself, and soon. Mary Ann would be visiting in two weeks.

New friends dropped by with loads of plants for me to adopt. Both were ex-nuns, together for at least thirty years, who worked at odd jobs that allowed them to live a simple life I couldn't imagine for myself. Structure and plans, two things I didn't now have, filled a need in me for a sense of safety. Their land was in a small town over an hour from me, their house off the electricity grid. They parked their car on the road and walked a mile on a path cut through the woods to get to their home in rain, snow, or blackflies. They chopped their own wood, used an outhouse, and grew much of their food. I visited them with friends to help stack wood, and I admired their courage and grit. A part of me wished I could do the same, but I knew there was too much "city" in me to follow their choice. My life, even now, in comparison to theirs, was like living in suburbia.

On a hazy, cool fall day, the earthy scent of smoke from other woodstoves drifted through the woods, reminding me of browning marshmallows by a fire. Three friends visited to help stack my wood pile, the pieces about sixteen inches long by six inches in diameter, not entirely seasoned but hopefully weathered enough to easily start a fire. I learned to stack "professionally," meaning ensuring when you take one log off the pile, the rest don't fall apart. We made a line, the four of us wearing gloves, bending, lifting, laughing, sweating, sneezing from the dust, piece to piece stacked securely as possible. We covered the pile with large blue tarps to protect it from rain and snow, pinning the ends down like a tent into the ground, but making it easy for me to access the wood as needed. The walk with a wagon to gather the wood was approximately six feet from the front door. It wouldn't be easy when the weather turned to snow and I had to shovel to make a path to the wood. A lesson for the following year's stacking: stack closer to the house.

After dinner with my workmates at a local diner, I slowly got ready for my first Maine winter in my new home. While the weather was cool at night, I brought in a handful of wood to practice how to best operate my new stove, following instructions from friends. There were initial screw-ups. One night I rushed to the screen door with my stove gloves holding a burning piece of wood and threw it outside on a pile of dirt. The house was smoky, and the cats hid. Fortunately, with snow on the ground, the wood was easily smothered, but it had to dry out for a couple of days.

Before the walls were painted, two friends helped me paint the downstairs subfloor medium brown. I bought rugs to cover most of the floor until I could afford to install pine flooring in the living room and linoleum in the kitchen/dining room. The walls were sterile, unpainted, without pictures, even after Frank finished the window and door trim. I was learning patience—a challenging lesson for me.

It was the student holidays, and I had four days off. Mary Ann visited, bringing with her two bookcases, a stereo cabinet, and an art table, all of which she had made. The art table surprised me. With a big smile she said, "I remembered you liked to draw and doodle, and I thought the table could go upstairs in your office by the light of the window." My smile was as wide as hers. Since my move, she had changed her career from paralegal to talented carpenter. We hugged, and our bodies blended into each other as naturally as they had years earlier. I breathed in her new woody scent from her carpentry work.

Together we built a box to hold my firewood, covered it with polyurethane, and nailed peacefully, with no one-upmanship. We were always bad at working together on projects, with our two dominant personalities. Now that I had some building skills, I had nothing to prove anymore. Even though the walls were unpainted, she helped me hang a few pictures as well as my outside wind chimes.

We didn't argue, a nice change of pace. But I quickly cut off any words she wanted to share about her relationship with Donna, the good as well as the bad. We chatted about my life here and updates of what was happening in *our* New Haven community. I missed my friends and the happenings of the area. We had no intense conversations, no further resolutions of the past. It was easier to let go of what we couldn't change. She cooked her delicious veggie and noodle stir-fry and corn chowder, hearty food I needed, perfuming the house with warm memories of meals in New Haven. We lovingly acknowledged we still cared for each other deeply. We were family, just a family that could no longer live together.

After we hugged goodbye, a few tears in both our eyes, I took a nap. Maya and the cats joined me in silence. The only way I knew it was windy outside was from the sound of the chimes we had hung. There were no shaky windows like in the New Haven house.

Relaxed, I unpacked my books, slowly putting them in the

bookcases, carefully placing certain topics together and holding some like prayer books, old ones with the musky smell that lingered lovingly until I sneezed. I recalled when I had read them and the different stages of my life at the time of reading.

Later at night, sitting on a small rug in the living room, I unpacked family and vacation albums, wistfully reliving memories. My father loved to take pictures: black-and-white ones from before my mother's death, some from the two orphanages, some with Fred and friends, others of my high school years, and some of our family trips after returning to live together. I laughed at how, as a teenager, I had sloppily reinforced them in albums with Scotch tape and staples.

I stared at my face in one photo, examining my eyes, trying to recapture what I'd been feeling. Luckily, I had saved diaries and writings from some of those years, which said so much more than the somewhat perfunctory smiles in photos. It was hard for me to look at the pictures of my brother when we were young; I saw only vacant eyes seeking understanding. I found forgotten pictures of visits with my cousins, aunts, and uncles. I spent so little time with them during my childhood, though more during my teenage years.

Also, there were many pictures of Mary Ann and me during our life together, fortunately more neatly anchored in albums than the ones from my younger years. Vacations with her mother to Cape Cod, trips to Puerto Rico, New Mexico, New York to visit my father and to Massachusetts to visit her mother, events and demonstrations in which we participated. Pausing, I inhaled deeply the joy and pain of memories and closed the albums, leaving them on the floor, not ready to put them in the file cabinet.

After a leisurely walk with Maya, I unpacked my diaries and journals. I glanced through my first diary, given to me by Effie, my Flanders cousin, as a gift at age twelve when we left the orphanage—a three-by-three-inch pink diary, now with a broken lock and aged white paper. I laughed at my penciled handwriting and the silly things I had written. Then I read my confusion, the bewildered emotions of my new life outside the orphanage, missing childhood friends . . . and closed the diary. I was not mentally prepared to go through them.

Instead, I put some small framed pictures on the two chimney mantels with some knickknacks, including the bones of a deer head and chin Maya found when we visited the property early on. I had transported from New Haven an odd-looking table found at a yard sale that was once a wooden cable spool and served as a coffee table when I lived with Mary Ann. Now it sat covered with newspapers and folders in front of my red-and-black-checkered, two-seater couch.

Though unfinished, the house was becoming a home!

On a gloomy, rainy Tuesday morning when I was supposed to go to work, Shadow, my sweet and loving dark-gray cat who had been with me since law school, had been chased up a maple tree and wouldn't come down. I called for help from my neighbor Jim. "Could you please come over with a ladder? I need your help getting Shadow down from a tree." He brought over the ladder and gently clutched fearful Shadow, safely delivering her into my arms. I hadn't the foggiest idea what scared her. Then, not soon after, as I prepared to leave for the office, Maya decided she didn't want to come back into the house, which prevented me from going to work; I couldn't leave her outside alone.

Maya's action turned out to be an omen or gift of sorts. Later that day as I sat on the couch, a drop of water fell on my shoulder, prompting me to discover what looked like a crack in one skylight. A surge of anger passed through me. I laughed so as not to scream, then prayed this wouldn't become a downpour before I got it fixed. I surely needed the day at home.

The following weekend brought hard rain. As I sat on the couch, the drop became an uneven sporadic stream, falling again from the skylight, washing over my hair. I became unglued, jumped up and placed a large cooking pot where my body had been to catch the rain, and wept. My mind filled with a scratchy noise, like crumpling aluminum foil. *What next?* I wasn't going to deal with this in the midst of anger. I'd make calls on Monday when I was calmer. It was more essential to concentrate on studying for the bar exam. Everything else could wait, almost.

My work hours were flexible, thankfully so, as Maya sporadically acted out, not springing into the house after our morning walk when I allowed her off leash. My fault. I should have known better. It seemed *I* was the one who needed training! Again, I called my neighbor Rose before she left for work. "Could you please come down to the house so I can get Maya inside?" She didn't hesitate, being familiar with this request. Maya became tail-wagging excited and walked in with her. My morning walks changed to always using a leash. Friends helped me build a pen. Someone gave me an old wooden doghouse, and I put it under the large end of the deck. Maya was a happy camper, loving the cold weather.

I tested Maya's attachment to me. In the woods, walking with a friend and Maya, I faked illness by lying down in a patch of leaves, whimpering in pain. She walked around me a few times and finally sat down against my body with apparent concern. I thought maybe she questioned the truth of the scenario, but at least I knew that if I were hurt, she'd hang around. Being alone, I needed that feeling of security.

There was so much stress and angst and joy these past few months. But with it all, I had a beautiful house standing tall and plumb, with no major disasters other than a leaky skylight. I was in debt but had my job, my house, my trees and blueberry fields, healthy and happy animals, new supportive friends, and general good health, body aches and pains aside. I still had to learn to slow down and to study for the bar, but I was content with the choices I had made.

As I rested on the couch, my mind relaxed from its never-ending thoughts. Then the phone rang, and the words on the other end shook my trust in my new Maine world, striking fear in my heart. An act of violence had been perpetrated on friends in a nearby feminist and lesbian community.

Chapter 28

Definitions

Dear Eva, Dear Mother,

You were my therapist before I knew what the word meant. Your wisdom always reached me through my writing, even prior to my ability to write, through talking to you in my head when I was crestfallen or angry. I am now both crestfallen and angry . . . and intimidated.

A friend's phone call rocked my new world in Maine. Fear struck a local feminist and lesbian community, many of whom are friends who live on a large plot of land in varied houses in a small rural town. They don't hide their lifestyle or choices. For that, they have been regularly harassed by several bigots or bullies who are distrustful of "the other" or can't accept people who are different— something sadly prevalent in this world.

From the beginning, the community functioned under stress, on guard, with only a few supportive neighbors. Now this ugliness had culminated in a local man pouring gas into one woman's well! Many in the town, who had generally ignored what was happening to this perceived unconventional and unorthodox community, succumbed to personal fear and became more sympathetic. I hope such sympathy turns into action to dispel the harassment my friends are still experiencing, but I know this women's community is stalwart and steadfast in its own vision. I wish I could be as well.

Settling into my home and excited to have fulfilled a dream to move to a rural town and build my house, I now live with jarring questions.

I think about a birthday card I received with a picture of a little girl looking into a mirror. It helped me feel positive and hopeful during a time when my life was the opposite. It had the following sentiment:

"You wake up every morning with the option of being anyone you wish. How beautiful that you always <u>choose</u> yourself." —Taylor Kent White

Now that saying seems shallow. I question whether we are free to choose. Do we really have the option in this world that constantly chooses to define and judge us?

This is the second jolt in my early Maine experience based on one's sexuality or how one chooses to live, the first being the killing of Charlie Howard, a gay man thrown off a bridge.

I'm not naïve. I knew in New Haven that hate and violence against outspoken women and gay people existed, but I was somewhat secure, protected, being an activist and feminist in a large liberal community. Even so, in my legal world, I was more circumspect about my relationship with Mary Ann, although never circumspect about my feminism.

My dear Eva, it's hard to admit to you my insecurities, although I know you understand. Early on in law school, it was awkward to be a feminist when I believed myself intellectually mediocre compared to the younger students, so I muzzled my anxiety by jumping in bed with various male students, giving me a visceral feeling of control. Of course such "control" was meaningless.

I didn't like myself, not until I started therapy, remembering the little orphan in me with the dreams and strength to survive.

It seems, as much as I fight defining myself, that I am a societal definition.

"You wake up every morning with the option of being anyone you wish. How beautiful that you always choose yourself."

I was never a little girl allowed to be anyone she wished. I wasn't like my friends, who seemed born eager to have children. I felt guilty lacking that desire. The closest I got to it was at age seventeen, writing in my diary a letter to my mythical daughter about why she shouldn't have sex at a young age, how to deal with boys at parties, and how to be a good girl in anticipation of her future marriage. Maybe what I was writing to her is what you wanted to convey to me. I guess I wasn't listening; I handled those years badly.

When I was with Mary Ann, I hid my life choice from relatives. But when they finally met Mary Ann at a family reunion, they liked her; she's someone hard not to like. I'm lucky our family lived in progressive cities, and not surprisingly, I soon wasn't alone—four other cousins in our large extended family came out as gay, all of us hidden at times.

Dearest Eva, in my twenties I still didn't picture myself being a mother. Maybe if I'd had you in my life as a role model, it might have made a difference. Who knows? I didn't play with dolls as a child. No time for that. I was like a soldier, or sometimes a thief, always watching my back.

In Brooklyn, after Dad's retirement, I watched his delight in playing with the neighbor's young son. I carried Jewish guilt that I hadn't given him grandchildren. I wept, recognizing he never had time to play with eight-year-old Fred when we left the orphanage *because he worked such long hours driving a cab. As for me, I was too busy redefining my life as well as being like you, the mother of our household, caring for Fred and worrying about Dad.*

"You wake up every morning with the <u>option</u> of being anyone you wish. How beautiful that you always choose yourself."

Option. What a loaded word for most people. In a world without definitions, whom you love would not be labeled or limited. You would just love. You wouldn't be typecast by the clothes you wear, your choice of partner, your level of education . . . on and on.

But I'm human. I struggle to be more than the one word that society, or I, assign me. It's not an easy struggle; it's better to say "search." So now, dear Mother, I continue to contend with the fear of those who are wedded to their definitions of others and search inside not to allow it to best me as I try to be "anyone I wish."

Your daughter

Chapter 29
Nesting

The saying is true, time *does* fly when you're having fun. Well, for me, it was true that time was flying but not necessarily true about having fun. I worked at the university and studied to retake the bar. The fun, or maybe joy, came from humanizing my home, making it reflect me.

Women to the rescue! My repeated complaints about insulation dust and my bloody nose reached the ears of friends. I hired a team of women painters who arrived to transform my bare walls. It was a rough couple of days to have my calmness and organization invaded, but I couldn't have been happier. I asked them if it was difficult for women painters to compete in a man's world, especially in Maine. The head of the team, thin and tall with long hair in a ponytail, nodded. "We've been doing this now for a number of years. At first we struggled with Mainers not taking us seriously. But over time we proved ourselves after neighbors of clients saw our work and our neatness in contrast to male painters, and we got more referrals." My bonus? The job was less costly than it would have been in New Haven!

As the painters worked, I envisioned a house coming alive with artwork on the newly tinted walls: my copy of Picasso's *Dove Peace Woman* hanging across from the couch and my favorite Picasso,

Mother and Child, in a place where I could see it from my bed. I pulled out a few original pieces from cousins and friends and some of my doodle art that I had framed and saved. I laid them out on the floor, creating a visual plan for each wall, particularly for the large wall adjacent to the steps, which is strikingly visible when one walks into the house. In one weekend, a feeling of home settled in. Much work was still ahead, but now I had the warmth of beloved art surrounding me.

I was ready for an inaugural house party. I invited ten friends to join me to celebrate my first New Year's Eve in Maine. Most dressed casually, not like a celebratory night. We played games and drank wine. Scrabble. Cards. Monopoly. The games were not the center of attention. Instead, it was the easy laughter of friends sharing stories and raising a glass, particularly laughter about my bug protection outfits. Oh, how I had missed having a party in my own home, remembering all the parties Mary Ann and I had, dancing the night away, all of us dressed up in silly, sometimes outrageous, clothing. To my disappointment, my first Maine party ended all too soon. I pleaded, "Aren't we going to dance—at least a little?"

Heads shook. A few said, "I don't like driving home too late in winter, and I have to get ready for work." I discovered time is different in Maine than in the city. My guests went home before the witching hour of midnight, leaving me alone. I cleaned the dishes and glasses, settled the animals, and sat on the couch, toasting out loud, "Here's to me," and lifting my glass as I welcomed in the New Year, wondering what it would bring. Had I turned the page on my relationship with Mary Ann? Would I be able to complete the rest of the house? Would I find love again? Would I pass the bar?

These questions rambled around in my slightly woozy head. One moment I was excited and happy about the new adventure before me.

The next I was sure I couldn't last through the Maine winter. New Year's Eve had released a particular pang of loneliness. It was my first New Year's Eve not in a relationship. I flopped into bed, and my eyes rested on Picasso's *Mother and Child*. Another pang. This one hid behind thoughts of "if only" and "what if?" This was a soul kind of loneliness, deeper, one that still hadn't healed.

Luckily, I had a job with perks—holidays, spring and winter breaks—allowing for travel. I visited Mary Ann in New Haven, staying with friends. I walked into *our* house. She showed me the changes she'd made, and my heart turned cold. We had a few days of superficial pleasantness, keeping busy by going out to eat and visiting with mutual friends. Then the spell broke, with hot and angry honesty, meaningless hurtful words. But like earlier times, when we danced together at a party alive with fervent memories and the joy of how well we blended on the dance floor, my anger tempered. The rest of the week was calm—open warmth with a touch of protectiveness in both of us. So much painful confusion sifted through me. My feelings of rootlessness returned. At times I saw the side of me I hated—the lonely side—and I wanted to hide but ended up running away in vivid, active dreams. Yet the two of us together made it through visiting my father and brother in Brooklyn, enjoying my dad's cooking, always his sweet, oily, succulent noodle kugel.

Nesting back at my home, I stayed up late at night, walked on the snow in my boots, the crunch and cold refreshing me, and viewed the moon in its full brightness, never so noticeable in the city. When the moon was gone, multiple stars lit up the deep dark sky, reminding me how small we humans are in the scheme of life. When it was too cold outside, before going to bed, I stared out my windows mesmerized by the night sky, with the backdrop of the bare trees standing out among the full pines.

The next evening on the way to a political meeting at a local restaurant, I stopped at the supermarket to pick up a few items. A straggly fortyish man sat in front of the store with a sweet-looking dog named Mandy, a cross between a short haired shepherd and a collie. I asked about the dog as I petted her. In a sad voice, he informed me, "I gave the dog to a neighbor and later found out he was in jail. He'll be out soon, and I don't want him havin' the dog. He's bad takin' care of her, even ties her up outside at night. I can't take her back as I'm gettin' divorced."

Sucker that I was, and not processing clearly, I agreed to take eight-month-old Mandy. I rationalized that maybe Maya needed a companion; maybe she'd listen better. I put Mandy in the back of my car and continued to the meeting. Leaving the meeting quickly when it ended I found Mandy relaxed calmly in the back seat. At home, the two dogs were friendly with each other. Mandy didn't bother the cats, although of course they were more restrained.

At three in the morning, I jumped out of bed. The dogs were barking and fighting in the living room. Rattled, I threw on a jacket over pajamas and ran out in the rain putting Mandy in my car, intending to return her. A few minutes later it hit me: *I don't know where the owner lives, not even his name.* In the morning, I took Mandy to work with me until I could figure out what to do about her. She was sugary friendly with my coworkers and actually listened to me. We went outside to the common area where students played with their dogs, and Mandy heeled off leash, ignoring other dogs, delighted in playing ball. This was the type of dog I wished Maya had become, I thought guiltily.

I didn't want to give her up. Over time the dogs became companions but not always agreeable ones. One day I returned home to discover a cyclone had devastated my new, large, beautiful, and somewhat expensive oriental rug. It was covered with cat litter and kibble, dirt from turned-over plants, dog and cat toys, vomit, and some books with torn edges. The stench took away my breath as I cleaned up the mess. From that point on, when I left for work and it wasn't too cold, I put them out in the pen where they could enjoy the southern sun to keep them warm, although husky Maya enjoyed staying under the deck in her doghouse or in the hole she dug.

My father and I spoke weekly. On my birthday he called to sing "Happy Birthday," a remembrance of his great singing voice, though now a little shaky. He never forgot to call and sing to me on my birthday, wherever I lived. In the orphanage, he always visited on our birthdays and brought us a cake to share with the other kids.

Now I called him with joyous news. I shrieked, "Dad, I passed the bar!" I uttered these words with a profound breath of liberation.

I sensed his smile and heard his tears as he said, in his soft, Brooklyn Jewish accent, "Sweetheart, I'm so happy for you. I knew you would." After the ceremony of being admitted to the Maine bar, my work life normalized, allowing for more participation in community life. My nesting life was settling in.

Chapter 30

Blossoming

Spring arrived: more sun in the evening, white and painted trillium budding in the woods, music of birds whose names I had yet to learn, and new unknown sounds from the woods at night and early morning. The dogs barked more at night. It was a relief that I had the pen for them to go in and out without worry, except one night when six bright eyes peered into the sliding glass door —a family of raccoons. Fortuitously, it was late enough that the dogs were sleeping.

One year in Maine. I'd amazed myself as well as my friends. At dinner with two Maine-born buddies, I said, "Hey, guess what? I just realized this is my anniversary. I've been here one year."

They heartily laughed, to my surprise. Then one said, "We bet you wouldn't survive a year here."

I proudly retorted, "You definitely lost that bet!"

Spring moved swiftly into summer. I looked out my kitchen window one early morning and—surprise!—a graceful, large, brown buck with six-inch antlers stood alone, nibbling on grass, leaves, and acorns. That was the first I'd seen in the front yard. I stood quietly, watching him for twenty minutes, until he walked off to find another tasty area. Thrilled, I called friends, sharing another initiation into

Maine life. Fortunately, the dogs were in the house unaware, so they didn't disturb my peaceful scene.

Mandy and Maya liked the residents of the great outdoors as much as I did, but their approach was to confront them. Like most dogs, they had no common sense as to what animals to avoid. This was how porcupines invaded my calm world, or rather, Mandy and Maya invaded the porcupines' calm world. On our walks, they confronted porcupines in the woods, including one that dared to enter the pen. Several times the dogs were hit by the quills on their bodies, faces, and even inside their mouths. One time, with Mandy anesthetized, I helped the doctor pull them out of her bloody mouth. I was building an extension to the vet's office with the expense of removing the quills. That was it for me. Much to their dismay, I subsequently walked them on long leashes, not an easy endeavor with two such sturdy and headstrong dogs.

Over time I made friends in the local and surrounding communities, joining with six straight and lesbian women to start a reading and discussion group, gathering every two weeks in each other's homes. These were spirited women from various backgrounds, a few of whom were married. I was the only Jewish woman, which made me somewhat atypical, except that most were "from away." In one gathering, we discussed mothers and daughters. We drew pictures of our views of our families, infinitely challenging for me. I drew colored blended circles representing my father and brother, surrounding the orphanage with black sharp lines running through boxes, representing death. I was dazed at my finished sketch; it was like a therapy drawing and so disturbingly different from the drawings of others, even when some had negativity.

In the group, I was again drawn to one of the women, Nancy, who was also involved in the local peace action group. We were on the same political wavelength. She was unconventional, funny and serious almost at the same time, easily speaking her mind as I did. Maybe that was from her life in Buffalo; like me from Brooklyn, we were city people. Most of the others were more reserved. Nancy was still involved in Spruce Run, the Bangor battered women's project, and continued to prod me to get involved because of my New Haven experiences. I seriously considered it now that my life had settled. As well, she still was involved in an on-again-off-again relationship with her partner of several years, so my mind didn't reflect beyond friendship.

The oppressive blackflies, my nemeses, were now fortunately gone, replaced by mosquitos, as one set of antagonists supplanted another. Mosquitos hadn't been much of a bother in my childhood or in my life in New Haven, but I now had to accept them as unwelcome neighbors. However, these neighbors also entwined with a multicolored kaleidoscopic of wildflowers—lupin, paintbrushes, Queen Anne's lace, lily of the valley, buttercups—and dancing yellow butterflies.

This summer season was in sharp contrast from the last when I was building my home, although I had workers fashion a banister for the steps, kitchen cabinet doors and drawers, and a sliding door for my bedroom closet. *My house is becoming a home.* I was truly settling in, making a rooted nest for myself, almost like the birds around my windows.

The warmer weather also brought visitors: Mary Ann, friends, and my brother. I became a leisurely tour guide rather than a housebuilder, even though the house was still incomplete. Fred's visit was a tornado of picture-taking, canoeing, movies, and swimming at the lake, with Mandy swimming and surfboarding. Maya wasn't a water dog. She waded at the water's edge, chasing small turtles, frogs, and other lake critters swimming between the underwater plant life.

It took until the fall for the dogs to get hit by a skunk. The house reeked, as did my clothes. I struggled washing the dogs in the tub, one at a time, as they shook their bodies and got water and skunk smell all over me. I then scrubbed myself in the shower, not too successfully. I went to work not realizing the harsh, rotten-egg scent of skunk still clung to my skin, even my shoulder bag. Paige and Gene, as well as the student interns, laughed at my predicament and stayed as far away from me as possible. It was so embarrassing, especially when clients came in, and I had to explain my situation. The embarrassment didn't last long, as everyone shared their own stories of what products to use the next time, though hopefully there wouldn't be a next time. It seemed not much fully worked—tomato juice, baking soda, dishwashing soap, and other home remedies were ineffective. I was grateful for the weekends when I aired out my clothes and shoulder bag. I even tried putting perfume in the bag, which only made it worse. I showered a few times a day and tried some of the suggested remedies, but the smell permeated the house for over two weeks, dissipating slowly.

Now the dogs and I were definitely nested into Maine life.

In the brisk air of October, my life falling into place, I agreed to join the Spruce Run board of directors after Nancy's regular entreaties. I'd also developed a better sense of her from conversations in our local women's group. She and I drove together to board meetings in Bangor, each trip sharing more of our history, including the end of her on-again-off-again relationship with her ex and my relationship with Mary Ann.

She was a lot like me, a combination of intensity and playfulness, never knowing when one or the other would set in. When she smiled, her whole face lit up, framed by her short dark hair and brown eyes. Her smile was open but protective. When she shared more, I understood why her smile was that way as she revealed her unresolved anger and sadness in her relationship with her parents. "They don't accept my lifestyle, particularly my relationship with Michelle, whom they met a few times when visiting here. They're Baptists. I'm not. We can't get beyond arguing." To my surprise, my internal reaction was, *Maybe they wouldn't accept me, this Jewish girl!* Wow, where did that come from? I hadn't consciously thought about a relationship with Nancy.

Before I could respond, she continued. "My politics are too radical for them. When I got married in college to a guy they knew, it made them so happy. He died of cancer early on. That's the only relationship they considered 'real.' My younger sister is the perfect daughter I never was."

When I returned home, I glanced at myself in the mirror, questioning. *Roberta, what the heck's going on inside you? You're not ready for a relationship with someone who recently ended one. You know her ex; she's in your community. Nancy just moved out of her house and bought a small house two miles from you. You're just settling into your own life, not ready for serious intimacy.* I was getting carried away with my thoughts; maybe it was natural for me to wonder if her parents would like me. I liked to be liked.

I shut down such thoughts. I wasn't ready.

Chapter 31

Nancy

I continued to repress the fire building in me as Nancy and I spent more time together. After a period on the Spruce Run Board, we determined it was important that the town of Ellsworth have its own battered women's shelter so that abused women in our area didn't have to travel to Bangor for protection. We, with others on and off the board, separated from Spruce Run and formed a new organization in our area, initiating a frenzied time of planning and meetings. Living so near to each other, Nancy and I immersed ourselves in the intensity and exhaustion of this new project, driving and having dinners together, our lives intertwined in this new aspiring adventure.

Between work and meetings, on sunny days we bundled up in winter coats and hats and walked together on the beach with Maya, Mandy, and Nancy's small older dog, Mitra, philosophizing about our work in the peace action group and the new battered women's project. We shared more of our histories, amazed at how similar we were in our outside endeavors. Since we didn't have family in Maine, our respite was sharing holidays with friends.

Nancy became more physically friendly with gentle touches, almost as if by accident. When our fingers touched, wisps of electricity flushed my cheeks. At a friend's Harvest Moon Ball party I helped plan, Nancy dressed as country singer Patsy Cline. I dressed as a Rockette, all in black: boots, tights, nylon shorts, silky blouse with white collar and cuffs, vest with tails, and a touch of silver jewelry. I needed to feel sexy and strong, in clothes different from those I had worn so long building my house. We all danced, sang, and became silly. We were busy, active women letting loose. Nancy released her carefree side, the side I hadn't yet seen, joking and singing. We danced naturally together, free-flowing to country and rock music. It was similar to dancing with Mary Ann, in unison with the emotional passion of movement even with our different styles. A few months earlier, I'd had a brief attraction to another woman, but when we danced together, she was so awkward and stiff that my interest immediately melted like icicles on a sunny winter day. Dancing with Nancy was the opposite. But my mind challenged my body, not yet ready for the passion sprouting inside.

Is this the start of "dating"? I wasn't sure. There was the general awkwardness of dating, but it was so hard to know with women—unlike with men where you knew what to expect and the intended result. The flirting was clear. Relationships/friendships with women seemed much more whole, making it hard to know the boundaries between friendship and intimacy. Maybe the caution involved in this lack of roles was healthy for now since I wasn't sure what I wanted or wanted to feel.

Winter was in full force. My private world, my house, was surrounded by eight inches of snow. It was eighteen degrees outside. My little bedroom, cozy even in the coldest corner of the house, was my cocoon of safety—white walls offset by golden pine-framed windows, door, and ceiling. Surrounded by dogs and cats, I found that the scent of burning wood in the stove warmed my bubble of protection.

During the beginning of the holiday season, I grew melancholy and missed holidays and birthdays with Dad and Fred, no longer a few hours' drive as when I'd lived in New Haven. Last year I had rushed around New York and New Haven like a busy beaver trying to see and do so much. Now I was spending relaxing Thanksgiving dinners with friends in three different homes. Nancy was at one of the dinners, and we shared energetic talk and laughs with no forced moments. I was slowly creating traditions in my new world.

Home alone, I weighed my life in the city and my life with Mary Ann and questioned whether belonging was really a state of mind, a state of internal connectedness, inner happiness—concepts at times only touching the tips of my fingers. I questioned too much, dreamed too much. Joan, my therapist, told me I needed now and then to let this innocent body and soul just enjoy living in the moment.

The next week after working on our peace action project, Nancy joined me with popcorn and soda in documentary bingeing: *An Early Frost* and *The Times of Harvey Milk*. Both of us were soon in tears, feeling anger at life's ugliness against gays. One we watched, *Silent Pioneers*, was more upbeat about gay men and women growing old.

When Mary Ann visited for a long weekend, I was in an exceptionally happy mood. At night, the winds howled; it was ten degrees outside, yet seventy-two within. Mary Ann appreciated the heat from the woodstove, until I noisily got up at four in the morning to add more wood to the dying fire. It was quite different from baseboard heat. Surprisingly, we got along like loving sisters, easily chatting and reminiscing, enjoying time with Maya and the cats, whom she understandably missed. I had finally accepted Donna in her life, allowing her to share with me the ups and downs of that relationship. I hesitantly shared with her, "I've made a new friend: Nancy. We're working together on a battered women's shelter." I knew Mary Ann would bombard me with questions. I think that's why I told her. I needed to express some of my confused feelings, and I knew she would be supportive, maybe relieved. When we hugged goodbye tightly, it was a contented hug, so different from the hug on the day I left her to drive permanently to Maine. I was no longer looking back. I was flowing into my new life not questioning my choices.

On a whirlwind of personal pleasure, I morphed from a caterpillar into a butterfly. I woke up one morning with the beginning words of a story idea in full bloom and began writing again, as I had in New Haven and when I was young. In the process of writing, I discovered how accepting I had become of myself. Therapy surely had helped.

To top off the year, Nancy hosted a New Year's Eve party in her small house where friends gathered in different rooms. There was wine and moderate drinking, with a few people dancing. Close to midnight, Nancy and I were alone in one small, dimly lit room, laughing as we fast danced, each trying to lead the other. The music changed to something slow. At midnight we kissed hesitatingly, then more fully. My legs weakened, like my first kiss with Ernie and then with Mary Ann. People left shortly after midnight after quick goodbyes. Nancy and I continued sensually dancing, slowly kissing, smiling, until four in the morning.

The next day, January 1, 1986, our friendship ripened into a budding romance, slowly, passionately, lovingly. I was grateful I didn't have to go to the office but had a week left on school break. I couldn't concentrate on much except this passion for and with Nancy. Oh, so delicious to experience these feelings again! I immersed myself in her, without losing my own essence as I had done in the past. My juices ran wild. At another party I savored our passion during dancing, feeling supremely sensual with the movements of the music. I loved leading her around the floor, gyrating to every sound, lost in the emotion of the music. *I think I've watched too many Ginger Rogers movies.* There were no more questions in my head. I was all into this romance, this relationship.

It was so freeing to experience my emotions. To learn patience. To again be enthralled with loving. I didn't run from being consumed; I ran *to* it—not to get lost in it, but to glory and grow in the freedom of such open passion and warmth. What a difference from early winter the prior year. All the therapy I'd done in dealing with issues after my breakup with Mary Ann and in living alone came to fruition. I was defined finally by *me*, at ease with myself. Contented. Accepting. My ego diminished. I didn't claim perfection; I wasn't leaving therapy. There were still issues to work on and explore and pain to express, especially connected with my childhood and family. Issues came and went. I saw the patterns and worked things through. I didn't feel debilitated.

The moon shone full on my cold winter birthday. This passionate love warmed me, leaving me with little sleep. Yet we both functioned in the outside world, working at our jobs and our political and social obligations. As we each had our own home, we shared time in both places with the three dogs, though we were more at my home because of the needs of my cats.

My lips were full and bloated, just like Mary Ann's lips had been when she'd returned from a day with Donna. I'd been so angry then, but not now. I'd come full circle.

We shared our challenging histories, Nancy not holding back the pain of her troubled family dynamics, which were particularly painful because she still loved them. Her sullen facial changes made it easy to discern her feelings. I understood her dark moods, as well as her recent embittered relationship and breakup. I talked her through the pain and didn't take her doldrums personally. I also shared in her playful silliness and love of celebrations. Because of her thoughtfulness, I sensed she wouldn't deliberately hurt anyone.

A short time after we got together, Nancy had described her on-again-off-again relationship with Michelle. "We were always arguing, even about meaningless things—having to prove ourselves. It was tiring."

Now I understood why she sometimes "tested" my love and endurance. Early on she groused about the way I drank soda from a bottle—an odd, petty comment. When I was younger, I would have boiled over, but now I didn't take it personally and just turned it into a joke. Nancy's sadness was translucent as glass, especially related to her family and her last relationship. We learned together, not arduously but lovingly, not having to test each other.

I sweetly needled her about her compulsive neatness. Everything in her drawers was folded neatly, even her socks with the same colors together—not like me, who tied the socks and threw them in the drawer. Later I grasped the benefit of folding. It allowed for more room in the drawer. I acknowledged that therapy had changed me for the better. The small stuff didn't irritate me, and my relationship with Nancy benefited.

In March Nancy spent two weeks in Nicaragua on a peace mission, living with a Nicaraguan family. I kept busy at the office, catching up on reading and doing my political work. It was hard to say goodbye and harder not to be able to talk for two weeks. She took my photo with her. I conversed with her photo on my dashboard. Her smile eased my busy day. Spring was approaching, even visible through twelve inches of snow. While she was away, I visited my dad and Fred for the weekend, and Mary Ann joined me in New York with much support for my new relationship.

Upon Nancy's return, we reconnected with fire and warmth. It was almost like a honeymoon, so short had the time been that we'd been together. I was almost constantly in touch with my body and my feelings. They were so different from the past. I experienced an intensity I had forgotten was possible, wanting more and more but knowing I must be patient. There was no rush; the means were as important as the ends.

Shortly after her return, Nancy strained her back and became a bedridden curmudgeon for a while. I took care of her in my house for a week. She wasn't the easiest of patients, but it didn't matter. Nothing made me run from her; it just brought me closer. Once she realized I wasn't like her ex, we settled into an easy, natural rhythm.

Finally, the wood ceiling of my home was finished, and I had a new ceiling fan from Hong Kong that my brother sent me. I now looked up to the warmth and beauty of wood, just in time for my first home-cooked Passover seder. On a calm evening, the setting sun sparkled through a prism sitting on a windowsill. Rays of colorful light bounced around the room, as eleven women shared dinner with me, using the Haggadah, which is the Jewish prayer text setting forth the order of the seder and the essential text used to conduct the seder meal. Except this Haggadah, this book of instructions, prayers, blessings, and stories, was nontraditional and had been expanded to be feminist in its phrasing.

We sat on the floor around long, low coffee tables pulled together, borrowed from friends. I was the only Jewish woman. This was so different from any seder I'd ever attended. I imagined some of my ancestors turning in their graves. I justified my guilt by the fact that I was introducing friends to the tradition of an unfamiliar religion. With wine, matzo, roast chicken, veggies, and potatoes, we toasted Passover. Before the main meal, we took turns reading from the Haggadah while tasting the symbolic foods that ceremoniously illustrated the story of the Jewish exodus from Egypt. My favorite was charoset, a sticky sweet salad made from apples, nuts, lemon juice, cinnamon, and grape juice instead of wine, for those who didn't drink liquor. It represented the mortar used by the Hebrew slaves to make bricks and the struggles of minorities and women to escape the control of others.

My guests, stuffed with food and conversation, slowly departed after three hours—except Nancy. She stayed overnight, her dog Mitra keeping company with Mandy, Maya, and the cats. Waking up the next morning, with Nancy and the animals still sleeping and light brightening the bedroom, I lay quietly and meditated on how blessed I was to again trust, again luxuriate in romance, again feel whole. Wrapped in my blanket, I rejoiced in my many dreamy expectations.

Chapter 32

Confluence

Spring brought cool night air in swirls of sweet-fern freshness and visitors. My brother came for a few days. Nancy's maternal grandparents visited, and I briefly met this five-foot-two, hunched over, old-world Italian couple in their late eighties, with gracious smiles and soft voices. In rough Italian, Nancy introduced me as her "dear close friend," and Grandma gave me a gentle hug. We chatted superficially—it was a little hard to understand their accent—but I walked away relieved that they seemed to like me.

As autumn arrived, Nancy's parents surprisingly chose to come to Maine for a weekend visit, which they hadn't done in many years. Nancy vacillated, afraid the visit would turn into a screaming match. They hadn't liked Michelle, and she was afraid they wouldn't like me. But she gave in, as I was resolute in my desire to meet them. I cleaned the house for hours, washing the floors, which were still painted brown and unfinished, dusting, and hiding the dog and cat toys in the closet. Nancy had warned me they were neatniks.

I was a nervous wreck. Hosting parents was never my forte, but in addition, we came from such divergent backgrounds. When I calmed down, I thought, *Well, in New York and New Haven, I lived in diverse communities and worked with clients of every type with dissimilar personalities and religions, so I can do this. Again, I can do this!*

I called my friend Emma, an expert cook. "Help! I need you to walk me through making pot roast with potatoes." The morning of the visit, she walked me through the recipe on the phone, step by step, confirming whether the salt and pepper should be a pinch or a spoonful, which direction to cut the meat, how small the potatoes should be. I didn't want to repeat the upsetting dinner I had fed to Mary Ann's mother many years before. To my relief, as well as Nancy's, the pot roast, colorful salad, and homemade cake (though not by me) were a success.

Nancy warned me they liked to play games, something I rarely did, except for cards. Her parents taught me cribbage as they laughed and petted the dogs and cats. To my surprise, they were quite down-to-earth. I hadn't known what to expect, given Nancy's description of her relationship with them. Mrs. J, around five feet tall, thin, with gray hair neatly coiffured, casually dressed in a skirt, blouse, and sweater, had a kind smile. Mr. J was about a head taller, also casually dressed, with thinning brown hair and a hearty smile. Mr. J asked questions about my house, the building of it, and seemed genuinely interested in the details as he enjoyed fixing up his own house. I showed him around, proud of what I had done. I knew the evening was a success when her parents said I could call them by their first names. For some unknown reason, I didn't feel comfortable with this, and I continued to call them Mr. and Mrs. J. When the evening ended, Nancy's smile extended almost to her ears. I slept that night like a baby.

After that successful visit, Nancy decided she was ready to go home and see more of her family for the first time in years. We drove from Maine to Buffalo to the house in which she had grown up. Her parents lived in a working-class neighborhood, in a small white house with a small front lawn and a garage adjacent to a small backyard. Her grandparents lived next door in a similar house. We walked into the mouth-watering aroma of hot Italian meatballs in sauce and a mix of homemade chocolate-iced cake and cookies. We slept in separate single beds in the downstairs finished basement. I tried to be physically close, but she was too nervous with her parents upstairs. Walking through the house, I saw pictures of Nancy's wedding and of her young, deceased husband, obviously a dream her parents wanted to maintain.

The two of us walked around town, Nancy showing me where she had gone to school, the church she'd attended but mostly avoided, where she had hung out with friends, and where she had cried and hidden from her family. The telling caused more tears as we sat on the swings near the church she no longer attended. We talked more about the difficulties of her life at home. She and her father had strong personalities and clashed a lot. "They didn't accept my relationships, except for my short-lived marriage," she shared. I thought about my father. We didn't really talk or clash. We avoided. I hated how I felt when I upset him.

Listening to Nancy, I felt my face redden in jealousy. As unhappy as she was, she had a mother who loved and babied her, a father who had taught her to use tools and build things, and a younger sister to tease—the typical American family I had so envied in my youth and maybe still did.

To my pleasant surprise, I again got along with her parents, as well as her sister. It was easy to chat. I genuinely liked them. Even though we had vastly different religious beliefs, I could relate to their working-class lifestyle and understood their need for a religious connection. That was my experience too. Her mother had worked as a secretary, and her father was a union man, both retired. They were unpretentious people trying to relate to their daughter yet strongly sticking to their beliefs. I then understood why they disliked Nancy's ex. As Nancy told me, she was "too uppity for them, whereas you're natural and nonjudgmental."

We dined on meatballs and spaghetti, played cards, and laughed a lot while eating cake and cookies. In the morning, I had no desire for breakfast, still stuffed from lunch and dinner the day before.

One evening, sitting in their neat and spotless living room, they took out family slides and pictures, and we viewed Nancy's childhood with her parents and sister. Nancy wiped away tears through a childlike smile, finally relaxed. They were outtalking each other, trying to tell me the history of the events in the pictures, laughing as they spoke. Her sister's baby was six months old. Nancy adored holding and playing with him, as did I. Stepping back, watching them in moments of playfulness, I felt such joy for Nancy. I also brimmed with more envy. Even with all the ups and downs of their psychodynamics, they were a family, with grandparents, who had done things together when the kids were young and supported each other during hard times. Or was that my dream?

We took a night ride to Niagara Falls. Nancy and her sister skipped on the walkway, holding hands like happy little girls, while I walked behind talking with her father, who shared with me his work, the beauty of the falls, and our laughs at watching his daughters act like kids. Mrs. J was home caring for the baby.

A few days later, with Nancy utterly relaxed, we drove back to Maine smiling and laughing at the successful visit. Gone was the tension from when we first walked into her childhood house.

December school break arrived. Nancy and I were about ready to celebrate our one-year anniversary; this was sometimes hard to believe but mostly so naturally right. The passion, excitement, and loving intensified. I was still open, alive, wholly me, not pretending or repressing. We drove to New York, first visiting New Haven and staying at my old house, now Mary Ann's, with Nancy and me sleeping in Mary Ann and Donna's waterbed. I initially tensed being back in the house, but my excitement to share my old life in New Haven outweighed my uptightness. I gave Nancy a short tour of the town, and we visited my old law firm, the latter a very special few minutes of smiles and hugs with my former law partners.

From New Haven, we drove to New York for Nancy to meet my father. Dad was at his peak, showing off his endearing humor about his women neighbors who now and then cooked for him and of course filling our stomachs with his homemade noodle kugel. I took her to the Christmas parade in Manhattan. She was like a kid in a candy store. In fact, she had the heart of a child. She loved holidays, decorating, and being playful, which allowed me to let go of my blasé attitude and enjoy the holidays anew. I showed her around town, including the street of my first uptown Manhattan apartment and my favorite restaurant in the Village, El Faro, where they made the best Chicken Villeroy, marinated in bechamel cream. It was still as tasty as years before. When I left New Haven, I asked the restaurant for the recipe. They gave it to me, but friends and I couldn't match the taste of eating it in the restaurant so perhaps the ambiance was part of the taste.

We drove back to Maine in high spirits and celebrated New Year's with friends, without the nervousness experienced the previous New Year. I couldn't believe how fortunate I was. I looked with love and affection at her eyes, face, and physical sensuality, like a teenager's first love but in an adult body and mind. Blissful and grateful, I savored a future bright with love.

Chapter 33

Thunderbolt

My journal writing had decreased until December 13, after Nancy and I returned to Maine from Buffalo. My last sentence was: "Living seems more important right now than writing about it." How right I was.

On a cold and snowy late January morning, I glanced out my front door, surprised to see my friend Emma walking toward the house, her round face pale and strangely serious. As I opened the door for her, a police car drove up and two police officers walked toward the house. The moments got blurry. Emma was trembling.

She blurted out, "Nancy was in a car accident. She died!"

I held onto the kitchen counter by the door. My body tumbled in slow motion. Emma grabbed me and kept me standing until one of the officers could hold me up. The lawyer in me tried to take in the facts from the police—facts I didn't want to hear. The police took some information and wrote down directions to the morgue, which turned out to be the bottom floor of a funeral home.

After the police left, the phone rang. I answered, hearing the sweet voice of Nancy's mother, calling from Buffalo. "Hi Roberta, I've been trying to reach Nancy. Is she with you?"

I looked at Emma, and her tears became mine. I panicked.

Why is she calling?! She never calls this early in the morning. It's Saturday.

"Mrs. J, I don't know how to tell you . . . I'm so sorry, but I just found out Nancy died this morning. Car accident. Icy road. She was on the way to her office."

My voice was shallow. I was having trouble forming complete sentences. Trying to hold back a swath of waterworks. *Shit, couldn't I have been less blunt?*

Silence. Then heartrending, high-pitched screams. Her father picked up the phone. My body shook as I repeated those macabre words and explained I didn't know more.

"I'm going to the morgue to identify her." I left out the word *body*. "I promise, I'll call you back as soon as I have more information."

I saw two other friends walk toward my house, this house I hoped would someday be shared with Nancy. My friend Jen, a geriatric nurse who had seen much death in her work, joined me on the surreal half-hour car ride to the morgue, Nancy's last resting place. Jen drove.

My mind was empty and full at the same time. In law school I'd had to identify my elderly uncle in a real morgue in Brooklyn when he died in a hospital dementia ward. *Nancy is only thirty-seven!* I thought of my mother's death at thirty-two, dying in a hospital. I never got to say goodbye.

My knees faltered as Jen held my hand and stayed close while we walked down a cluster of deep steps, not fully grasping this would be the last time I'd see and touch Nancy. The room was sterile and as cold as snow on flesh. Her body was nude on a steel table with a thin white sheet covering her, except for her face. I saw a few scratches and dried blood on her forehead and hands, but her face had a look of calm, peace, not fear; her lips were pursed almost in a smile.

I held her hand, slowly and lightly kissed her on her lips and forehead and slid my other hand over her damp hair, staring at her face, scared I might someday forget. I couldn't decide whether to stay longer or leave. I didn't want to move. *How can I leave her on this metal table?* I held myself so tight to keep from collapsing on the floor. *I am a strong person. I will be strong.* Jen also gave her a gentle kiss on the forehead. I forced myself to say goodbye with a final touch, a final tearful look.

The coroner informed me she had died instantly. He was confident in his assessment as, to my astonishment, her accident happened right in front of his house. He spoke gently. "The road was icy this morning, and the car skidded and turned over, hitting a pole."

I should have been relieved but was operating on empty until he told me where he lived. I recoiled, as if struck by a thunderbolt. A week earlier, we had been driving home from a movie at night on the same road as the accident. Nancy was driving fast. My stomach somersaulted and my forehead knotted like a rope, noticeably at the spot where she died. I had screamed angrily, "Slow down—you're driving too fast—my head is burning!"

Jen and I returned to my house. I walked into a roomful of friends. I was loved. Nancy was loved. I fell to the floor and cried, and friends surrounded and held me.

When I was ready, I called her parents. Mr. J answered, his normally animated voice toneless as he told me they'd be flying in tomorrow and made arrangements to rent a car and stay at the local motel. I could envision him slumped in his big green stuffed chair, the chair he sat in often when I visited with Nancy.

I gave a friend the key to Nancy's house to go in and find her picture albums. I pulled out my albums of us together—our skiing, day trips, visit to her family, political events, time with friends—memories to share at the memorial.

Sitting around my dining room table and living room, friends helped me plan the memorial service. Someone put food on the table, but I had no desire to eat. I looked forward to Mary Ann arriving later that night. I trusted her to hold me, to care for me. I could let go with her in ways I couldn't with other friends. I couldn't call my father or brother. They wouldn't know how to relate to my pain, although my father would say a few supportive words; that would be for later.

After the planning, I sent my friends home against their protestations. I needed to be alone. The animals were quiet, surely sensing the mood of the day, but I held Mitra tightly against my body, feeling she knew something was off. I fell into an on-again-off-again sleep. At one point, I opened my eyes and unmistakably saw Nancy's round smiling face, her deep brown eyes gazing lovingly at me. I jumped up. Was I imagining? Hallucinating? *No, it is real.* I smiled back, sensing she was okay. But I wasn't.

When Mary Ann arrived, she was tenderly supportive and protective like a dear sister as we cried together. I was so glad she had previously met Nancy. With all that we had gone through in our relationship, Mary Ann was still family, the person with whom I could still be wholly open and trusting.

The following afternoon, before Nancy's parents arrived, the lawyer in me took over. Nancy had made a will before she went on her two-week solidarity trip to Nicaragua to visit and work in our Bucksport's Sister City. She wanted to be cremated, not embalmed or laid out on display. As I was responsible for handling her affairs, when her parents arrived, I had to explain her wishes to them. We sat around the table, the same table at which we had laughed and played cards, and I gave them further distressing news. They wanted her body to be buried in Buffalo, not cremated. I hated to disappoint them; they'd been through enough. I decided to compromise. Nancy would be dressed and put in a casket so her parents could see her one more time before the memorial, and then she'd be cremated. I learned from being part of so many deaths in my family and working in hospice, as well as in my legal work, that rituals of death are for the survivors, not the deceased. I chose to fulfill Nancy's wishes without alienating her grieving parents.

Nancy's death and lack of serious reconciliation with her parents fostered intense conversations between us. They lived with much guilt and anger and too many unresolved feelings. I tried to be loving and supportive, but I also grieved.

The memorial service was in a local Methodist church and was an eye-opener for her parents. They sadly didn't know about her life in Maine and now discovered more about their vibrant and committed daughter, her brimming sense of humor not much seen at home. About two hundred friends and acquaintances attended, including her ex, Michelle, with whom I casually got along. At least thirty people spoke about their connections and experiences with and about Nancy. Beside tears, there were stories that created much laughter, like the one of her going to the legislature to fight for a bill wearing lobster earrings, thinking it would make this Buffalo girl fit in. We also displayed pictures of her life, covering all the places and people important to her—including her family, Michelle and me.

Mary Ann stood by my side at the service, with Nancy's parents on the other side, all of us holding each other up when we had to stand. My neighbors attended the service, and Rose gave me a big hug. I had never spoken with Jim or his wife Rose about my personal life, so the hug was a welcome surprise. All our friends were supportive of Nancy's parents, who were clearly overwhelmed by the outpouring of love and respect.

Nancy wanted her cremains to be cast in the ocean. Her parents wanted some to bury near their home, near other deceased family members, to be by their own remains when it was their time. I understood and gave them half the remains, remembering that my mother's body was buried in a cemetery on Long Island, New York, one I no longer visited.

At the end of the day, about eight of us, including her parents, shared dinner in a local restaurant. The owner, who knew Nancy well, treated us to the dinner. Before her parents returned to the airport the following day, we visited Nancy's house. It was so barren, with not much furniture. They walked around each room gazing at pictures on the walls, including some family ones. I walked around, remembering where we first kissed and how we had decorated some of the rooms, particularly the bedroom.

It was painful to say goodbye to them. Part of me wanted to go with them, console them, but I wasn't the person for that. They would be returning to their remaining daughter, who couldn't attend because her baby was ill.

Back at my house, I sat alone, except for the dogs and cats. Nancy's dog, Mitra, appeared as lost as I but was comfortable in my home, having spent much time there. I took a few days off from work, even though I got calls from the paralegals.

I wrote in my journal: "Nancy is dead. So easy to say, so hard to believe. No kisses, no more touching, dancing, laughing, loving, planning, folding sheets together, bitching together, working together."

Sitting on the couch, the sun shining on me through the cold February air, I ruminated on the heartbreaking but meaningful conversations with Nancy's parents, as well as with friends. It was all raw emotions, an intensity that belonged deep in the soul.

I moved my body on the couch and petted Mitra, who was sitting by my legs. I looked up and out. *Where are you, Nancy? Who are you in the bigger life of the soul? What part do I play in this life/death drama? There must be more to life than just a sad death.*

I suddenly had the need to connect with people in my life with whom I should reconcile in case *I* soon would die: friendships that hadn't ended so well. During the next few weeks, I wrote letters, including ones to my father and brother, explaining my pain. In the evenings, I achieved momentary solace reading all the sympathy cards received.

I returned to work and moved like a zombie, with tears ready to flow at any kind word. My emptiness made work difficult. I wanted to lie in bed and call Nancy to me—to see her, talk to her, and ask, "Why now? Why couldn't we have had more time together? Why don't I deserve more joy? Why couldn't the bigger struggles wait a little longer so we could continue all we had?"

The travel to and from work was an easy place to contemplate, process, and feel relief that I had no regrets for things unsaid or undone. I just wanted more of all the luscious fun, joy, tenderness, and caring she gave me. I wanted to be selfish; I wanted more time. Sometimes I yearned to melt away; to let people take care of me; to do nothing but stare at her pictures. But that wasn't me. It was not the Roberta she loved. I would move back into the struggle—work, laugh, function, but bleed hollow for a long time.

I dealt with Nancy's possessions, her finances, and the new house she barely lived in, sometimes yielding to bouts of anger at her for making me go through this. At times I wanted to keep material memories of her, like her shirts with her coffee or woody scents, and other times I wanted nothing, but my hands couldn't give away most of her clothes. I needed to breathe her in when wearing them.

My office wasn't far from the state police barracks where Nancy's belongings were being held. I dreaded going but knew I must. "Hello,

I'm here to pick up the belongings of Nancy J. I'm her personal representative." (I couldn't say, "I'm her lover.") I showed my identification and took her laundry basket, with the laundry she'd planned to do at my house that day after work and the odds and ends from the car that someone had put in the basket.

I drove to the garage where damaged cars were held. I faced the ugly remains of her brown Subaru Outback. There was blood and cracked glass on the front window. The front end was smashed in. I was able to look inside, and the one thing I noticed was a figurine of a small silver horsehead. The other one I knew she had wasn't there. I was disgusted with myself; I couldn't recall what she planned to do with them. I only knew she enjoyed having them in the car. On the way home, my memory returned—she was going to use them as knobs on her car radio. *How could I have forgotten something so meaningful to her?*

With my remaining strength, I doggedly drove the road on which she died. I stopped in front of the coroner's house, set back from the winding road. I saw what appeared to be dents in the telephone pole. I talked to Nancy, hoping she'd somehow contact me. *Nancy, send me a sign. I need to know you are here. I want to see the smile you gave me the night you died.* But nothing.

Her ashes sat in an urn on my bookcase. Sometimes I passed them, forgetting for a moment what they were, what they represented, and tears overflowed from guilt. When I first picked them up, it was so significant. I was holding, in a different form, the body I had held to mine. Now it was a box holding my torment.

Over the next few months, my dream life was active and repetitive. I had dreams about Nancy returning—that we'd buried her too soon. She wasn't dead, just on vacation, but we weren't connecting. I tried to call her but had forgotten the number or couldn't make the connection; or she had left me, breaking up our relationship, not dying, and I didn't understand why. And in the dreams, I screamed and bellowed, "How could you! Why? Why couldn't we have had more time together? Why don't I deserve more joy, more time to experience this love?"

Feelings I hadn't experienced since my mother's death overwhelmed me. Then, I had been a child who didn't understand how family and home could be ripped away so suddenly. Now it had happened again—my dreams of love, family, and home gone in a flash on an icy road.

One early evening, I had a particularly anguishing dream while taking a nap on the couch. I was on my knees in the kitchen, crying, or more like wailing from the depth of my soul into eternity, like the piercing mourning cries of Middle Eastern women, hearing the echo, but nobody around me heard my anguish. In the dream, I intentionally didn't stop wailing as I needed to feel the pain and maybe connect to the "why" of so many losses. It was like being on a mountain listening to my voice bellow into eternity or through eternity. When I woke, my mind was remarkably relaxed, sensing it was real, like I had experienced those cries more times than I ever could have fathomed.

The dream reminded me that, on the day before Nancy died, I noticed she seemed a little aloof in her actions and attention toward me. She didn't want to sleep at my house, which was unusual. In the morning she brought Mitra to stay with me as she was going to her office for a few hours. Maybe on some unconscious level, she knew we would not be touching or seeing each other again. *Am I imagining this?*

Another dream repeated a few times in different forms. I was driving without control of the wheel, not knowing where I was traveling and scared at first. Then I lifted my hands from the wheel and trusted, speaking out loud to myself that I didn't need physical control, that if I let go, I'd be okay, trusting the guidance I couldn't now see or even feel. In the dream I lost my fear for a while but then woke up in a sweat.

As my thoughts spiraled, I was struck by how so many of my interactions with Nancy reminded me of others in my life, such as Ernie (my boyfriend in New York) and Mary Ann. I remembered them both with joyful smiles, especially thinking of when we danced. The Italian-ness of Ernie and the political energy of Mary Ann were so like Nancy. Sometimes, the similarities blended in my mind with other friends as well, almost like we were all born from the same large soul family.

Ernie had kept in touch with me over the years, still calling me "Sherry" from the song he wrote for me. He sent me yearly birthday cards. He accepted my relationships with women. One month after Nancy's death he called me, very distraught.

"Sherry, I just had to call you now. I had this upsetting dream that you were in a car accident! In the dream, I was crying, and when I woke up I was sweating. I'm so glad you're okay. It felt so real!"

"When was the dream?" I asked.

"About a month ago. I waited to call you; I was afraid."

It was the time of Nancy's death. I was blown away! I guessed we really were all connected in some way. When we hung up, I was enthralled with something greater than reality, but I still felt like a bundle of wet crumbled paper.

For the next eight years, my life with Nancy continued through my relationship with her parents and the exploration of my spiritual side.

Chapter 34

Endurance

Nancy's parents and I spoke regularly. I needed their concern and connection as much as they needed mine. In one conversation, Mrs. J tried to comfort me. "You should be open to another relationship; you deserve love." I was shocked by her openness, as well as her acknowledgment that Nancy and I were in a relationship. I told her, "It will be a long time before I can think about that." She also sent me homemade cookies and candy, her way of sharing her heart.

I looked over at Nancy's smiling, jovial face in the photo on my dresser, taken while cross-country skiing in the fields, and smiled. Other times I gazed at pictures and felt hollow, like an empty tree, knowing there would be no more pictures to take. I continued wearing her shirts and jackets, recapturing her musk oil scent. I listened to her favorite radio station to connect to our memories.

There were so many things that needed to be done: Work on the house. Rewrite my will. Send letters to friends and family. Put my files in order. Prepare for the inevitable, just in case I died soon. But I was numb, exhausted, and not eating much. *I must remember to eat.* I lost six pounds, which may have been the saving grace of this horror. I looked forward to mail, receiving cards and letters that awakened my sleeping spirit.

Nancy had always bought lottery tickets. One day I decided to do the same and won $500! I laughed out loud. "Nancy, couldn't you have added a few more winning numbers and made it a million-dollar win?"

I dined with two close friends at their house, the same house at which I first met Nancy. Holly spoke about the effect of Nancy's death on her relationship with Kelly. She hesitantly shared, "It's odd to say, but Nancy's death is a *gift* to me and Kelly, in the sense that our pain is forcing us to reevaluate what's important to us, more than the day-to-day craziness we go through."

I found it healing not to feel alone in this grief. When loss was shared and expressed, my grief was less of a burden. There was a community grieving and a community healing.

I appreciated the word *gift*. Nancy had given me the gift of exploration into my spiritual side on a deeper level than I'd ever done. There were inner depths I hungered to access, but fear and the busyness of life, or the excuse of it, had blocked me. Her death shook me into the urgency to break through the fear. Now I shifted to a different level of growth, almost like the eight stages described by psychologist Erik Erikson.

Walking the dogs on our barely used dirt road, questioning myself, trying to make sure I wasn't blocking grief, talking in my head to Nancy, I saw the backside of what appeared to be a political button on the side of the road in the brown grass. I picked it up and read with a laugh, "Wild Women Don't Get the Blues." A coincidence or Nancy's fun-loving sense of humor at work? I preferred to think the latter.

On my birthday, a group of friends surprised me with a party—a surprise since they knew I had no desire to celebrate. They stopped me as I turned to leave. To my astonishment, I learned that before

Nancy left for Nicaragua, she had personally designed a sensuous heart-shaped silver pendant on a silver chain to be made for me by a local jeweler. She finished the design but hadn't yet taken it to the jeweler. She gave instructions to Jen to have it completed in case she didn't return from her trip. At the time of her death, it wasn't completed, but it was finished for my birthday. Nancy hadn't yet paid for it, so all these friends and a few who couldn't attend did that for her. It was an enduring gift of Nancy's promise and hope.

At a Holly Near concert at the university, I wore the pendant, silver against a blue turtleneck, to stand out for friends to view. The tears were hard to shy away from, especially when Holly sang "Over the Rainbow," a song I associated with Nancy and a song I'd never heard Holly sing.

Nighttime came more alive for me than daytime. I was having experiences that shook me with both excitement and trepidation. I had an out-of-body adventure flying with Nancy. After nestling myself to sleep in my comforter, imagining how exciting it would be to romp with her free of our bodies, suddenly in a hazy sleep my body was in motion, arching and lifting. I tried to speak but my words were garbled. As my body elevated, I perceived a presence and the strength of an arm holding my right wrist. I heard myself saying, "Okay, I'll relax," as I concentrated on slowing my breathing. My eyes were closed, yet I saw a dim pink light. I was flying, knowing I wasn't alone. Nancy was with me. I couldn't deny that reality, that connection.

After this captivating and eerie experience, I recalled many past flying dreams, not sure then if they were real. They had never before been with another person. I'd written about them in my journals, sometimes writing I wished they happened more often. Now they were.

For someone who gets nauseous on planes, I delighted in this feeling of flying, even when not with Nancy. I was like a bird soaring, sometimes on a carpet, traversing over cities and ocean, across open land, dipping and rising, passing through clouds. We had conversations of a sort, with her dressed in colorful, almost childish, clothes, fitting her human personality. I sensed she was experiencing a new type of learning, but I also upset her with too many questions.

I recorded these dreams, these experiences, in my journal. They were almost more real than the dream house I built, a measure of what I clung to; a conduit to understanding; a grasp onto hope. My sleep life had become as important as my waking life. I didn't share this with friends. It was too hard to explain, and they probably would have looked at me with sympathy and confusion. This was not the Roberta they've experienced.

While the pain of loss and memories jumped between worse and better, the depth of inner growth I discovered through the pain expanded and healed me. I always believed there were reasons for everything. This belief had helped me accept my mother's death and endure living in the orphanage. I attempted to take every experience as a challenge to my growth, recognizing the "why" of it, opening to the pain, growing through it, becoming more compassionate toward myself, and hopefully finding the universal connection, not separateness. Now this challenge weighed more heavily.

I sat by my cozy woodstove with Mitra, who was partially asleep, her breathing like a gentle wave through her body. I read Nancy's poetry and stories written after the death of her husband, who succumbed to illness in his late twenties. She expressed so many questions and so much impatience in her search for answers like I was now. Nancy called John her teacher and felt perhaps their purpose together was for her to learn from him, just as now I was learning from Nancy. Over time the challenges of the outside world over-whelmed her. I hoped I would learn to balance it all.

I drafted the paperwork for filing Nancy's will in probate court, feeling like two people—the grieving lover and the impersonal lawyer. I was like a puddle of water sitting on frozen ground with no place to go. The heavy convulsive tears diminished, then suddenly again crushed me, especially while driving to work listening to songs on the radio.

One night I woke up, and my inner voice kept singing songs from *The Wizard of Oz*, one of Nancy's favorite movies. I clearly envisioned her smiling face dancing on a rainbow. I adored her childish excite-ment when we watched the movie on TV. My childhood experiences didn't include that movie.

I met with friends, sitting outside on the grass for two hours of gifted conversation. We performed a sharing vigil for women trav-eling to Nicaragua with the Witness for Peace group, the same trip Nancy went on this time the year before. We read poems. I read some of Nancy's Nicaraguan journal. Her last words in the journal choked my voice. I didn't read them out loud: "Can't wait to kiss Roberta again." We questioned our work, life's meaning, optimism and pes-simism about human nature, and our ability to effect change. It was healing. *Healing*, a word I used often now.

I had conversations with friends as to how we wanted to die. Some said, "In my sleep. I don't want to suffer."

I stated, "I want notice in advance of when I'm going to die, even if the advance notice is a painful illness. This way I'll have time to find homes for my animals, get stuff in order, and hopefully die in my home, sharing with friends and family around me." Then I quipped, "Like a TV movie."

As an attorney, I advised clients to put their affairs in order so they didn't leave the hard decisions to those suffering their loss. I recognized I hadn't done all that for myself. I had a will and medical and financial powers of attorney, but that wasn't enough. I needed to talk in depth to those I'd asked to make decisions for me if I were unable to do so myself. I'd done that superficially, and I should know better. My mother died too young. I'd known clients younger than me who'd died.

A few days later, after dinner at a friend's house, I drove home slowly in slushy snow. Relieved to be out of the car, I listened to music and did my own form of hatha yoga, then poured a little wine into Nancy's two special, tall, thin wine glasses, hoping maybe the wine in one would disappear on its own. The dogs and cats were quiet, reading my mood. I lit one candle, turned the lights off, then danced in the dark to the smooth jazz singing of Sade, our favorite. The outdoor light was on. I watched the snow fall, seeing myself reflected in the window, alone.

I appreciated receiving letters or phone calls that said, "Take your time, we understand; we look forward to connecting when you're ready. If you need us, we're here." So simple and reassuring. My dream world continued actively, like a night of watching movies. I woke up often and recorded many dreams on tape to write in my journal the next day. No wonder I was more tired than I should have been. I had a desperate urge to see the Barbra Streisand movie, *On a Clear Day.* I bought the video, watching it three times with different friends. Each time Barbra sang, I imagined I could see Nancy in the far reaches of forever.

My days floated in and out of memories and the stuff of life that needed to be done. My mind briefly stopped pondering expectations and memories as my wood floor was laid and finished. There were days of noise, sawdust, and dirt. Also, latticework was completed around the house and a more secure dog pen. The floors shone beautifully, but my heart shone only during my new nighttime experiences. The work on the house was perfunctory, even though I was excited that Nancy's family would appreciate the improvements when they arrived shortly; maybe her parents wouldn't even notice—they were as numb as I.

I met the potential buyers of Nancy's house, a home barely lived in yet holding the savory energy of some of our brief sharing.

I had conversations with Nancy's mother and sister, their pain so heavy and surely more mournful than mine, for all they hadn't been able to share with her.

On May 10, Nancy would have turned thirty-eight. I went through more of her history with the help of friends. They took items I didn't want to give to strangers or keep for myself, like her old records and games. It made me want to take everything I owned and dump it so those I left behind wouldn't go through this emotional state of absurdity.

In mid-June I was sitting in my living room at three thirty. Nancy's parents, her sister Angela, and her husband and baby Gary were sightseeing in Camden. I couldn't join them, feeling too physically and emotionally exhausted. The dogs and cats were recovering from baby energy and clatter. My eyes were watery and red listening to Nancy's music tape on which she sang and played her guitar, a gift for her nephew made before she died.

I enjoyed their company, especially being "Aunt Roberta" to her nephew. We shared warm and open conversations. Angela told me I reminded her of Nancy in many ways. I didn't ask what ways—hopefully they were positive ones. Because she hadn't been able to attend the funeral, this was her first time here. Her father liked to be busy and helped me with some minor jobs around the house. We shared laughs and tears, cherishing the connection between us. The family brought outrageously delicious Italian desserts, and Mrs. J cooked for us. The scents of food and diapers in the house were as alive as Nancy was when we visited Buffalo, seemingly so long ago. I told them, "I'm eating two pieces of cake cause Nancy's making me eat one for her!"

When they arrived, we first drove to Nancy's house for Angela to see it. Buyers were moving in shortly. Then we visited Spruce Run, the battered women's shelter she helped start, and the office of Parents Anonymous, her last job. I broke down and cried on the shoulder of Nancy's secretary. On Saturday we had dinner at a friend's home. I bawled in Angela's arms after listening to her mother talk about Nancy's childhood. There was so much I wanted to share with her and so little time we had.

Nancy wanted her cremains to be scattered off Cape Elizabeth, Maine, not making it easy for us. We drove two and a half hours to Portland and rented a boat to take us to Cape Elizabeth for the scattering. Nancy's ex, Michelle, and two friends, Sally and Karen, joined us. I felt a little uneasiness between people who superficially knew each other, but we focused on the purpose of the trip—and seasickness.

It was foggy, with the waves as choppy as the emotions between us. Because of the weather, we were forced to stop halfway to the Cape for the ceremony. Karen and I vomited a few times. I had taken Dramamine beforehand, but it didn't help. We all laughed with the thought that Nancy was laughing at us. Maybe she didn't want us to be too serious. We scattered the ashes through the ocean wind with some of her body dust blowing back on us. To our shock, some of her cremains were unexpected chips of bone. Sally brought wildflowers from her garden that she let loose to cascade through the wind and rough sea. Karen sang a song, Michelle read a hymn, and I read two of Nancy's poems, written in 1970. We shared stories of and about her and returned to land famished, sharing a late lunch. This was the first and last time this group of mourners would be together.

After a few days, Nancy's family was on their way home. I missed them, even the busyness. The house was peaceful, orderly, but cheerless. It still smelled of baby powder. It wasn't easy to say goodbye, especially for Nancy's father. He cried as he hugged me. I was left with an album of pictures to pull together.

As I returned to my routines, work, exercise, and meditation, I now had an extended family with whom to share my loss.

The effects of Nancy's death on me had become as enriching as the effects of her life with me. The irony didn't escape me that all my life I had longed for the family that was taken from me. Now I had a family, but it had come at the expense of another loss. Nevertheless, it was healing—healing me in the present and healing the child of the past.

Chapter 35

Mourning

With Nancy's parents back in Buffalo, my days flowed one into the other with office work and nighttime indwelling—searching for understanding and answers while knowing questions and answers changed constantly. Nothing was static, especially my constant dreaming and nighttime experiences with or about Nancy. I still questioned what I was experiencing, yet so desired them.

I spoke infrequently to my father and brother, not wanting to burden them with my emotions. There wasn't much change in their days, so our conversations were superficial. I was numb anyway.

My outside world was warm with a gentle breeze. I drove to the nearby lake to swim, walked on leftover winter leaves and gravel in the winding woods along the water's edge, and arrived at my favorite spot, hidden by trees with a cluster of rocks to sit on after swimming. The water was calm and cool. Having the lake to myself, I lay on my back, watching the movement of clouds in hope I might again see Nancy's smiling face as I did on the day of her death. The night before I had a short dream of us making love. The passion welled up in me to the point of almost fainting, so much so I had to stop to breathe. I woke up thinking if I couldn't share with her in real life, such a dream now and then would keep both of us alive.

Driving to work, I listened to a tape from last year of a presentation at a hospice meeting. The speaker, a psychic named Arlene, spoke about the light that people see who experience near-death. She equated it to fireflies. About a month ago before dozing, I was trying to visualize a protective light around Nancy and me and my house, using the fireflies analogy, when I recalled a peculiar white light seen in the corner of my bedroom one late afternoon upon waking from a nap. Its shape was like a moving star but with many points. I thought it might have been light from the sun or a car, but the sun, or other light, doesn't hit that spot in my bedroom, and cars don't pass my house. Thereafter I pictured it as Nancy's light, a light I hoped to see again.

I called and met with Arlene at a spiritual center where she lived, which was comprised of old houses in the countryside. I breathed in the blended scents of worn wood furniture, wild flowers, and mixed cooking spices I couldn't even name, an environment that folded me inside it. Arlene was tall, friendly, older than me with long gray hair, calmly self-possessed. We sat in a private area, chairs close together around a small table. She did a "reading" with me for over an hour, which I recorded. I had generally been a skeptic on psychic tales and advice. Once in Connecticut, I saw a psychic whom people raved about. She told me surprising things that did come true, but I wasn't trusting, thinking perhaps she just got lucky.

After general introductions and small-talk, Arlene confirmed what I was experiencing with Nancy's family, even though I didn't discuss that with her. The skeptic in me was protective in what I disclosed, yet she startled me by saying, "You are standing in Nancy's shoes, sharing her unfinished sentences, her unfinished emotions, in a way that she couldn't do during her lifetime, and in the process, *you* have a new family."

She also shared, which I found strange, that we would author a book *together*, with Nancy being on a different plane from me. "There is learning to harmonize your two vibrations." Then she added upsettingly, "People are going to think you've absolutely flipped your lid; they are going to think, okay, she's been grieving too long."

I hesitantly asked, "What do I do with what people think about me?" Her response hit home. "You share with people in your group who will understand. It's important to maintain an inner balance of stability."

I was astonished. Arlene knew nothing about me, especially that I was in a group—a group of friends that included Nancy. She also didn't know that I wrote, nor that I daydreamed about writing a book, even before Nancy died. Sentiments of trust enveloped me. She further affirmed my experiences. "There might be times when you see and feel her clearly, other times you will sense her. Sometimes she will try to catch your vision by perhaps some things not being in their usual place."

I was stunned, recalling the political button found on the road by my house, "Wild Women Don't Get the Blues."

Arlene also announced I wouldn't have another meaningful relationship for eight years. "Use the years for learning, growing, writing." Now as I look back, how right she was.

I walked out of our conversation in amazement, wondering if I could share this with friends but sensing I had better wait. This level of spirituality wasn't something I had previously discussed with anyone.

Back to the reality of living: most of my friends were in relationships. Over time my loneliness surged as I watched couples being couples. There was an awkwardness when we ate out. The waiter asked, "How are you all paying?" I said, "Just me," as friends in couples said, "We're on one bill." It was the same after Mary Ann and I broke up. I decided I'd be more conscious of this in the future if I'm ever a "couple" again.

In Augusta, Maine, an hour and a half from home, I presented a legal workshop at the Gay/Lesbian Symposium and was sympathetically embraced with hugs by many people I knew and who had known Nancy. I couldn't stay for the whole day as I walked through it emotionally numb, easy to tears, even with friends. Maybe it was just PMS. The conference brochure was dedicated to Nancy and another person. I initially considered toughing it out, but when I thought about the dance to be held in the evening and how I'd miss dancing with her, my pain stung too hard.

As time moved on for others, it did less so for me. I sometimes sensed I was a burden on friends. At one holiday picnic, I suddenly had a need to talk through my pain. My friends wanted to have fun and not be sad, but they tried to be supportive and listen. *How much can I throw at them?* After that I decided to process more on my own, to pull back somewhat from talking about what I was going through unless information was solicited. Even being excited about some of my experiences and wanting to blab on and on, I controlled my enthusiasm and anxiety and dealt inwardly. I also recognized that accepting death as a hospice volunteer was significantly different from accepting death when it hit home.

On returning from the picnic, I called Nancy's parents and spoke to Mrs. J. It was so easy to share with her; we grieved the same loss. I planned a visit for the following month.

I began reading unfamiliar books, driven to understand the world's thinking regarding death and dying, reincarnation, out-of-body experiences, near-death experiences, and how they fit into Judaism's mystical side, the Kabbalah. The reading brought me a little closer to comprehending my dream experiences, appreciating being connected with something beyond my human "self."

My dad called. His voice unusually nervous and labored. "Molly died." Molly was his landlady and friend, someone who I knew well when I lived there. "She died last night," he added. He lived in a two-family house, he upstairs and she downstairs. The house was on a tree-lined block of similar houses, friendly neighbors, and away from the bustle of the shopping area, to which he could easily walk. I had concern for my father but didn't have the energy to mourn Molly. He had found her dead in the morning when he went to check on her. He'd called the police, stayed with her body, and waited until her daughter arrived.

He was in soul-stirring pain, nervous about his future, and willing to talk about it. He worried what would happen to him, softly whispering, "Molly's kids will surely sell the house. Where will I go?"

I had no answer. He wouldn't come to Maine; I had offered. He'd miss the city and his Jewish culture. His life was suddenly uprooted again, a reality that often rattled his sleep. I could easily commiserate—father and daughter bleeding loss, feeling rootless.

I made plans to fly to Brooklyn for a long weekend.

Together, we processed the options for a move. I was relieved that he had time to find a new place and didn't have to leave immediately. He and Fred would do the search. He didn't want to hear me talk about death and dying. To him, it was "stupid." He believed we die and go to the worms and nothing more. Fred, when studying biology, once "educated" me on that point. His words convinced me to be cremated. I abhorred bugs, although this was less of a fear now after living in the woods. I knew I couldn't force my beliefs on my father. I tried to be supportive. The encouragement and concern I received now came from Nancy's family.

While visiting my father, I found and read letters I'd saved and forgotten about from as far back as 1957, ones I hadn't taken with me when I left New York. Some I threw away. Some were from my deceased Uncle Morris, with whom I had lived on the farm after my mother died. I sent them to his son, Aaron; I couldn't destroy them. I kept some silly letters from my friends in the orphanage.

I also found letters from my favorite counselor in the orphanage, Lea, my mother substitute. I smiled with soft-hearted memories; she was my protector. She called me her "honey bunny." I forgot that we had communicated for a few years afterward. I wondered if she were still living, not having any idea of her age. Earlier I had tried searching for her, but no luck.

I returned to Maine with the letters, to my house, dogs, cats, and work, as I ran around trying to get everything in order so I could travel to Massachusetts the next day for my first retreat experience at the Kripalu Center.

Life was wonderfully strange. Upon my return from New York, I found a letter from Mrs. J. She wrote, "It's so surprising how we felt connected to you from the first time we met." Adding, "Maybe that was Nancy preparing us for her death." They hoped so. I believed so.

Chapter 36

Spirit

Six months after Nancy died, I was in the registration line at Kripalu, a retreat and wellness center in the mountains of Massachusetts. It was my first visit, and I was greeted by an enormous red brick building, previously a monastery, unnervingly reminding me of the Yonkers orphanage building. I was startled to see so many parked cars, so many people signing up, not having considered all the workshops happening on the weekend. I unexpectedly sweated, not from a hot flash but more likely from a sense of claustrophobia. I hadn't been in a big crowd since Nancy's funeral. I also hadn't pre-registered for any workshop, wanting to be unfettered and to attend what interested me with no obligations.

My private room faced a mountain. The door had no lock; it was a trusting environment, not something this city girl was yet used to. Everywhere I strode in the building, my nostrils were pleasantly suffused with zestful blends of citrus, spices, balsam incense, and flowers.

I arrived in time for dinner. The dining hall was spacious with floor-to-ceiling windows facing mountainous trees and greenery. We carried trays, perusing a variety of food to choose from, which was beneficial for my limited palate. I didn't eat spicy food, having grown up on meat, potatoes, canned vegetables, and Chinese restaurants on Sundays, although my taste had expanded some. I had my first pizza at age twenty-one. Now I tried to be daring, for me. Much of the food was pleasingly natural and delicious; I stayed away from anything with pungent spices. I wasn't threatened walking in, as I had been in the high school dining hall. Here we didn't know each other and ate quietly, meditatively, with no conversation.

I signed up for the Kripalu Experience, the title in their catalog. It was truly an experience for me. Instead of just reading, I was taking the frightening steps of publicly practicing yoga and meditation, sitting in awkward positions against which my body rebelled and which afterward required a rewarding deep coconut cream massage. I daily walked slowly around a labyrinth, surrounded by statuesque trees, vibrant gardens, and vistas of mountains changing shape from sunrise to sunset. At the end of each day I participated in a free-dance workshop, just letting go, not paying attention to the other participants. During breaks I sat in a recliner chair facing the gardens and distant woods staring through floor-to-ceiling windows. Before breakfast I sat by myself outside on the deck appreciating the morning sun.

In my early years in the orphanage, I believed the pain of life had a purpose for my soul, even if I didn't understand exactly what "purpose" meant or what a "soul" was. Now I knew pain was part of my soul's growth. Without pain, I couldn't appreciate pleasure. It was the yin and the yang.

I surprised myself, relieved to be out of my home, my corner of heaven. I needed space, newness, a place to process.

I read somewhere that the real goal of meditation is to come home to parts of ourselves that we'd lost in the rush of life. This was a challenge for me. I lived actively, sometimes obsessively. I hadn't possessed a natural inner calm. Nancy's death changed me. My soul peeked out and roared, "Finally, you noticed me!" I didn't need to be Superman's daughter anymore as I had in the orphanage, which was something I told myself a lot, maybe now believing it.

Before Nancy's death, I grieved an emptiness I couldn't name. Now I could. As external successes came to me, they were exciting for a while but didn't penetrate soulfully. Over time I became confident that the answers were deep within me. Hopefully, I would "be" the experience I sought, without giving up the person I was, yet still be centered in the balance of the two. The word *yoga* meant union. I was working on the union of my external and inner selves.

One morning at Kripalu, I woke up with song lyrics in my head: "If you're feeling sad and lonely . . . don't be afraid, you can call me." I couldn't recall the name of the song or all the lyrics, but those words surrounded me like a mother's hug—or my bare remembrance of my mother's hug.

After four days at Kripalu, I drove home, praying these experiences would stay with me when I returned to my regular day-to-day life. The first night home, loneliness set in but also a calmness and a more trusting sense of place.

What I didn't expect to confront on my return was how my new "enlightenment" affected others. The changes I was undergoing and my enthusiasm were threatening to a friend of many years. Since Nancy's death, I saw life through a wider screen, viewing it in a long-term way, seeing connections on a spiritual level not just on a personal level. This spaciousness released a lot of my anger, particularly around politics. We have roles in friendships, and change can be disturbing, especially if it appears we're moving in opposite directions.

One morning my friend came over for an hour of conversation, she sitting at the kitchen table and me in the rocking chair. I learned the angst causing her to be distant—her fear of my changes—and how to reconcile our different paths to continue our friendship. We shared without anger, knowing we respected and cared for each other. I told her softly, "The discovery of my spiritual side is multicolored. I'm struggling to let go of anger at the world, at politics. I want to challenge issues but not get lost in them. I'm not perfect doing it, but more and more I need to see life and politics through a wider prism and find a greater purpose." She was quiet, her normal way, always difficult to read. I continued, "I hope my challenges, my search, will deepen our friendship, not the opposite." She listened, speaking minimally, sadly leaving the conversation incomplete.

Later I conversed with another friend who brought me back to a healthy clarity and perspective. I acknowledged that my changes and journey might be scary for some friends, who were experiencing me so differently now, like a husband who fears adjusting to his wife's new lifestyle after feminist consciousness-raising. I hoped we'd continue conversing and she'd become more open. I didn't want to lose our friendship. But I couldn't return to who I was before Nancy's death to make some people more comfortable. I reread Peck's book, *The Road Less Traveled*, to remind myself that the spiritual journey is not easy, understandably so.

I was hopeful my friend and I would work it out. I asked myself, *Isn't the richness of growth to work through painful struggles?* Maybe if I kept repeating those words, like a mantra, I'd totally believe it, yet our relationship was painfully superficial for a few years.

Settling back in after Kripalu, I became aware of how my body was being affected by events and feelings during interactions with others. After two weeks back in reality's busyness, the tightness and tension in my neck and a pinched nerve were palpable. I didn't have an appointment with my chiropractor, so at night I lay down on the living room rug, soft music playing, animals quiet, and concentrated on the pain, questioning why I was experiencing it. I recognized my anxiousness and disappointment that my friend and I weren't connecting. I acknowledged she likely sensed the possible loss of our friendship, as did I, albeit differently. After forty minutes of pondering that realization, the pinched nerve no longer pinched.

As enthusiastic as I had been at Kripalu, believing I had more control over my life and schedule, I sullenly acknowledged I wasn't living my day-to-day life in the "Kripalu Experience." I grasped how easy it was to fall back into routine and a bustling life, including the peaks and valleys of missing Nancy. I worked through them as I was able, accepting I had a long way to go. In my *real* world, it was challenging finding a compatible balance of the inner and the outer. At least now I had a healthier set of skills.

I found a book that helped my healing. In reading the first story in Stephen Levine's *Meetings at the Edge*, dialogues with the grieving and the dying, the words of a woman who lost a child to cancer expressed what rang so true to me: "I have never felt so bad or so good in my whole life."

I was stepping onto unfamiliar paths without handrails. At times I floundered. In fear I reached out, knowing I must reach more within, driving on the eternal road, going into the eternal cry I had experienced in a dream shortly after Nancy died—going home to a place I'd been longing to find. Now I knew it was there. I saw the hazy opening of the door and was slowly, slowly, making my way through the fog. At times I took several steps in. Other times I was lost in the blinding fog and couldn't see the door.

Getting ready for Mary Ann's visit later in the day, I meditated, relaxing my tense muscles from traveling so much for work. I visualized sending healing energy to friends and family. Next I moved the energy beyond that, sending it to the universe, to cover everyone and everything, the way I had prayed as a child, never wanting to leave anyone out, my list of names eventually propelling me into sleep. I envisioned a healing light of blended colors surrounding and penetrating the earth, then spreading like an aura to the rest of the universe. To heal my body, I pictured the sun's rays spreading into loving, warm arms and hands massaging me, hugging me. My muscle tension lessened. When Mary Ann arrived, a tearful extended hug and her homemade soup softened my pain.

At three thirty Sunday morning, I drove with Mary Ann and some friends to the top of Cadillac Mountain in Acadia National Park, for the Harmonic Convergence Ceremony, to experience an event I've never before attended. Approximately three hundred people attended, all trying to connect with the energy of others around the world. Some brought musical instruments, others sang. My body filled with peacefulness moving with the music. Afterward, famished, we stopped at a local restaurant for breakfast before returning home.

At night I dreamt we were at Cadillac Mountain for the ceremony, standing in a building waiting for something to happen. Suddenly the sky opened. First I saw amazing designs of constellations in white light against a dark sky changing forms and shapes, followed by varied gigantic moving scenes of history combined with different colored circles zooming all around me. Swirls of purple light, like a cyclone, descended next to me. Unafraid, I leapt into its hot and powdery texture. I breathed easily, moving amid the swirls and lathering the powder all over me. Since no one else had touched it, I placed more on my hands and spread it on others nearby. Music played, and the sky opened again, with circles of color zooming around to the beat of the music. I woke in calmness, body relaxed, not wanting to leave my bed.

Mary Ann's visit continued to be supportive and warm. We spent time with Jen and Emma, just like the old days, when we were two couples. Of course, this was different, like trying to bring back the past, especially when we started reminiscing about the fun times the four of us had together. It was a nostalgic weekend, but nostalgia far removed from the present.

To my surprise, Ernie called. "Sherry how are you doing?" After all these years he still liked calling me Sherry. "I hope you don't mind my calling. I still have the vision of the car accident." I told him, "I like hearing your voice. I feel lost a lot, but it's nice to know you have a deep connection to me and Nancy. How otherwise could you have had the vision of me in a car accident at the time Nancy died in her car?" He agreed. We chatted some more and I smiled as I hung up.

After Mary Ann returned to Connecticut, I called Arlene, the psychic, to wish her well with her upcoming surgery. It was pleasant to speak to her without having to ask for something. In chatting she mentioned she had been born near Buffalo, and when I asked what town, it was the same town in which Nancy grew up. We both were amazed. Clearly, Arlene's connection to Nancy wasn't coincidental.

Imperceptibly I discovered some balance and acceptance, knowing my invisible internal world was just as present in my life as the visible anguishing hurt I was experiencing.

Chapter 37

Synchronicity

Back in Buffalo with Nancy's parents, I stayed in their home. I likely gained five pounds with all the delicious meals and goodies teasing my sweet tooth. I ate plenty, especially Mrs. J's meatballs and lasagna. I slept in the finished basement, the place where I'd slept with Nancy on our last visit, this time hoping her parents didn't hear my sobs. At times, my memories of being there with Nancy choked my calmness, but I needed to be there, almost more than in my home.

Her parents took me to the Canadian side of Niagara Falls. We strolled the walkway, enjoying the beauty of a rainbow and flowers scenting the air with a trail of roses, lilies, and gardenias. I was engaged with the faces around me, content with the universe and Nancy's family, experiencing the joy of sharing and giving easily, yet not pressured to act beyond my natural self. I took pictures of them and our surroundings to hold onto those memories.

Nancy's words, said through Arlene, haunted me. "It's time for the switchover." I believed, in some way, I was standing in Nancy's place in her family. I had thought I was in her family's life to help them reconcile their feelings about Nancy. I'd since come to believe the "switchover" had an additional meaning—that her family was here for me. Mrs. J was the mother I never had. They were the complete family life I never experienced. I had barely lived with my mother, nor with my father and brother until Fred and I moved back with him when I was a teenager. This epiphany was like a reincarnation, a rebirth. I lost my family when my mother died. Now I had been reborn into this family.

One late night, while I was sitting with Mrs. J at her round kitchen table eating homemade muffins with tea, she timidly said, "Sometimes it's scary for me and Mr. J, these strong feelings we have for you, at the same time wondering if we're substituting you for Nancy."

I responded, "It doesn't scare me." I added as sincerely as I could, "Mrs. J, the obstacles you couldn't or didn't have time to work out with Nancy, you can talk about with me. I'm here to share with you, as you share with me your love and laughter. I don't want to be intrusive in your family, but I believe Nancy needed us to do this."

It was heartening that even though she and her daughter Angela professed not to believe in reincarnation or necessarily understood all I tried to share with them, they seemed to have an interest in hearing about it. I shared with them my psychic experiences with Nancy, with added humor, and we joked and laughed. My words seemed to give Mrs. J a sense of peace, especially when I said Nancy was sharing in their struggles and growth, trying to understand and work through the pain and love of their tumultuous relationship. I added, "The uniqueness of life is in the willingness to forgive our so-called mistakes, like I believe God would do."

It was difficult to easily talk about Nancy with Mr. J. One afternoon when Mrs. J was out shopping, I sat with him in the den, with a football game on the television. He suddenly opened up, sharing how he and Nancy worked together on house problems. "She had a knack for the work. I taught her, and we hammered and fixed things—about the only times we didn't argue." He looked at me, resettling into his recliner, and burst into tears. I wanted to hug him but didn't want to intrude into the tears he needed to release. He quickly changed the subject. But when I was ready to get on the plane for my return trip, he gave me a strong hug.

In between serious conversation, I rode Nancy's bike around her suburban neighborhood, remembering what she told me about her life in Buffalo. I laughed and cried with her family watching *My Fair Lady* on the lawn of the Art Park. There was lots of girl-talk between her mother, sister, and me—deep conversations about life and death, the differences between men and women, tolerance, and being Aunt Roberta.

Nancy's grandparents shared lunch and dinner with us and, upon leaving, gave me gifts of homemade Italian cookies and hand-made pillowcases.

I so desired that her parents' connection with me would facilitate some type of reconciliation with Nancy, an acceptance and forgiveness of their challenging relationship. It was a privilege to help ease their pain, together with my own.

I returned home and relished letters and conversations with them, including a package from Mrs. J of malted balls and banana chips, as well as dog treats.

Waking up one morning I profoundly grasped the reality that I was alone, though surrounded by the dogs and cats. This journey was an intimate adventure, not easily shared with others. I couldn't push it on them unless they asked to share it with me. I was open enough about experiencing my captivating newness.

Shortly thereafter, a friend called asking me to help mediate discord and friction for a group of her longtime friends who owned land together. The session was to be held at my home. These were caring women with whom I'd shared friendship on and off over the years. I was anxious, not wanting the meeting to be a typical legal mediation only resolving a property division, but more so a safe place for opening, letting go, and trusting, so friendships could be renewed. In sharing with them, I wasn't confident I knew how to fulfill my non-lawyerly intentions.

Days before, nervous that I hadn't decided on my approach, I sat on the couch, envisioning their pain and loss of friendship and their fears. I abruptly experienced a clarity of mind and heart, and ideas streamed in as to what to say and do to make the process purposeful.

I opened the meeting at my house asking each to share how they met and how and why they decided to buy the property together. They emotionally shared their memories. I then asked, "What are your goals for this meeting?" Their answers to the questions added a softness to the conversation. Together we changed the negative energy into positive ways to resolve their burdensome issues, leading to embraces with welcome tears. When they left, I plopped into bed, relaxed with relief and fullness.

As an attorney I've mediated divorces, financial settlements, and family arguments. This mediation was different. I was able to set aside my ego, something hard for me to do when handling legal matters. My heart expanded, and words emanated from a wiser part of me, not just from my intellect. This experience reinforced for me that all the answers are already inside us when we open to them. The reading and learning I'd been doing was the inspiration to help reach into what already existed, the "infinite wisdom" of the universe that was accessible to us, albeit not easily. I affirmed to myself that going forward, I would try to bring this compassion and warmth into other emotionally difficult experiences, including those at work.

There was a time when I laughed at this way of thinking,

dismissing it as corny, "touchy-feely" stuff. At moments I still questioned, but each new opening decreased my skepticism. I hoped that the inner urgency of my search wouldn't let me go back to my old way of being.

I was amid an internal struggle, trying to understand ego, its place—or absence—in spiritual awareness. Book reading acted itself out in my dreams, sometimes centering, other times the opposite. It was hard to learn to accept confusion and patience; it must have been the lawyer in me. Lots of internal walls needed to be broken down. Because I knew the depth of some of my reading was beyond my comprehension, I needed to stop expecting intellectual understanding and accept that insight would mainly come through something more than mind analysis, even though I did appreciate the intellectual stimulation.

Occasionally I wished help from a guru, or "spiritual friend," a term I preferred. While working at the university, I learned of some professors meeting to discuss spiritual issues. I had lunch with Kyriacos Markides, a professor who wrote *The Magus of Strovolos*, a fascinating story about a spiritual healer in Cypress with whom Kyriacos had spent time. I then met other teachers, as well as people outside the university, who were forming a group to discuss spirituality, reincarnation, mysticism, religion, and whatever extended from those conversations.

Euphoria warmed my body—meeting people who enjoyed delving into the depths of what I too desired to examine. When Kyriacos presented a workshop titled "Spirituality and Healing," I was like a kid in a candy shop!

As the group grew, we named it the Center for Noetic Studies and became a nonprofit organization, the mission of which was to provide a forum for the discussion of traditional and nontraditional approaches to personal and spiritual growth. Our first public conference was scheduled to be on exploring mysticism in religion.

I would be presenting a workshop on Jewish mysticism. A friend gave me the book, *The Thirteen Petalled Rose*, which was a discourse on the essence of Jewish existence and belief. This fed my hunger for insight and was perfect timing in preparation for my presentation, which thankfully was eight months away. Throughout my life, I'd been caught in an internal dichotomy about my religion. Well, most religions. Now I was taking on the challenge of finding a more impassioned approach to that relationship.

The excitement of my learning didn't unbind my connection to Nancy. One Saturday I participated in a Sister City kick-off celebration in Bucksport, thinking back to my shared work with her in helping start the Sister City project between Bucksport and a town in Nicaragua. A little girl wore a sweater with a giraffe on it, Nancy's favorite animal. A friend dedicated a song to Nancy, and a dog howled during the singing. We laughed, joking that Nancy's spirit was with us. So many memories stuffed me like a tasty meal, especially of Nancy's slide show presentation of her experience in Nicaragua that she shared with friends when she returned.

Driving home, I turned on my favorite radio show with Marian McPartland. She and her guest were fooling around on the piano playing "Over the Rainbow," the song I connected to Nancy. Then they played a Duke Ellington song called "I'm Beginning to See the Light." I laughed. It was more than coincidence. Synchronicity was real.

Chapter 38

Bonding

Nights were challenging. It was painful to fall asleep, especially on Fridays, when Nancy and I looked forward to an enraptured weekend after busy workdays. Nine months since her death, she was still in in my interminable thoughts and dreams. I sat in bed dazed, struggling to process too much, as if all the answers would pop into my head. It was too uncomfortable to talk to friends or family. I hadn't much shared with them, sensing their awkwardness in not knowing what to say and believing they'd think I was losing it if I shared my nighttime communication with Nancy. My experiences as a volunteer hospice worker helped me understand my own fluctuations, as well as appreciate the feelings of friends.

When clear-minded, I grasped the so-called spiritual facts of life, realizing I needed to move on beyond Nancy's humanness and knowing we are more than our humanness. Yet as I nestled in bed remembering our physical oneness, I continued to function in the present. Thinking of the future seemed meaningless.

My desire to embellish my house, my corner of heaven, was hollow; my inner needs had priority.

I continued learning from my dreams. I read a book called *Lucid Dreaming*, which helped develop my skill of being awake in dreams, raising my awareness, and controlling the dream to a degree. I discovered many people had recorded and analyzed their dream experiences as I was doing, reducing my aloneness.

I sometimes berated myself for not letting go of Nancy, not wanting to pressure her at the beginning of her new journey. I just wanted her a part of *my* journey. When clear-minded, I accepted our connection on the soul level, with larger goals than just this human connection. *But oh, how strong was that human connection!*

I attended an inspirational workshop by Joan Borysenko, who wrote *Minding the Body, Mending the Mind*, as well as a second workshop led by Kyriacos. Both centered me—at least for a while. At Kyriacos's workshop, we did a chakra meditation sending healing energy to a woman in the group who had breast cancer. This was new to me. I'd never studied chakra centers in the human body, energy centers that were well-known in Indian spiritual traditions.

That night I dreamt I lived in a building that had a "Chakra Center," surprised that I didn't know there was such a place in my building. When I awoke, I realized that the "building" was really my body.

In another dream the same night, I was flying and able to control my movements. I saw a sign that said, HALL OF SECRETS, and was excited to fly into it. But as I moved closer, it was revealed as a deception, an empty hall. When I woke from the dream, I sensed my dream-self was reminding me the "Hall of Secrets" was not outside of me, but inside.

Days later, while I was driving home from a visit with friends and listening to oldies music on the radio, a man called in and requested to dedicate the song "Heatwave" to someone in Nancy's hometown. That night I woke from sleep several times, finding myself singing "This Magic Moment," by Jay and the Americans, a song I had never sung but knew a lot of the words.

Driving to work the following day, feeling joyful talking to Nancy in my head, the song "Heatwave" came on the radio, immediately followed by "This Magic Moment." I couldn't stop laughing. I wasn't alone. As I searched for a parking spot at work, which took longer than usual, "Over the Rainbow," sung by Judy Garland, began to play. I guessed Nancy found music, which she loved, an easy way to communicate. That empty pit in my stomach was full for a while.

The winter holidays arrived, nowadays emotionally distressing. I had a mother-daughter, friend-to-friend conversation with Mrs. J. Nancy's parents were going through a rollercoaster of memories, good and bad, especially remembering the last joyful visit they'd had with Nancy and me.

Mrs. J shared, "I couldn't sleep last night. I got up and reread all the letters you sent us. Thank you for your support." I told her, "The thank-you goes both ways."

A few days after the call, I received a letter from Mrs. J, saying I could call them Mom and Pop instead of Mr. and Mrs. J. I cried cloud-nine tears for Nancy. Her parents had genuinely accepted me into their family. I doubted I'd use Mom and Pop. Somehow it felt awkward. I never even called them by their first names, accustomed by now to Mr. and Mrs. J.

Early on New Year's Day, I visited my father. He was happy in his new apartment but not used to living in a tall building and taking an elevator. The last such building he lived in was when my mother died, a three-floor walkup.

He met some friendly neighbors, mostly women, and gave up his car. He enjoyed walking to the stores and restaurants rather than having to drive. We attended a family bar mitzvah. I enjoyed seeing relatives but couldn't share my pain, as I knew I'd cry. So it was all superficial conversation. Some of them knew Mary Ann but had never met Nancy.

I returned home to another letter from Mrs. J. She wrote, "It must have been in God's plan for you to be there for us when Nancy died."

I read that the Buddha was once asked why a man should love all persons equally. He answered: "Because . . . in the very numerous and varied life spans of each man, every other being has at one time or another been dear to him." The words invigorated me.

I received a surprisingly warm letter from a male cousin of mine. We were the same age. I had written him about Nancy's death and my relationship to her. That was the first time I came out to him, although he had met Mary Ann once at a family reunion. His response ushered tears, especially when he shared he had cried after visiting us in the orphanage with his father. I never knew my brother's and my circumstances had touched him so.

Marking one year since Nancy's death, friends and I held a service of remembrance at a church. We advertised it in the paper with Nancy's picture and a poem I found she had written long before her death. Appropriate words: "Life is a beautiful secret. Why is it whispered? It should be shouted and lived fully. . . ." As she had tried to do. Mrs. J called and asked me to buy flowers for the service. When I picked them up, the shop owner gave me an additional gift bouquet as his remembrance of Nancy. I sat in the car, graceless sobs choking my breathing.

Reliving my memories and experiences from *after* Nancy's death were almost more real than those before her death. I couldn't recover the year before but could hopefully continue to maintain the unique contact we had. The past year's happenings were alive in my thoughts, especially the image of her smiling, peaceful face filling my room the night of her death. I also relived the night when we shared our aura colors. She smiled like an eager child seeing my colors, as I could see hers—a sparkling blended variety of blues, greens, yellows, fuchsia, and more.

One evening I guiltily confessed to myself that if I had the chance to go back in time to our human togetherness *before* she died, with the price of having to give up all that I've learned and experienced *since* her death, I didn't know if I'd want to. This was unsettling. It was so harsh a thing to admit. I wanted what I couldn't have—both together.

I had come to unquestionably believe that love and bonding expand beyond our physical lives. We share the knowledge of our union in eternity. They connect us to family and friends, here and there. I was not alone in my sorrow.

Chapter 39

Harvesting

Dear Eva,

Four years in rural Maine, and I'm still a city girl. What have I harvested? I pick blueberries in the fields, but that's just bending over and breaking your back—for a few berries mixed in with a bunch of leaves. I don't grow vegetables. I plant flowers, but they don't bloom like my friends' gardens. Maybe because I don't like working in the dirt.

My contentment is being in the woods, cutting small bushes and brush to make way for the dogs and me to walk and find kindling for my woodstove, enjoying the animal tracks but praying the dogs won't chase porcupines and be quilled.

What I truly harvest—or attempt to—is my mind and spirit. I harvest my energy into writing and meditation, thinking and philosophizing. Since Nancy's death, I'm relearning how to live. I sit in my sunny house and harvest words. I use words to harvest memories, dreams, and fantasies. I harvest the memories of pain into learning.

As the frost of fall chills my body, I harvest the glow of fire and friendship keeping me warm during the winter. I remember the losses. *Too many early deaths: Nancy, friends from our local discussion group, and of course, always, you.*

I harvest the quiet of my soul, to hold the stillness lovingly, expanding it into fullness.

I don't pick and grow fruits and vegetables, but at each eating, I harvest the taste of their skin and juiciness.

Harvest means to savor, to hold, to extend the life of.

So dear Mother, I harvest my life for you. I try to live my life fully, deeply, for the shortness of yours.

Your daughter

Chapter 40

Engaging

I woke up with the astounding realization that it had been four years since I'd moved to Maine. It seemed like an emotional lifetime. I'd loved and lost, but the breakup with Mary Ann in Connecticut was so opposite to the terminal loss of Nancy, gone now for fourteen months. Mary Ann and I were dear friends. I'd become part of a new family—Nancy's. I still grieved, but also healed, one day, sometimes one moment, at a time. My job at the university was pleasantly easygoing, yet I was thinking about a future change to private practice. I was connected to a supportive community of friends, active in a local women's group, a Sister City project, and the Center for Noetic Studies.

Even amid bouts of stumbling pain, when I'd shrink into myself, I hadn't stopped living; that was not me. At the same time, I wasn't ready to even think about a new intimate relationship. Some friends would rejoice if I did find a new partner, but I recalled what Arlene, the psychic, said: I wouldn't be in a relationship for at least eight years. That was fine with me. This solo journey was what I needed.

I returned to volunteering for hospice, as I had in Connecticut. The training was exhilarating but at times emotionally depleting. When home in bed and sometimes in the group, I'd relive some of my losses: my mother, my aunt Nora on the farm, separation from my father and brother while living in the orphanage, loss of friendships when I left the orphanage, Mary Ann's mother, and, of course, Nancy.

In hospice training we listened to a presentation by Bernie Siegel, the doctor who wrote *Love, Medicine and Miracles*. He talked of patients' rights, of standing up for ourselves and making our own decisions when doctors weren't receptive. This was similar to the way I spoke to clients about legal rights, especially when we discussed spousal rights, children's rights, and government agencies.

The Connecticut hospice where I volunteered was a non-institutional building for the dying. In Maine, hospice services were delivered in the home. I sat with patients to give family members a break so they could work, shop, relax, sleep. Some of the conversations cheered my soul.

One of my first visits was to a small wood house heated by a woodstove in a rural area of Maine. Twice a week for three weeks I sat with a hospice patient, eighty-one, on dialysis and oxygen, with liver and heart problems. She'd been in bed for over a year fighting death, in and out of lucidity. I sat by her bed in a semi-dark room. The antiseptic smell overwhelmed the rusty aroma of the woodstove. She told me she communicated now and then with her deceased sister. It brought her contentment. I also had intense conversations with her husband, Gordon, age seventy-six, who was dedicated to his wife's care. He shared with me his out-of-body experiences. I shared mine.

When I learned his wife had died the week before, I called Gordon to see how he was coping. The conversation was arduous, his suffering painful as his voice leapt between wails and dread. He confessed, "I'm gonna marry again; Donna told me I should. I love her, but I don't think I can live alone." He kept busy, avoiding grief, although he allowed himself to cry. He invited me to visit, but it was seven thirty at night and he lived almost an hour's drive away. Besides, his desperate desire for a wife made me think it wasn't the right time for a visit. We spoke on the phone for an hour, and I told him I'd visit soon.

At my visit he opened up emotionally, acknowledging his feelings of loss, allowing his tears. He was endeavoring to trust the future and spending time with supportive family and friends. Over time he moved back into life, enjoying doing things he couldn't do while his wife was ill. He participated in a hospice bereavement group for surviving spouses, enabling him to process his loss and be supported by other survivors.

With the intensity of hospice and my own life transitions, I learned to find balance in sharing with people. I acknowledged I couldn't take away someone's pain or shorten their growth experience. Sometimes I lightened the load a little, but it was their personal work that mattered, not mine. My ego desired to solve the world's problems, but my enthusiasm and helpful words weren't really what was needed. Instead, I learned to be loving and patient with people while they struggled, or at times didn't struggle, with their relationships and, sometimes, their negativity or passivity—just as I had to be patient with myself as I worked through the vestiges of my own negativity.

My work as a patient volunteer led me to join the hospice board and train to facilitate bereavement groups. In the groups I gained as much as I gave.

At the same time, my office work at the university was busy—not as easygoing as I had expected—while I also continued to handle some private cases. I represented a middle-aged woman going through a divorce. Her husband earned excellent pay with a solid pension. She had been a homemaker, brought up the kids, cooked, socialized with him and his coworkers, and supported his work so he could move up in business. She hadn't worked outside the home and had no job experience. The children were grown and out of the home.

At trial I had a financial advisor testify to the husband's earnings and benefits. In addition to receiving alimony, I argued she should receive a portion of his pension. The judge didn't accept my argument on the pension issue and, in addition, granted a paltry amount of alimony. I appealed to the Maine Law Court, the highest court. That was my first argument before this court, which was a little intimidating at first, but then my ego eventually delighted in responding to questions from six judges. It had been a while since I'd handled such a challenging case. Several months later, I learned the court agreed with my client. The decision became precedent, making it easier in Maine for women in long-term marriages who hadn't worked outside the home to receive a meaningful share of the "marital" pension, as well as adequate alimony. I once again felt alive as an attorney.

A warm May bloomed through leftover snow and rain, the time again for blackflies, mosquitos, mowing, cutting brush, and putting some new flowers in my small garden. I dressed in my battle fatigues: white pants tucked into my socks, which tucked into my high boots; my green top with netted hood worn over a long-sleeve shirt; and, finally, a wide-brimmed hat to keep the netting off my face. And, just in case, some blackfly spray.

Mary Ann visited and unexpectedly invited me to join her trip to Germany and Russia the following year. I hesitated at first but ultimately agreed enthusiastically. It would be something to anticipate. We were lucky to have friends in Germany who had visited Connecticut and whom Mary Ann had visited. I soon started studying tapes of both German and Russian while driving to and from work.

It would be a spiritual challenge for me to travel to these two countries, wanting to visit where my father grew up although doubting we'd get to Ukraine, which was then still a part of Russia. Visiting Germany could be a form of Jewish reconciliation for me, considering the horrors of the Holocaust. Our women friends from Germany spoke the language in gentle tones. They were politically active and had confronted their parents about their inaction during World War II. Before hearing my friends' soft voices, I'd only heard German spoken loud and rough in movies or harsh by a teenage boyfriend of mine talking to his mother. My father's German was mixed with Yiddish and many words I didn't understand, but his voice was never sharp, being as gentle as his personality.

July arrived—sixteen months since Nancy's death. I seemed to measure my life by her death: before and after.

I visited my father and brother and kept myself in generally good spirits with lots of affirmations. New York's noise and frenzy were my spiritual test. To my surprise, my dad suggested we take a family trip to the Bronx Zoo, like we had before the orphanage and later when we moved back home. I was ecstatic, like a kid again. At the zoo, the heat and clatter didn't bother me. My mind wandered through my few childhood memories of Sunday afternoons with a balloon in one hand and my dad holding the other, seeing seals, bears, and scary tigers and eating sticky popcorn and cotton candy.

During my visit, I walked with him to his local park where a conglomeration of Russian Jews, Holocaust survivors, African Americans, and Hassidim shared the day, many playing cards and chess at stone tables and benches. I missed this diversity living in Maine. My father spoke Russian and German with some of his friends. I tried practicing Russian with him, but his words were very different from the tapes, more informal. Sadly, his memory no longer held much of the vocabulary with which he had grown up.

I read books on the Kabbalah and other Jewish wisdom of the sages in preparation for my presentation at the conference in early April. Jewish mysticism and other writings gave me a connection to historical Judaism, as opposed to current organized religion.

I recognized my ability to persevere was so connected to having been born and brought up in the Jewish tradition with its suffering and its laws on the ways of living and being. Reading various books on the Kabbalah, I experienced the greater portrait of my heritage, discovering where I connected and where I didn't. I learned how many religions, philosophies, and mystical traditions blended into each other. The goals were the same, the choice of ways diverse, as measured by time, place, and need, coming out of personal experience, just as mine did, blending the personal with the historical and finding a place and way that felt right. Yet I still had difficulty with the stories in the Bible. Long ago when babysitting for a friend's son, I read to him from a child's Bible story book and abruptly stopped. The words were so violent. What had he been hearing? Not the meaning behind the stories, but the violence—the same violence that was on television, in the movies, and in war. So much to weigh and contemplate, like my younger self questioning the rabbi.

Back in Maine, my home was still surrounded by rough terrain and crabgrass, enhanced by a tiny vegetable garden sprouting eight tomatoes and two broccoli plants. The irises I planted were blooming, and the trim on the outside windows had been painted blue—a picturesque sight for a city girl.

During the summer, I was visited by two sweet grown-up daughters of my cousins, Diana and Effie, whose parents had the farm we briefly lived on after my mother's death. I hadn't seen these second cousins since they were around nine years old. We shared life stories, the pain and joy of similar losses. Diana had died at age thirty-two, like my mother, from cancer. She had left four young children and a husband. Her husband was financially secure, able to hire help to care for his children, so the kids weren't separated from each other. Sadly, Effie now had cancer. I felt as if the past walked into my present—a warm, loving period of the past, with much sadness.

In late August, I visited Nancy's family to celebrate her nephew turning two, bringing a musical present for him, knowing Nancy's hand had helped pick it out. The joyous visit was intense with laughter, serious talk, memories, closeness, food, and people overload. My style of living wasn't constantly active without quiet breaks in between, but this time I didn't mind. I helped them set up for the birthday party, including moving chairs and furniture. We sat outside in the warm sun, with more people than the immediate family. I'd never seen so many gifts as her nephew received, like a child's Christmas explosion. I cherished the short nighttime moments of quiet talks with Mrs. J. In a soft voice, staring down at her hands, she remarked, "Children shouldn't die before their parents." All I could say was, "So true." After a short visit, they drove me to the airport. When we said goodbye, it was like saying goodbye to Nancy—repeatedly.

Shortly after returning home, I was in a scary automobile accident on my way to dinner at a friend's house. A woman in a pickup truck was driving erratically and looked like she might hit me head-on. I stayed steady and managed the car well. She lost control and dented the side of my car. Only my car and my emotions were scarred, except for a little soreness in my right arm. I hadn't always worn a seat belt, but this time had automatically done so. After the accident and exchange of information, I continued to my friend's house. The car radio was on, and a Nancy song surrounded me. When I arrived home, there was a call on my answering machine from Nancy's mother, ending with, "We love you." Yes, maybe Nancy was with me.

Time reminded me of wounds as well as love. I recalled having dinner with Nancy and her family, celebrating Christmas with them and going with her to her childhood church. I wiped away her tears at the time; I couldn't wipe away her memories. Now, I relived her past by looking at the family pictures at my house and remembering two sisters playing, carefree in their youth. I waited until the day after Christmas to open my gifts from her family, now my family too, and to chat on the phone.

I had reengaged in life. More and more I discovered that remarkable experiences materialized as I needed them, not by coincidence. That recognition made every moment more meaningful and understandable.

Chapter 41

Belief

It was the second anniversary of Nancy's death. What an odd word, *anniversary*. To me, it's a word of celebration, not death. Yet two years had passed with much growth and mindful touching upon the lives of others, almost as if I had been reborn since that tragic day. I gazed at her pictures and wondered, *Did I ever actually hold and blend with this smiling face?*

Then, a jubilant surprise! I learned I wasn't alone in my connection to Nancy. Angela wrote to me, sharing the details of her conversation with her two-and-a-half-year-old son, Gary, who had a visit from Nancy as he waited in the car for a minute or so while she ran into a store. When she returned and started the car, Gary announced, "Nancy."

Angela was stunned. She reacted, "What?"

He repeated Nancy's name.

She asked him, "You mean Aunt Nancy?"

He nodded his head.

"What about Aunt Nancy?"

He said, "Nancy in car."

Angela asked again, "What, Aunt Nancy in *this* car?"

Gary again responded, nodding his head.

Angela looked around and then asked him, "Is Aunt Nancy *still* in the car?"

"No."

Angela was in disbelief, but also, maybe, in belief.

What a lightness the letter added to my day.

Soon thereafter, in planning for my visit to Germany and Russia in late April, I developed an intestinal problem debilitating my body, making me tired and weak. I couldn't eat. I tried to understand its meaning on a deeper level, but the answers weren't coming. While I couldn't figure out the "why" of it, I told myself I'd try to learn from it. *What can it teach me? The reality of not being in control? The acceptance of physical pain?* I didn't have the strength to contemplate the answers.

My illness lasted four weeks. The doctor tested me to death. People wondered if I had cancer. Lonely and scared late one night, I called my brother to chat, hoping to release my anxiety, and his words briefly helped. Later at one in the morning, feeling worse and experiencing chills and difficulty getting up from bed, I called a friend who worked with homeopathic medicine. She and her partner drove over and stayed with me until morning light. Her tinctures, as well as her caring, eased my pain and fear. I visited the doctor the next day. Finally, I was given the right test: a simple fecal smear. I had giardia, an intestinal parasite usually found in contaminated water. How I had swallowed contaminated water was beyond me. I was put on a regimen of meds but still lacked strength.

At the same time, I was attempting to work on my presentation on Jewish mysticism for the upcoming daylong workshop. My mind wasn't fully robust as I sat cross-legged on my couch. Yet I discovered when I closed off my analytical brain and instead sat calmly, asking for guidance, I sometimes received it. I trustingly summoned support on how to present my complex material. The next morning, numerous ideas and stories revitalized me while driving to work. I hoped I could remember them all when I got home, knowing if I stayed centered and meditated beforehand, asking for help, I would recall what I needed.

In the weeks leading up to my trip to Germany, my lovable gray cat, Shadow, now twelve, was dying, dwindling away. She had a hyperthyroid problem. Her weight was down to four and a half pounds. She cried to eat all the time, an unbearable wailing that broke my heart. I was unable to calm her, even while constantly holding and feeding her. My other cats and dogs were flustered. I grievously worried about her care when I had to leave. Giving this burden to a house sitter who wasn't familiar with Shadow would be immense.

I finally made a crushing decision to put Shadow to sleep. She'd been with me from my days in law school. Two weeks before leaving, I took her to the vet. I so didn't want the responsibility of this decision. My mind agonized, debated, quarreled with itself—the right, the wrong, the moral, the necessary, the quality of life. *Who decides?* Through a torrent of tears, I grasped that *how* I came to the decision was as meaningful as the decision itself. I tried to release my guilty mind, but it was far from easy.

In the morning I took Shadow to the vet and stayed, petting and talking to her, as he gave her the shot and her soul released. She passed peacefully and was cremated. I buried her ashes in my garden to become part of the flowers of spring. I took a nap and had a vivid dream in which Shadow was cuddled right next to me on the couch as she always did. I petted her, and it felt so real. *What is real and what is illusion?* In the dream state, the emotions were very real.

The Exploring Mysticism in Religion conference was finally here.

To add to my unease, it was April and snowing! I drove to the university in a spring snowstorm. Even though I often spoke publicly on legal issues, this talk was momentous to me, since I had never made a presentation on this subject—I'd only discussed it with friends who shared my interest. My talk explored the Kabbalah, the spiritual teachings of how the universe worked and how it affects our lives. I was far from being a lifelong student. In fact, I was a novice and had never studied the work in Hebrew. Kabbalah was that part of Judaism hidden from lay people for centuries—mystical, complicated, connected with the beauty of the tree of life.

The night before the presentation, I had a humbling experience that evolved into my opening comments. Even after all I had studied and meditated on, I felt ill-prepared, imagining that what I had learned and attempted to experience in the past year had been absorbed only intellectually, not in the heart. Maybe I'd falter, get confused, or be incoherent—all the fears of the ego. It was hard to control. On one level, I knew a lot of what I studied had become part of me and I should be able to easily speak about it, even with my insecurities.

I meditated, asking for help from the Baal Shem Tov, a Jewish mystic rabbi considered the founder of Hasidic Judaism, a sect originally formed in Ukraine, where my father was born. From reading, I admired his way of being, which included laughter and freely dancing as a part of moving deeply into spirituality, even though at that time only men had permission to learn. Women, of course, were excluded. I visualized his energy and knowledge surrounding me, standing beside me as I spoke, feeding me a little of his wisdom.

That night, I dreamt of ten tall, large, bronze-skinned women, taller than humans, dancing in a circle high in the sky with me in the middle, my hands outstretched, swirling around and around. Their faces glistened with devotion and protective smiles, like a mother's smile. I awoke energized and ready to face my fear.

I stepped out of my worry as I gave the workshop, relaxed, my notes not that necessary, ideas and thoughts easily expressed, even those I hadn't considered before. The questions were challenging and thought-provoking, with supportive feedback. I decided to continue reading and learning and find what felt right for me, without feeling I must accept it all.

I was ready to enjoy Germany and Russia with Mary Ann.

Chapter 42
Insight

The trip to Germany and Russia was my first journey to the other side of the world. Our German friend Gudrun lived in the Hunsrück area, with its farmland and wine country. Everywhere we glanced were vistas of lush green fields dotted with small towns, grazing land, and rolling hills. People walked from town to town over the countryside. I thought that any moment I'd see Julie Andrews pop up singing songs from the movie, *The Sound of Music*. My imagination joined Julie running and twirling in awe on the lush green mountainside. Gudrun lived in a collective of eleven women friends in three houses, each colorful house in a different town. They made their own cheese and bread, grew most of the food they ate, and raised goats, using the goats' milk for cheese-making. The past year they also produced four hundred bottles of apple cider. Mary Ann and I frolicked with the goats and held the baby goats in our arms. I was like an innocent child, no worries in the world, prodding my childhood memory of visits to the zoo.

On our first day, we took a half-hour walk along the rolling terrain to the next town where the collective baked bread in the town's bakery. The fresh hot aroma of the bread filled the street and set off my desire for a cream cheese and jelly sandwich with tea. That sanguine thought plummeted as I walked in, viewing two deep, long ovens. My legs wobbled as I suddenly felt nauseous. The ovens reminded me of how I imagined concentration camp ovens. That reaction and my reflexive unease at seeing the trains along the Rhine were the only two connections I linked to my Jewish heritage. Some friends expressed concern I might respond negatively to Germany and its people; I had wondered that myself. Would I see only the past? I didn't. Our progressive German friends openly discussed their feelings with us.

The train ride to Bonn was an experience out of an Agatha Christie movie—my first trip in a train with private rooms, soft couches, doors with shades, and small writing tables. We rode into history along the Rhine with the chugging hum of the wheels on the tracks and views of steep mountainsides, castles, and multicolored towns. In another historic town, Trier, we traversed Roman ruins and baths that were over two thousand years old, still partially standing, as well as the house where Karl Marx was born, now a museum. But in the middle of the town square, we also saw a McDonald's!

Experiencing Germany with friends was laid back compared to the intensity, contrasts, and powerfulness of our eight days in Moscow and Leningrad. With Gudrun's ability to read Russian and comprehend maps and my limited ability to speak Russian, we held our own. Through a contact in the States, we met with two women: Galina, an interpreter in Moscow, and Zina, a research scientist in Leningrad.

In Moscow, Galina helped me find an Orthodox synagogue, one of only two, which was dimly lit with dark brown benches like many old traditional American synagogues. I chatted with a young rabbi who spoke a little English. He described the synagogue's history as well as his contact with Jews in New York. The synagogue had existed for a hundred years and had a small congregation. I was hoping to find my last name listed in their records but wasn't successful the way my uncle had been years before when he visited Russia. Within twenty minutes of researching various synagogue records, my uncle had found his and my father's eldest brother, who hadn't come to America as he was married with two children. I was then sixteen and corresponded with our new cousin, who knew some English, for about a year, but this soon ended as it became difficult with the language disparities.

Galina also made reservations for us to eat at one of Moscow's best restaurants—a surprise, a Jewish kosher restaurant! Before our vacation, Galina learned that Mary Ann did carpentry, so she wanted us to meet her carpenter friends, who were excited about meeting a "woman carpenter." When we arrived at the restaurant, which was on the bottom floor of an apartment high-rise, Galina hadn't shown up. Fortuitously, earlier in the day, we had met a friend of Gudrun's, Gabriella, who'd been studying Russian and shared the evening with us.

We waited outside the restaurant, not knowing the people who would join us. Two old-fashioned Cadillac-style cars drove up, and out stepped eight young men, smiling nervously, and initially reminding us of the Mafia as portrayed in a movie, all in dark suits and wearing fedoras. We were apprehensive. But when we noticed them holding bouquets of pink roses, our bodies relaxed.

For all of us to participate in the conversation around a long table, the men spoke Russian to Gabriella, who then translated into German to Gudrun, who then repeated in English to me and Mary Ann. Back and forth we gabbed about carpentry, the building of my house, life in Moscow, life in the States, their work and relationships. I was known by my friends for a tendency to ask blunt, indiscreet questions that shocked people, although it was always mainly out of curiosity. In chatting about relationships, I asked the guys, "Since some of you live with your parents because of lack of housing, where do you make love with your girlfriends?" That roused animated conversation, including stories of making love under the bridges, like a movie made in Paris. It was the first time I could recall having such a conversation about relationships with a group of men, especially in three languages! It was a few hours of hilarious sharing.

We ate chicken, gefilte fish, salads, various appetizers, and cognac, the latter of which was not to my taste. We brought with us some carpentry magazines, peace buttons, seashells, and other small items to give to them; they were much appreciated. One man gave me his expired bus driver photo. The evening finished with a speech by one man about how meaningful it was to break barriers and get to know each other beyond national stereotypes.

In Leningrad we joined Zina, a friendly, humorous woman in her forties. She invited us to her small apartment and fed us a parade of delicious food, more than our stomachs could handle. While she had a small refrigerator, she kept some food cold on the porch, a common practice in Leningrad. We met her two friendly children and husband. The apartment building, with a view of the river and harbor, looked just like the tall projects of the Bronx. She gave us a tour of Leningrad, taking us to a circus, an opera, and an exhibit of a modern painter recently deceased. She showed us the ballet school where Baryshnikov studied, which was the building in the movie *White Nights*. At night we walked the busy lit streets, where many people sold their wares. I bought a painting of an open bridge at night. The artist explained it had been painted at the time of the White Nights, as the drawbridges in Leningrad were only open at night.

During the trip, my energy wasn't at full strength, even with the meds I was taking for giardia. Upon returning home, I had another bout of diarrhea and serious intestinal pain, debilitating me six days later and requiring more tests. Friends came over with food and to hear stories, but it wasn't easy for me to eat. I was comforted, upon returning to the office, to find that work was a slow pace back into routine.

The trip was a pivotal one for me. I wouldn't call it a vacation. Vacation connotes carefree pleasure. This experience was walking through history—a little of my family's history as I recalled my grandparents' and father's painful childhood in Russia before coming to America. I was learning not just about others but also about myself, which was a healthy challenge to some of my life concepts and perceptions of lives in other countries.

With some perspective of time, I strove to clarify my understanding of my encounters so as not to be culturally biased, especially appreciating how much was not experienced. I shared this with a friend who not long before had visited the Soviet Union. I experienced only an exceedingly small part of the lives of a few people in Moscow and Leningrad. Why should I measure their lack of privacy needs by my desire for privacy? I thought about Japan and some Latin American countries, where people lived together in tight quarters and accepted it since they were used to or perhaps preferred it. Who was I to judge? I could only say it wasn't the way I'd want to live because of how I'd been used to living.

I finally found out I had an intestinal infection, minor in comparison to giardia. It didn't require any treatment, just patience and a bland diet for about ten days. I presumed I'd gotten it on the trip. But even so, I found the strength to type a nine-page letter to family and friends that shared my insights and experiences abroad.

While taking care of the remnants of my illness, I dwelled on how

I related to food during my life. For many years, much of my behavior was connected to my childhood in the orphanage and fear of not having enough to eat—or as much as I wanted rather than needed. I still experienced this, sometimes unconsciously. Attending an event or a brunch, many times I'd be at the food station early on filling my plate, usually taking too much. I noticed I also ate too much when I was restless or when socializing and not enjoying myself. Sometimes I used the phrase "stuffing myself." *What am I really stuffing, or what am I trying to avoid?* These were questions I hadn't yet fully answered.

The hardest to balance was my desire for chocolate, potato chips, and sweets and my fear that I wouldn't get enough. I knew what was happening but couldn't stop. I daily tried to be more conscious of my habitual relationship with food. Over the years I changed my diet and ate healthier with fresh foods, such as grains, veggies, whole wheat, and much less meat. I had grown up on bland or simply cooked meals with veggies from a can. I couldn't recall eating fresh vegetables until much older. Understandably, my stomach couldn't take hot and spicy foods, much to the chagrin of my friends.

I knew my intestines had been damaged from these past few months of infection. I needed time to heal and care for my body. Another insight—I must care for the body wherein my soul resides in this lifetime.

Chapter 43

Renewal

I found myself writing more: stories, fantasies, poetry, and prose. Some evenings I'd sit and wait, and words flowed. Not just my words, but words of spirit, guiding my thoughts, surprising me. It was a blend of me and my spirit friends, or self and higher self. I wasn't sure how to describe what was happening, but I delighted in it. I sat and asked for sharing, and it birthed, like a child I never had. I loved that I was writing again in addition to journaling.

The Center for Noetic Studies was planning another conference, this one on science and spirituality. The guest speaker would be Huston Smith, author of *The World's Religions*. My workshop would be on reincarnation, which I'd been reading about for a while. I discovered in the university's library a trove of fascinating documents by Dr. Ian Stevenson, a professor of psychiatry at the University of Virginia Medical School, who had a team of investigators traveling the world to meet young children and detail their memories of past lives. The actual conversations were in books in the library. Stevenson wrote a book for the public, called *Children Who Remember Past Lives*. I further discovered that Carl Jung, in his book, *Memories, Dreams, Reflections*, wrote eloquently of his belief in reincarnation related to his life. As to my own recent experiences, the reading was supportive.

In July I received a call from Nancy's mother, saying, "I'm glad you're coming *home* in August." I doubted she sensed the effect of her words. I was blanketed in motherly love, pondering how my life experiences might fit in with Dr. Stevenson's findings.

As my mind created room for more sun and fewer clouds, I understood why it's said that each season has its own emotions; summer in Maine is about outdoors and nature and conversations and people and movement, even in the heat and humidity. My stomach was satiated from eating blackberries and raspberries just picked from around the house, and I was exhilarated to be surrounded by color and tastiness, to have it part of my environment. To my surprise, it was again a time for dancing and playfulness, energy joyfully spent sharing ideas, wisdom, and healing.

It was also time to play with children, seeing the world through their eyes, watching their challenges, sharing in their exuberance, tears, and smiles. With my three new little neighbors at the top of the road, I embraced their excitement over each moment's discovery. We were now a small neighborhood: me, this new family, and the family who lived here when I came, whose two children were now teens. I took the three young ones for walks with the dogs down our dirt road. We listened to the sounds of nature in the woods and fields. We drew pictures at my kitchen table. I loved to share with them, to help influence their thinking, hopefully giving them a broader view of life—things I had missed in my childhood.

Visiting New York to be with my dad and brother became another spiritual challenge of love. I wasn't expecting any deep support for myself. I was there for them, to acknowledge and support the life that brought us together. *Come on girl, you know you want some support!*

My father complained of burning in his ankles. "Dad, I'll take you to the doctor," I said. "Maybe the doctor can release the pain as he did once before." But he didn't want to go. He didn't believe anything would help. He just wanted to complain and live with the suffering, perhaps still unconsciously believing he deserved it.

My visits with my father and the conversations with my friend who had difficulty with my changes since Nancy's death both supported my struggle to release negativity and pessimism, aspects of my childhood experiences. It had been so easy for me to get into that mindset. I needed to be on alert and not let it best me.

For a change of perspective, I made another visit to Nancy's family, which was as joyous and intense as previous visits. Her parents took me to an impressive interactive science center in Toronto. In the center stood a large cardboard statue of a famous Canadian woman runner and an area that gave attendees the ability to run fifty feet to see how their speed matched the runner's speed. I watched kids take the run and reminisced how I had loved to run in my teens and how good I had been, even beating a male cousin.

Without thinking and not paying attention to the fact that I had menstrual pain, I attempted the run bending, but not doing a lunge at the beginning as runners do. Problem was, I had never done a lunge before a run. When I stood up and sprinted, I slid and fell flat on my face after a few steps, sending my glasses flying. I saw the shock on the faces of Mr. and Mrs. J as they rushed over to help. The child in me didn't let a fall best me. I quickly rose, picked up my glasses, and started over, *without* bending, and ran to the end, not bothering to check my time. The three of us walked away, me walking like a bowlegged cowgirl who'd just gotten off a long horseback ride, with bruises on my legs.

It was also Nancy's grandfather's birthday. At the kitchen table,

I gave him a gift box of handkerchiefs. He cried, saying I reminded him of Nancy. Mrs. J and I spoke about how the manifestations of loss changed over time and how the reality of time and the busyness of life were there to deflect the loss. She shared that her husband was afraid to face the depths of his emotions, and he often cried, holding onto feelings of guilt around his relationship with Nancy, sadly unreconciled before her death. I reminded her, "Nancy was so happy being with all of you on her last visit. She was energized with memories as we drove back to Maine."

And me? Where was I after visits with my family and adopted family? Learning balance within imbalance like circles within circles. Even when I felt stretched in many directions like the rays of the sun, I was still connected to the center of the sun while active in each ray simultaneously. I was clearly not in this incarnation for pure peacefulness. That wasn't my purpose and shouldn't be my expectation. Instead, I would try to find peace of mind and balance in the lives of my sun's rays. My energy was devoted to these discoveries and not yet energized to concentrate on beautifying my home.

It was soon mid-September with the splendor of yellow, red, and orange foliage and cool breezes. I continued my study and simple meditative practices of Jewish mysticism, knowing it was intimately connected to the Torah, which I was both drawn to and repelled by at the same time (especially the secondary status of women in Torah and Kabbalah teachings). My challenge was to cultivate for myself more egalitarian and humanistic interpretations. I attempted to understand the symbolic and allegorical hidden meanings behind the historical facts. I finally grasped some of the diverse levels of meaning in the biblical stories. The stories were material, the hidden meaning spiritual. I began reading more egalitarian interpretations of the hidden wisdom of the Torah written by women.

I recalled the words of the rabbi in the orphanage: "Rivka, the Torah is God's words. The stories have a deeper meaning beyond the words on paper. That's why rabbis study so much and pray so much. We look deep into God's words."

I presented my workshop on reincarnation, as well as smaller workshops on Jewish mysticism. I discussed my ambivalence with a woman friend who was studying to be a rabbi. The learning rejuvenated and supported my psychic experiences and my need for further learning.

While I was still on the fence about what I believed, I was certain I had many lifetimes to come to figure it all out.

Chapter 44

Navigating

Years passed quickly like day into night. Another January. Another year with the house still unfinished. Livable? Yes. But finished? No. It was as if the house remained in the state it had been in when Nancy died. If the house wasn't moving on, would I? Truly?

Nancy and I first kissed at the beginning of one January, and she died toward the end of another January. It was still an emotionally hard month, and I was no longer seeing New Year's as a happy time. I continued having nighttime dreams and experiences with Nancy—less often, but each time surprising and profound—of us flying together, sharing words and gentle touches. I recorded them, but not as much as before; I woke up overly tired too many times.

I put my procrastination on finishing the house out of mind and took the plunge to return to private practice, another step in navigating my unexpected path.

I opened my own law office in Ellsworth, twenty minutes from home. I found space in a building in town, which had been a two-story house, now rehabbed for business. I was nervous financially but willing to take the gamble. I moved in and advertised my practice, handling divorces and general matters; then I added estate planning to my practice, as well as elder law, a rising area of the profession regarding protection of the elderly and their right to services. I spoke at a Bar Association seminar about the pension case I had previously won and advertised my new practice. In the process, I developed contacts through the organizations I'd been a part of, so business flowed in.

I taught a family law class for students who wanted to be legal secretaries or paralegals. A week before the class commenced, I had a dream about teaching it. In the dream, thirteen people attended, and I made an introductory speech about family law. The speech was so vivid that when I woke, I recorded it almost word for word. Later in the first session of my *real* class, I read it to them. And surprisingly, there were thirteen people in the class! After Nancy's death, so much of my life became more than coincidence. In the class I delighted to not only impart legal lore but also to share my life experiences and spiritual insights related to family matters. The two now went hand in hand for me.

My world outside of work was deep green with splashes of colorful wildflowers cheering my spirit. When I walked the dogs early in the morning, I marveled at the nearly hidden intricate cobwebs connecting bush to bush to tree limbs, even in the blueberry fields, like lives connected but many times not recognized. The voices of the children in my "neighborhood" melted my heart. The wagging tails of my dogs and cats warmed the house and gave me jubilant company as I navigated my solitary journey into deeper consciousness. My teacher was life; my practice was moment-to-moment-living, trying to be mindful in relation to everything.

In September Maya discovered a black kitten on the doorstep! Loving, warm, playful. The vet thought he was about five months old. There were no signs anywhere that he was missed. Of course, I kept him as part of the Crumblesweat family, naming him Midnight. All my pet names started with the letter *M*, even Nancy's dog, Mitra.

I joined the YMCA in Ellsworth and befriended a woman in the exercise class. We chatted about dancing. After a few meetings, we decided to teach a dance class: mambo, cha-cha, jitterbug, and waltz. I bought dance videos to help me teach and learn new steps. At night, with the outside lights on, I watched myself practice new steps through my south windows, again alone, wondering whether that would be the way of this life for me.

I took a few lessons from a local professional dancer at least twenty years my senior. I floated with him during the waltz, foxtrot, and tango, again feeling like Ginger Rogers—a real-life Ginger, not my dream Ginger. I laughed to myself, thinking perhaps the spirits of Uncle Sam and Aunt Florence, who had danced in the Roseland Ballroom in New York, were with me. Thirty eager dancers attended our class, which we relished teaching for a few months.

Even as an attorney, I was still connected to my past as a legal secretary unable to separate myself from that part of me. It helped keep me balanced. I wrote an article for the Maine Legal Secretaries Association called "The Ruminations of a Lawyer, Ex-Legal Secretary," supporting legal staff as I had while in law school but now with a weighty grasp of how definitions had controlled my life. I ended with the following:

> *People generally define who they are by what they do. "I'm a lawyer," "I'm a secretary," "I'm a mother," "I'm a garbage collector." But we easily forget there is more to us than our job description. We are more than the power, or lack thereof, our job gives us. We are not better or more professional based on the money in our pocket or the power we wield, whether it is a lawyer over a secretary . . . or a secretary over a receptionist. The depth of who we are is deeper than our external definitions. This is easy to forget*

as we play our societal roles. When we don't see beyond our defi-
nitions, we allow those definitions to control us, not the reverse. In
so doing, we either live in fear of the loss of our definition or glory
in its false power.

The never-ending world madness of politics and conflict affected my daily life. The country was at war in the Persian Gulf. Watching the fighting on television chilled my spirit. The utter helplessness brought the peace movement back to life. I steered myself into action, especially remembering my participation with Nancy on political issues. How could I not? I made phone calls and attended vigils and demonstrations. Not that the war would stop because of our action, but we felt less helpless and a little more hopeful doing something. I questioned, *Will I be alive for the day when the human species takes the leap from violence as a means of conflict resolution to positive and peaceful means?* This life is a human schoolroom of choices. I hope the earth survives our failed tests.

I came to analyze my life by asking if what I do and how I am in relation to others and the world adds something meaningful and positive. It was far from easy, but I kept trying.

Since childhood I've had grandiose dreams of saving the world, mainly to protect the lonely, scared little girl I was in the orphanage. Since then I've gained self-assurance and self-control, with less fear. I kept the guilt about trying to save the world and always felt guilty that I should do more. The words *guilt* and *should* still reared their presumptive heads now and then, perhaps as part of my Jewish heritage. I consciously tried to separate shameful guilt from healthy guilt, the healthy guilt being the wise questioning and realistic assessment of what I could do, allowing for my limitations, and letting go of the fearful need to control. I worked to accept and trust that there's purpose to it all and that whatever steps I take are important, even if my steps aren't that of Gandhi or Peace Pilgrim.

A welcome brief surprise popped into my busy and emotional life. Nancy's parents drove from Buffalo to visit me for a few days. I took time off from work to show them the parts of Maine I loved, as well as those Nancy loved. We laughed, cried, and tried to persuade each other that life moves on and we'll do well. A few months later was the sixth anniversary of Nancy's death, and I sat on my bed crestfallen, pondering whether Mitra, her dog, would die soon. She was weak, disoriented, and breathing heavily. I prayed she would die on her own. I didn't want to have to put her to sleep. I'd done that with too many pets. I sat listening to Mitra's labored breath after having spoken to Nancy's mother. She had tried to comfort me, saying in her sweet, kind way, "You need to do what is best for Mitra. We can't hold on; let go and trust in God." She was such a religious person. But were either of us letting go of Nancy?

A few days later, I made the tortuous decision that it was time to call the vet to my house. After he left, I sat with Mitra's body while her spirit moved on. She'd been with me since Nancy's death. I imagined Nancy's spirit welcoming Mitra's spirit as they romped in the freedom of no time and space. Mitra was a loving and affectionate dog before deafness and disorientation affected her.

After Mitra was cremated, my little neighbors, Debby and Jason, five and six years old, helped me bury her ashes in my small, modest garden. We said prayers and goodbyes, and the kids took two carnations from their house to plant on the grave site. They weren't afraid to hold the ashes and put them in the ground. Little Debby liked to talk about death. "Who's going to die first? The dogs or you? I'll take care of the dogs if you die first." She talked about her grandparents dying. I talked about renewal and spirit, in simple terms.

It was a pleasant spring and summer, weather-wise, not ridiculously hot. Contentment flowed through me, even wearing my bug protection clothes when I walked through the woods and into the fields, eating wild berries, to a tree laden with apples ready to be picked. I was again cutting small trees and brush to allow light for stronger trees, designing a landscape jointly with nature, making it look like a park. I cut with a hand saw and clippers, carried or dragged trees and branches, and piled them up in hidden areas of the woods.

Winter arrived in its blustery, stormy way, and Nancy's grandfather died on Christmas Day, a special holiday for their family. I was comforted by having seen him when I visited on his birthday shortly before he died. As I spoke on the phone with Nancy's mother, she reminisced, saying, "It was God's will that you came into our lives. Before Nancy died, you helped give her back to us." I smiled and shed gratified tears.

I had navigated the ups and downs of the seven years since Nancy's death. Time allowed for acclimation and acceptance. However, I wondered if someone would ever come along who brought out the feelings and boundless energy in me that Nancy had.

Chapter 45

My Voice

Dear Eva, dear Mother,

At age seven, after you died, my voice bellowed, demanded, expected to receive all that I desired, no holds barred.

When I was nine, in the orphanage, my voice held back a little, reticent, aware of adult voices drowning out my own. I recognized that my voice could get me a corner chair, a slap, or denied seeing Dad.

At eleven, my voice again bellowed, ignoring the punishment. I was a tough kid, a tomgirl, even when in girls' dresses, with most torn by the end of the day.

As a teenager, I got my period, seriously discovered boys as an attraction rather than an annoyance, and my voice sweetened, cajoled, plotting my moves.

From there my voice went downhill through my teens and twenties, getting coarse and throaty from manipulating rather than demanding. It was stuck on the word "yes" and holding back "no."

I was a feminine female; angry and confused inside, sweet outside, not knowing who I really was. Feeling society's expectations, my stomach held my voice and locked it in continuous pain.

Then feminism hit the bookstores and the streets, and my voice shot out, taking back the night, singing in marches, blabbing on and on in Feminism 101 meetings.

My voice gained strength. The stomach pain slowly disappeared. And who I was again was redefined by a new culture.

Now nearing fifty, my voice is sometimes loud, sometimes subtle, sometimes even silly, and mostly thoughtful. I'm unafraid to stand up when necessary. I'm not defined by others. I no longer experience the dreams in which the ocean overtakes me. Instead, when the waves come, I dive in, hesitant, but not frightened.

Dear Mother, the little, hardened, lost girl is still in me, but that's okay. When I get too full of myself or too busily involved in life, I remember her. She helps center me. I wipe her tears, and we move on.

Your daughter

Chapter 46

Bernice

It was almost eight years since Nancy's death. I hadn't been in an intimate relationship for eight years. But that's a limiting definition of "relationship." I'd had conscious, profound relationships with spirit, my higher self, with Nancy after her death, and her family, as well with friends and nature—life itself.

Now something was shifting inside me—sparkles of holiday spirit, in a sensuous, almost sexual way I hadn't experienced in eight years. I again enjoyed partying with friends, dancing, letting loose— and became attracted to someone.

The name of that someone was Bernice. One October evening, I joined friends at a potluck gathering at the house she shared with a woman lawyer I knew. I walked in with two friends, placed the dish I made on the kitchen counter, and looked up to see a beguiling squarish face with dimples and deep brown eyes surrounded by stylish short brown hair. She introduced herself. We joked a little about her carrot dish and my pasta dish; mine I baked, hers was bought. It was a superficial conversation, but when she tilted her head to the side with a welcoming wide smile, warm shivers tangoed inside me. During the evening's chatter and laughs, all twelve of us sitting casually in a circle on cushioned living room chairs, a couch, and some on the floor, I kept a subtle eye on Bernice, who was friendly with everyone, clearly comfortable with herself and her whimsical wit.

Driving home from the potluck, I recalled an unexpected dream I had with Nancy a few days before meeting Bernice. She was letting go, moving on, freeing me to rekindle my sensuality. Remembering the dream, I understood and accepted it was time for both of us to move forward.

During the next few weeks before New Year's Eve, it seemed Bernice turned up everywhere I was, at various gatherings and dinners with friends. We shared different circles of friends, but now the circles blended over the holidays. We chatted casually. I recognized my intense delight but was not aware if she felt the same way. At one event she arrived with another woman, whom no one knew. At that point, I acknowledged my vulnerability and disappointment, but it didn't stop me from getting to know her.

Mary Ann and her partner of two years, Sally, visited for the holidays. Every new year Mary Ann would ask me, "Well, have you met someone?" I always said, "No, I'm not ready." This winter, as she helped me gather kindling in the field, she didn't ask her persistent question. I jumped up with kindling in my hands and burst, "Mary Ann, every year you ask me if I've met someone, and this year, when I have, you don't ask!"

Well, that outburst caused a challenging, but caring, interrogation of me about Bernice from my four closest friends. At the next holiday gathering, these dear friends, my protectors, cornered Bernice and gently probed her with questions about her life. At that point, they learned more than I knew. In our short chats, I hadn't asked the questions they posed, trying not to be my too intrusive self! They told me she was originally from New Jersey, was of Irish and Italian descent, had married briefly and divorced, and had come to

Maine with a partner but they'd parted ways a few years before. She was currently not in a relationship and worked as business manager of the WoodenBoat School in Brooklin, which was at the tip of my peninsula.

After Nancy died, I had written in my journal that New Year's Eve would never be a happy time for me. Hesitantly, I now wrote, "How wonderful to be proved wrong."

On New Year's Eve, bundled against unforgiving wind and light snow, we all attended a party at a friend's house with dancing and games and conversation, warmed by a woodstove fire. The mixed aroma of pizza, vegetable casserole, chocolate cake, and fresh baked bread made me dizzy with hunger. I had to control myself; I knew how I could get carried away taking more than I can eat.

Bernice was there, impeccably dressed, creases in her jeans, brown boots, and a wide-brimmed hat. I asked her to dance. We danced the same style, New York Lindy and cha-cha. I breathed in her subtle scent of earthy sandalwood oil. We both liked to lead and laughed as we took turns, dancing mainly with each other under the living room's soft lights. Being about the same height and body type, our bodies blended like warm marble cake and icing. We joked how we missed the variety of New York/New Jersey food. But I missed more of the Jewish food and she, the Italian. It was small-talk, nothing serious. At midnight, we hugged and kissed lightly, and then hugged and kissed others. Sometime after midnight, I drove home with friends. They approved of Bernice.

Mary Ann and Sally stayed at my house before returning to Connecticut. We skied and snowshoed until a surprise storm with raging winds dumped over a foot of snow. We lost electricity for seven hours, so we cooked on the woodstove and had dinner by candlelight.

After they left, I sat nervously on the couch but braved my unease and called Bernice for dinner at my house. In our conversation, she admitted, "I got your number from my roommate and was planning to call you." Relief flitted through me like a tranquilizer; I guessed I was reading the cues correctly.

Before making the call, I sat with my fear of giving up my accustomed routine; it is so easy to settle into one's past ways and habits. Making a new friendship—or something more—disrupts the known status quo. But then I thought of the Buddhist "don't know," that healthy state of mind allowing for growth and risk-taking. At night I dreamt how spirit and sexuality blended in a natural way, reminding me they didn't have to be separate. I had recently been reading a book by Thomas Moore called *Soul Mates: Honoring the Mystery of Love and Relationship*. Good timing.

A week later, I had my first sensual kiss in eight years. I delighted in Bernice's deep soothing voice, so different from my somewhat high-pitched one. Her New Jersey accent surfaced now and then, as did my Brooklyn accent. Her smile was open, not protective. She easily made me laugh with her quick wit and humor.

Five hours of talk preceded that goodnight kiss against her car. It was honest conversation on relationships, intimacy, death, spirituality, politics, and more. We were on the same wavelength and agreed on much, sharing our past relationships and losses. There was no need to impress.

The flowers of my soul were again reopening to the intimacy of life, and the colors of the flowers were the ones Bernice had brought me on our first "date." After she left, I looked over at Nancy's picture and sensed her smiling for me, the smile that knew the secret humor of life, the play that was being acted out. I could step outside the play and see its direction and connection while still being fully part of it.

On Sunday I tried to do some work, but my body fought me. This reawakened energy wanted to be acknowledged. Bernice had just left after sharing lunch and a short walk, followed by five minutes of kisses. Those kisses sparked samba dancing inside me. I rested on the couch for a half hour and relaxed into the feelings I'd waited this long to experience once again.

Over the weeks, my friends were a cheering squad of well-wishers. I did get some office work done, as well as drafting my fiftieth birthday party invitation. A few months earlier, I had decided to celebrate my fiftieth with a big dance party. I also had registered for my first eight-day meditation retreat in Massachusetts, departing the day after the party, and was looking forward to the retreat.

Bernice and I talked nightly. It was so delicious to hear her voice on my answering machine. I was supposed to go to Buffalo to visit Nancy's family in a few days but had a bad cold and was physically miserable. Also, a snowstorm was expected.

Then to my surprise, Ernie called. He said hesitantly, "I've been having this repeated negative dream where I see you in a house, and I smile and say hello, then suddenly I turn for a second, and you're gone."

I thought, *Maybe I'm not meant to travel.* He did dream about the car accident when Nancy died, afraid it was I. Possibly his dream meant something else, but he asked me not to go. I listened and put the visit off to the spring.

My cold slowly retreated, giving me more time to spend with Bernice. Even with my cold, we talked and cuddled, being patient. The sultry pulsations in my body intensified.

I thought about the comparison in getting together with Nancy and then Bernice. Both relationships started around New Year's. My lusty feelings reawakened suddenly each time before we got together, as well as the almost immediate knowledge of the rightness of our connection—a sense of such compatibility. In many ways with Bernice, the sharing and commonality felt more mature. Well, we *were* older. Nancy at the time had a lot of unresolved emotions, having recently broken up with her ex, as well as painful memories of her family. Bernice had a loving connection to her sister and brothers; her parents were deceased.

Maybe on the soul level, these two Italian women and this Jewish woman were playing out our "oversoul" learning, with subplots along the way. I thought about the book I read not long before by Jane Roberts, *The Education of Oversoul Seven*. Maybe I was being too dramatic, but no one could tell me these "coincidences" were meaningless. As I further pondered the connections, I recalled that Nancy had gone off to Nicaragua for two weeks in early March, as now I would be going off to a meditation retreat for eight days right after my birthday party. Hopefully, this relationship would last longer than Nancy's sudden death. I had to let go of hope. Everything had its purpose, and I could live in the "don't know" ebb and flow.

As I hadn't traveled to Buffalo, the extra few days allowed luscious leisurely sharing. Bernice gave me a tour of her work environment, which overlooked Penobscot Bay, a place for active sailing. We discovered we were both animal people and laughed at the adorableness of their capers. She had one cat, Steffie, a lovable black-gold Scottish fold, a captivating breed I had never seen.

We kept moving forward lovingly and lustfully—a lust based on openness, vulnerability, and trust. I melted into her body, not letting go of the gentle closeness, while at the same time not losing self; it was a oneness that combined soul, spirit, and body experiencing its oneness, knowing its distinctiveness. Fun, an essential word, was an integral part of our bond. We both sensed the spirit part of our connectedness, its future potential, but we didn't feel pressure or expectation—just a simple acknowledgment of reality, wherever it took us. We held an innate acceptance of each other, of not needing to change the other, of understanding human nature. I intuited Nancy smiling broadly for me, with me, with Bernice.

We both continued our volunteer activities. I was on two boards and attended a weekly writing group; Bernice was a big sister to a little girl through Big Brothers, Big Sisters. In time, she would leave her job at WoodenBoat School and become a case manager at BBBS.

We took our first sightseeing vacation together to Colorado and California, visiting my cousin Effie, whose cancer had worsened, and her two daughters as well as my Home kid friends, Josie and Leslie, and Josie's two daughters. A week before we traveled, I had been shocked to learn that Josie's husband was shot to death by a disgruntled employee. With a heavy heart, I also learned she had early-stage cancer. While we visited she endeavored to function like all Home kids did—clench your fists and tough it out. But at least she was able to share her stress and fears and to cry with us.

What an entrance for Bernice to meet my extended family! When I sometimes felt sorry about my early life, I reminded myself that, in comparison with my loving friends, I was the lucky one.

At times I was able to step back from my daily busyness and "witness," as the Buddhists say, the parts and characters being played out in this drama that seemed to last forever, but was, in spiritual time, only a second of the whole experience of our lives.

Bernice had given me a new January. Now January turned back into love and fun. There was so much to be grateful for—for Nancy and all she had given me spiritually and for Bernice and all that I was now receiving. I shed crystal tears for the specialness of it all—tears that came from the depth of sadness and loss transformed into the depth of joy and love.

Chapter 47

Rapture

Suddenly I was speaking in terms of "we." It had been a long time coming for me to say that word again and being a "we" to other people. This "we" was passionate, loving, comfortable, and fun. Bernice and I regularly spent at least a half the week together, outside of work.

On a typical frigid February day, grateful there was no snow, we celebrated my Half-Century Positively Young birthday party. Bernice helped me prepare. Mary Ann and Sally brought decorations. Jen and Emma, Gudrun from Germany, and other friends helped decorate. I rented a local gun club, the only place big enough. However, the club had taxidermized animal heads and bodies hanging on the walls. We covered them as best we could with decorations. I hired a young woman DJ who chose a variety of old and new dancing music.

Bernice was mildly nervous. This was her "coming out" to my friends, like a debutante ball. There were so many new people to get to know. I wasn't worried as she was naturally ultra-friendly. Out-of-state friends came earlier in the week, meeting Bernice in a more relaxed environment.

I decided to wear something a bit funky. We found a secondhand store, and I rented the perfect dress—hot red flamenco/can-can style, with a choker and garter made of the same red satin and black lace as trim. Sexy and fun—that was the way this fifty-year-old felt.

Ninety-nine people attended, a mix of young and old, office friends, out-of-staters, neighbors, and children. Some arrived with delicious cakes and other food to share, almost like a Maine church potluck. The kids had fun hitting two piñatas and knocking the candy out of them. Emma and Sally videotaped the event, garnering words on tape of love and laughs about me from guests—for posterity! The last slow song was "Lady in Red." Bernice and I danced alone after most people had left. It became our song.

The next day I packed for my trip to the Buddhist silent meditation retreat. Bernice stayed at my house caring for the dogs and cats. Before leaving, I had a carpenter build the banister on the upstairs walkway; I didn't want any falls—human or animal. I phoned my father and brother to let them know I wouldn't be calling for the next eight days, as we usually spoke a couple times a week. Kissing Bernice goodbye was like surrendering a sugary piece of watermelon on a hot summer day.

I felt enthusiasm mixed with nervousness about what to expect as I arrived early in the evening at the Insight Meditation Society in Massachusetts. I sat with others listening to intros by the teachers, then got settled in my two-person room, each bed with a night table and lamp and nothing more. I experienced my first forty-minute sitting meditation and ate dinner in silence, relieved I didn't have to make small-talk. My neck and shoulders were on fire from the pain of sitting as well as the seven-hour drive. Getting ready for bed, I found my mind returning to the achy emotions from saying goodbye to Bernice. I relived those long, not-wanting-to-let-go kisses, but also knew that, starting the next day, I needed to release my world and be in the stillness and silence of each new moment in this retreat. At the end of my first day, I plunged fully and completely into a deep sleep.

I learned I wasn't the only first timer of the sixty-eight participants, which reduced some of my uneasiness. After breakfast, everyone had to choose a daily job. I chose salad making with others in the
kitchen. They had friendly faces. We didn't talk; we just concentrated
on the cleaning, cutting, and draining of lettuce. The first full day I
broke from routine to catch up on sleep with a few naps and two outdoor walks after meals. Our teacher said we shouldn't write. Writing
was only memory; therefore, we weren't living in the present. Yet,
knowing myself, I knew I might yearn to write, so I brought a journal
with me, along with a book I'd been reading, *Nothing Special: Living
Zen*, by Charlotte Joko Beck. The lawyer in me always prepared for
eventualities.

My roommate and I didn't see much of each other. We barely
spoke late at night in our room. She was unforgiving about her meditation deficiencies, crying some. I tried to be supportive, but my
words didn't help.

Early on I experienced melancholy not being able to smile now
and then as people walked in the halls and rooms, their heads down
in individual concentration, the apparent purpose of the retreat. I
further grappled with how hard it was for me to move slowly. My
body needed to walk at a quicker pace; it was the city girl in me. Yet
I soon realized when I walked slowly, I concentrated more—up and
down steps, outside the building, stretching in the yoga room.

Initially, my mind wouldn't rest. It repeated, compared, reviewed
the past, thought of the future, and enjoyed memories. Now and then
it stayed in the present, especially when I ate, chewing each bite consciously and drinking slowly. The food was delicious—all natural.

I did smile and laugh quietly when cutting lettuce with other
workers. I acknowledged I needed to smile more at work, even when
I was tired.

When I privately met with one of the teachers, she explained that the traditions of some teachers, like Thich Nhat Hanh, approved of smiling. That seemed more pleasant than the glum state of not smiling or avoiding looking at others, though I understood the goal of turning inside oneself. The evening talks provided perspective. I recognized how my mind judged and compared, no less here than at home. Maybe that was the attorney in me or the insecure part of me. It was another issue to contemplate upon returning home.

Soon I was sitting for fifty minutes four times a day! In one sitting, I became aware that the first weekend was over, yet time had moved more slowly than normal when I didn't want it to end. Time was definable. It slowed as I slowed. I was now used to my little spot in the meditation hall. Routine set in. Sit, walk, and sleep repeated, with forty-five minutes of salad making. I admit I slinked into a room that had a phone and made a short call to Bernice and then to my dad. I needed to hear Bernice's voice and as well reassure my father that I was well; I had inherited his tendency to worry.

Faltering in my concentration on the breath during a sitting, my desire for Bernice popped up, which I allowed some leeway while thinking about her smile and the flowers likely waiting for me. Suddenly an easy, natural smile expanded. I must have looked like a child sneaking a piece of chocolate candy. I remembered how Nancy, when she went to Nicaragua, wrote in her journal, "I think of Roberta and smile." So now full circle, I think of Bernice and smile.

In my room, I sporadically read snippets from *Nothing Special, Living Zen*. At some point in the reading, I surprised myself with the thought that I'd like to write a book with the reverse title, *Everything Special, Living Joy*. This would not be contradicting Beck's book, just taking a different approach, a somewhat more joyful one, with the recognition that we could enjoy life without becoming adversely attached. Attachment was life's firebrand. I also thought about Jewish mystical history and the Baal Shem Tov—dancing the joy of life, even dancing its sadness.

My next sitting unearthed a major shock wave. Such humbling thoughts and insights soared around the subject of specialness, even a poem. My sensations were animated, and time passed quickly; if only I had the paper and pen sitting in my room. Over dinner, I laughed inside remembering that many writing ideas had floated through me. I'd recorded them in my journal, but most were unfinished. What I hadn't done was make time for writing, as I did with many dreams and poems when I sat in concentration after Nancy's death.

I accepted I had a busy mind, a thinker's mind. I didn't need to push it away; just let it rest. When it rested, the wisdom behind the busy mind unlocked. The soul mind shared its wisdom, delivering some momentous surprises. First, "a room of one's own" to write. One morning such beautiful grace came to and through me. I sat on the bed in a casual, calm frame of mindfulness, and spirit spoke. I was glad my roommate wasn't there. *Everything Special* was writing itself. My body welled up in love as I wrote. I asked myself, *Is this corny?* No! It was an awareness of grace almost as written in the Book of Psalms. Sometimes I experienced a passionate feeling of wholeness and gratitude. I continued as the words came and danced off my pen. A surprising thought hit me one late evening. I recalled what Arlene, the psychic, told me: I would write a book with Nancy. Was that now actually happening? I didn't know, but it was a pleasant notion.

Another realization came from the retreat—I was learning more clearly what I wanted in life. Silence may be golden, but so were smiles, friendly faces, loving faces. Even though I wasn't meditating on schedule—sitting, walking, sitting, walking, always following the breath, not looking at people—the love and joy pouring out on paper was still from the experience of this retreat. I wasn't an admirable student in the way the teachers expected, but I was learning and arriving at that peaceful state of mind sought in meditation. I was just getting there through my writing.

I broke silence one morning to talk briefly to my roommate, asking how she was doing. I sensed her suffering, her trying too hard. It was her first time, like me. She wasn't giving herself a break. I got her to smile, and she glowed. Hopefully, for a few seconds, the smile relaxed her body. I saw many faces with beautiful smiles; every now and then, someone forgot.

My next nighttime writing became the intro to my book, so quickly. *Boy, was I getting carried away!* I laughed at myself, so as not to take it too seriously. When I started thinking and writing like this, my melodramatic mind took over, seeing my death looming close. I couldn't let that happen, remembering all the delight I planned to share with Bernice for a long time to come, and the specialness and joy that remained to experience in this life. It was one thirty, and I hadn't stopped writing while my roommate slept. I tried to sleep, but words continued to pour out nonstop. I trusted my soul saying to me, "Hi, it's about time you noticed me. Let's share."

I enjoyed the evening dharma talks. The teacher explained the need for balance between faith, energy, mindfulness, concentration, and wisdom. Wisdom flowed automatically from the other four. You could never have too much mindfulness. I thought about joy, which was not mentioned. Maybe that's a state of mind you reach when all else was in balance.

While on a walk one morning, the wistful little child in me reemerged, bringing some tears. To stay alive in her tough, frightening environment, she imagined herself above it all as a protection against hurt. I hugged her memory. What would have happened if she, and every child, had been given unconditional love, been shown their specialness, and allowed the joy of spontaneity? How much more easily could we then *give* love and open our hearts? I hoped my little book could be shared with others. I returned to my room and wrote a poem about the majestic soul cradling our pain, the child's pain.

In this writing experience, I was learning patience. Sometimes words poured out. Sometimes I sat and waited. Sometimes a gush of beauty enveloped me.

The last poem became a direct experience in connecting with my breath. For the first time, I saw my breath as an "ancient partner" taking the soul journey with me. A friend and confidant, it knew me so well, all the "me's" of the past. It was as if this poem had been revealed to grasp the essence of the soul we carry around with us over our lifetimes. The breath and the soul were one. All my incarnations were in my breath. After writing the poem—or it writing me—I sat with my breath in the meditation hall and experienced a whole new understanding of connection and love. I hoped I could hold on to this fervor when I got back to my busy pace. I wouldn't even dare to say that perhaps I could slow the pace—that would be too much expectation.

The retreat was over. I wished "an enjoyable journey and much mindfulness in life" to my two friendly co-salad-makers and my roommate. I took a last walk through the woods. Tomorrow I'd spend time walking the woods of Crumblesweat with Bernice.

Chapter 48

Home

Bernice moved in with me in May. At our age, it felt so right. I had no problem sharing or giving up space. My eleven years of living alone in Maine had been long enough to have this corner of heaven to myself. Even though the house was finished to live in, there was much yet to do, especially around the grounds. I was pleased that Bernice enjoyed gardening, which was not my forte. My emphasis was on working in the woods.

We had both had our share of disappointing relationships, as well as a meaningful amount of therapy. When people asked why we blended so well, we lightheartedly told them we had each come to this relationship with "an overnight bag, not a steamer trunk." We'd learned how to recognize and work through issues.

Life was calmly fragrant, like the aroma of allspice. We couldn't foresee that a double-sized steamer trunk would soon be rolling into our home and a more profound meaning of Crumblesweat would make itself known.

I received a call from my brother, who still lived in New Jersey. "Roberta, Dad's in the hospital again."

I flew from Maine, and Fred picked me up at the airport. We sped to the Brooklyn hospital, a vast and busy monstrosity. Fred wasn't sure of the room as it had been changed. We asked directions from anyone who wore a hospital badge. My breathing was heavy from the harsh medicinal smell as we rushed through the noisy halls.

I recalled how my father and I had cried together watching movies. *I hope he's not crying.* It was mid-August, and I'd already been to see him twice this season, watching his eighty-five-year-old body barely able to walk but stubbornly holding onto its independence.

We walked into his room, and I first observed a deep, wide hole in his cheek from surgery to remove a large cancerous mole. He'd also had surgery for a hernia problem. He'd been under anesthesia for four and a half hours.

He was hallucinating and delusional, having been given a drug that shouldn't be given to older people. His hands were flailing, and he saw people talking to him on the walls and through the window. My heart hoped my mother was talking to him, but then again, that would likely have made him calmer. Fred said he had been this way the day before as well.

The nurses weren't helpful, being busy with other patients. The clanging and ringing of hospital noise reverberated in my head like the sound intensity I experienced during an MRI. I fought back tears and tried to ease my dad's confusion. His sad and disoriented face, the one that once looked like Clark Gable, was weathered from pain and tears. Fred wept quietly. I wished I could have been a comfort to him like I tried to be in the orphanage. This time it wasn't us in need but our father.

I called a friend in Maine who was a geriatric nurse. She suggested the doctors try a lighter drug, like Haldol, especially if he'd not been eating well. Luckily, his doctor agreed. The new drug worked, and the hallucinations dissipated over a few days of reduced doses.

The doctor privately told us our father had melanoma, a skin cancer on his face that had likely metastasized elsewhere. He didn't have a long time to live. The word *cancer* again rocked my world.

I became his part-time caregiver in the hospital. He was like a child, lying in his own waste until the nurse got around to cleaning him, even though I handled some of this, understanding he was embarrassed. My once handsome, strong father now weighed only 134 pounds.

My brother returned home to New Jersey, emotionally exhausted. Since I had moved to Maine, he had visited our father every other week, taking him out to eat and shop and watching TV together.

While my father was in the hospital, I stayed at night in his small fourth-floor, one-bedroom apartment, which was far from clean. Luba, his cat, kept me company, as well as some unwelcome roaches. I slept on the couch, restless, and woke up thinking I was hallucinating, but it was the roaches crawling on the walls. He hadn't allowed the building exterminator to enter his apartment, worried Luba would run out the door. This meant the roaches remained in occupancy.

After he returned to his apartment, I realized he couldn't live alone anymore. We stubbornly argued. I wanted him to live with me in Maine. He wanted to stay put. Fred agreed with me. For a few moments I became the six-year-old innocent me listening to my parents argue whether my mother should stay at home or go to the hospital.

"Dad, you can't live here anymore. You're falling a lot. You don't cook much or keep the apartment clean."

He responded with a shy, coy smile, not lost with age. "My neighbors look out for me, especially the women. They help me down the elevator so I can sit outside with them. Sometimes they even make me dinner."

Now *I* smiled.

My mind and heart couldn't bear the thought of putting him in a nursing home, recalling the dreadful experience had by one of his brothers while I was in law school. I had been forced by the family to be appointed my uncle's guardian. So with much trepidation, I called Bernice to discuss my dilemma. She had just moved in with me, and now in August I had to startle her with, "Guess who's coming to dinner—and staying!" I prayed this wouldn't be the death knell of our young relationship. This major life change would surely challenge us going forward. Mercifully, she agreed. We discussed some of the logistics, and I hung up, relieved.

Despite his horrific days in the hospital, now that he was home in his apartment, my mellow father was still handsome with his gray mustache and full white head of hair, the latter of which I inherited. Since he was no longer hallucinating, his hands moved like a gentle sonata when he spoke. He dejectedly settled into the reality of his situation and agreed to move to Maine, acknowledging, "I know it's hard for me to care for Luba. Anyway, I'll die soon."

He had given up driving his car, frustrated by having to move it daily to comply with alternate-side-of-the-street parking regulations. He was afraid he'd get a ticket. Over the years he'd become more isolated and fearful.

As a retired taxi driver, he had ruinous osteoarthritis from sitting in a cab ten hours a day for over thirty-five years. He wasn't the tall, strong man of his early days. Now his body was hunched at the shoulders, almost modeling the shape of his cab seat. My heart suffered, recalling how hard he had worked when my brother and I moved back home with him from the orphanage.

My grieving mind ran rampant with memories. He was no longer the man who loved long swims in the ocean when we went to the beach—no longer the man who, when a passenger in his cab held a gun to his head for money, slammed the gas pedal to the floor, headed into the middle of a four-way intersection, and jumped out of the cab, forcing the thief to run away.

I tried to make him smile. "Dad, do you remember a few years ago when Mary Ann and our German friends came to visit you?"

He grinned like a little boy. "They came to meet me, the man who makes the best noodle kugel."

My friends had given him an audience. He spoke a mix of German and Yiddish with them. I didn't understand the conversation and wondered why they were laughing and smiling. Later I found out.

"Dad, what did you tell my friends that made them laugh? All I understood were the words *hospital* and *traveled*."

"I told them about when I was in a German hospital while waiting to come to America. I went to the hospital because my knee was painful, and the male doctor flirted with me!"

I was astonished he had shared such an intimate story. It reminded me of his joy in storytelling and his subtle sense of humor.

He revealed he missed his previous apartment in a two-family house. He had an outdoor porch used for his love of sunbathing, but his long years of doing so had required several surgeries to remove cancerous moles. During that time he was more active, driving neighbors when needed. He loved to care for some of the neighborhood kids when they played on the street, and he shoveled snow for Molly, his landlady, until she died and he had to move.

My memories made me feel guilty and callous. I didn't want to take away his independence. But now I was in the role of parent and protector. I wanted to care for him and give him some joy before he died. I suddenly became excited; I could share with him my life in Maine. My brother was relieved.

Fred rented a minivan, to be filled with my father's limited belongings and little Luba. I walked down memory lane in his apartment, packing three of his old, worn suit jackets, in whose pockets dollar bills were still hidden. A drawer was filled with his white, neatly folded handkerchiefs, previously worn in his suit breast pocket. There were two worn fedoras. When he wasn't driving a cab, he always dressed like a gentleman. We also took his favorite few dishes and teacups, a small night table, his citizenship and marriage certificates, cab card with his picture, and leftover family photos.

Fred kept busy packing the van while I washed dirty dishes, swept, and cleaned up. I looked out my father's windows, which faced a busy street with people sitting in front of buildings, kids playing, loud conversations, a few small trees, and a rush of cars and police sirens. I felt a sense of ease as it hit me how relieved I was to no longer be living the city life, even if at times I missed it.

I reminded my father that my partner, Bernice, lived with me. He and my brother hadn't met her, although they briefly spoke with her when they called me. Now he was on the phone with Bernice as I cleaned. In his friendly, shy voice I heard him say, "I'm sorry, I hope you won't be upset with me living with you." He told me Bernice reassured him she wouldn't. We visited his only remaining sibling, Aaron, who lived nearby, so he could say a painful goodbye. The brothers were so close. He also said goodbye to neighbors and friends, and on a Friday morning, the three of us and Luba drove to my home in Maine.

During the ride, I wondered how my dad and Bernice would get along. She'd had the experience of caring for her mother before her death. She was more of a people person than I was. She knew by name most of the workers in the supermarket, restaurants, and local stores, causing us to add on an extra half hour wherever we went. I coveted her openness. I was more circumspect with strangers.

Bernice, our two dogs, and four cats greeted the caravan. The first week was emotionally and physically exhausting. We moved furniture and clothes and started the week-long project to make my father's downstairs space handicap accessible, while we moved to the upstairs guest bedroom, shopped for winter clothes for him, and made doctors' appointments. My brother returned to New Jersey after helping us unpack and get organized.

My father was fine with Bernice calling him Abrasha, his Russian name. Over time, he called Bernice Neesee, leaving off the "Ber."

Settling in was far from easy. The house temperature regularly varied. It became cold even in the fall, as the wood in the stove settled into ash in the mornings. The electric backup heat wasn't enough for his needs. Shortly after he arrived, we converted from electric heat to a whole-house propane furnace. We added a TV and radio in his room. At night he listened to the New York radio stations and ball games.

Our new Sunday routine evolved into Bernice and me sitting at the dining room table on a cool and sunny September morning, with my father relaxing in the new La-Z-Boy recliner, his feet up, watching *Meet the Press*. The appearance was of a typical family. This was so simple to state, but not simply done. At least I was at peace, not worrying about him being alone in his roach-infested apartment eating poorly. I took pictures, keeping a record as he went uphill before he started downhill.

I obtained a walker for him, which he didn't appreciate using. We hung a homemade canvas bag from the front of the walker to hold his phone for easy reach.

Three weeks after the move, I received a call from his New York doctor, apologizing. My father didn't have melanoma; he had squamous cell skin cancer that hadn't spread. He wasn't dying. I eagerly told him the good news. He quietly shrugged his shoulders. He knew he couldn't go back to Brooklyn. As well, I still had a need to make him happy, to help him discover picturesque Maine, and to meet new people.

So many clients had shared with me their hardships and raw stories of caring for elderly parents—the effect on their marriages, their children, their finances. As well, elderly clients shared their frustration and loss of control living with their adult children. I was supportive and advised them of available services as I gave legal advice. Now I was in their position.

I regrettably accepted being in the role of the parent with my father, the child. Wanting to feel helpful, he tried to sweep, and later shovel, the deck while using his walker. It didn't work and upset me. "Dad, you could fall! I don't want you to hurt yourself." I hated myself when I said those words. I took away his freedom. I watched him look out the windows, seeing only grass, trees, squirrels running around, birds at the feeder, and Bernice's new colorful gardens. I knew he missed watching the pulsating multiethnic world that had been his life.

He and I had breakfast together every morning before I left for work. Bernice left much earlier in the opposite direction, a half hour away. We made lunch for him, leaving it in the fridge, and put a chair by the counter nearby so he wouldn't have to move around too much to eat.

The three of us had dinner together. Bernice cooked, frustrated, as her love of spices was contrary to my father's diet and, to a major degree, to mine. She maintained her patience with both of us. He tried eating some new dishes. He didn't complain, just pushed away what he wouldn't eat. He wasn't demanding. But over time I bought food from the Jewish deli a half hour from home.

On the Jewish holiday of Chanukah, he sat at the table and gave directions to Bernice on how to make latkes, which are fried pancakes made of grated potatoes and onions, usually eaten on this holiday. Bernice asked him to help and brought the bowl to the table for him to mix the ingredients while she heated the frypan. I watched his face light up as he participated; he and Bernice naturally connected. I knew how to make latkes, but I sat quietly with a contented smile on my face.

My father decided he wasn't comfortable eating with his false teeth. He said the dentist hadn't made them right but never went to get them adjusted. So now he took them out at dinner, putting them on the table. Bernice stared at me with an intense look, and I gave him a bowl for his teeth. But she wouldn't be defeated and maintained her optimism.

He wore sweatpants for the first time in his life, also quilted flannel shirts, thick socks, and warm slippers.

He sat in the living room at night and watched *Jeopardy*, even though he had a TV in his room, choosing to be with us and the pets. We were pleased he liked to watch the news, but our ears throbbed with the level of volume he needed to hear the TV.

He delighted in petting the dogs and calling them to him, but they wouldn't enter his bedroom. Every time one of the cats passed his room, Luba hissed, and her body backed up ready to protect herself. I entered quietly and calmed her.

I hesitantly told Bernice it was fulfilling to care for him. She agreed. I took a leave of absence from two nonprofit boards to appreciate this time before his health faltered. But by early evening Bernice and I were exhausted. My office work never felt under control.

It soon worsened.

I took my father to a senior center to meet people and share in activities. He attended once and wasn't interested, saying he'd had a nice time but didn't want to return. I surmised the experience was so unlike his city life and Jewish culture. On Fred's next visit, he stuffed our freezer with bagels and knishes.

The doctor recommended some exercise to strengthen his legs. After a few tries, he objected, and "fired" the physical therapist because the soreness after each exercise was too severe. He wouldn't accept the added pain to become stronger. His belief that he couldn't get better had dried up his desire to try. I brooded, thinking he must want to suffer. A close cousin told me it was a "Kuriloff thing" to suffer, part of his inheritance from his Russian childhood. I understood.

A few months after he moved in, Luba died. We tried to save her, but she had age-related problems. My father was devastated, even though he tried to hide it. Fred visited, and we buried Luba on our property, in a small pet cemetery.

Caretaking had become more arduous for both me and Bernice. It felt like a full-time job on top of our actual full-time jobs, especially when added to caring for dogs, cats, a fish tank, and the house. I struggled to remain confident that our relationship would survive the test, questioning whether Bernice's love and patience would withstand the burdens upon our love.

Chapter 49

Challenge

My spiritual practice, my life, became a series of moment-to-moment challenges as I tried to maintain compassion within frenzy. I asked myself, *Can I make it?* Bernice and I jointly asked, *Can we make it—together?*

At the office I handled a particularly complicated divorce case, like the movie *The War of the Roses*. I asked another attorney to take over the financial aspect while I concluded the child custody piece. When he said yes, my body released months of stress.

Bernice was still a volunteer for Big Brothers, Big Sisters. In addition to her job, she volunteered to spend a few hours each week at a local school with a young girl during lunch break. She loved her time with Jody, playing games and being a supportive listener to her preteen joys and problems at school and home. She thought about pausing for a while. I said, "No way. You can't! This outlet is so necessary for you and important to Jody."

Our emotions splattered like broken glass. Sometimes she became as frustrated with her reactions as I was with mine. We harbored guilt, questioning whether we were too hard on my father. He had difficulty hearing, but even when he could hear, he didn't listen. I became exasperated when he didn't show appreciation for how much

Bernice did for him, how concerned she was for his needs. I explained this to him after some of her frustration erupted. All he said was, "I'll be better." These were sanguine words but hard to believe.

Bernice and I struggled to live in the present, releasing our expectations. It was a demanding but positive effort, making the next time easier . . . but there were too many next times. I found a reprieve from the stress in talking with Nancy's mother. We kept in touch regularly, and she shared words of wisdom from experience as her own parents' caregiver.

My father loved to sit outside. I surprised him. "Dad, we're going to build you a screened-in porch on the sunny south side of the deck."

He shrugged his shoulders. "Why do I need one? I can sit in a chair on the deck."

"It will protect you from bug bites as well as direct sun. We don't want you to develop any more cancerous moles."

"Roberta, what does it matter? I'm going to die soon. I'm eighty-five."

I didn't let him thwart me. We built the porch anyway. I should have known better. It took him ten minutes to settle on the porch with his walker, and then he repeatedly opened and closed the door for the dogs. After a week, his legs were bloody with blackfly bites! He no longer used the porch. Instead, he sat on the deck, bites and sun ignored.

One sunny day we took him with us for a ride down the coast, where we had previously ordered twin gold rings, each with three curves that bonded at two corners, representing our bond. Now the curves had a secondary meaning—the sudden curves our life was taking during this journey. One night when he slept, we sat on our upstairs bed by dim light and did a commitment ritual. We read a section from Gary Zukav's book, *The Seat of the Soul*, about spiritual relationships, and Shelley's poem, "Love's Philosophy," drank French cider, and ended with special words to each other as we exchanged rings.

That night I had a hazy dream about my mother. I woke not remembering details, but I deeply sensed she had held me softly, the way she would have held me as a baby. It gave me the impetus to find her wedding band and place it back on my pinky finger. I hadn't worn it since leaving my New Haven house. Bernice supported my desire, and to my surprise, a few days later my father noticed it and smiled.

Bernice and I traveled to New Jersey to celebrate Fred's birthday, a stress break we desperately needed. We hired a friend, Kim, to live in while we were away for a few days, as my father was fond of her from previous visits. But I quickly received too many calls. He worried about his constipation and that the animals weren't being taken care of. Kim was frustrated with his grumpiness and at a loss about how to ease his worries.

While we were out to dinner, Bernice's discontent rocketed with all the calls I made and received. Fred was caught in the middle but grateful we had visited. I cried in the restaurant bathroom, feeling like a rag doll dragged in many directions at once.

Arriving home, we found my father smiling, laughing, more relaxed, and enjoying Kim's cooking. We started saying grace before dinner.

When he smiled, his face lit up. At those moments I saw the father I knew when I was young, when he took us out of the orphanage to live with him again. Then he enjoyed being part of the world, singing at family weddings and bar mitzvahs. He danced the cha-cha with me at my cousin's wedding; read the news; was a strong Democrat; played cards and went to the races with friends.

The new vibrant life Bernice and I had together became vastly curtailed. We needed to ensure regular meals and medications. We couldn't just easily leave. It was like having kids. My father now had an overactive imagination and worried all the time when we were late coming home. Through his tears, he'd say, "I was so worried. I thought something happened to you." I heard those words often and related them to his fear of being left alone in a strange place, having experienced that same fear in the orphanage after times out with him, when he turned us over to the counselors, his head down.

With our care, he soon became physically stronger and more sensitive to his need to care for himself. He showered, made his bed every morning, and washed his lunch dishes, except that washing for him was just rinsing them in cold water. So we washed them again.

We learned that a good friend of ours had cancer. We endeavored to be supportive of her while we cared for my father.

At the last minute one morning, he and I squabbled over my plans for an afternoon trip. I had arranged for us to visit some elderly friends who spoke Russian. Along with giving Bernice the house to herself for a while, I wanted him to meet new people. He backed out at the last minute claiming his legs hurt too much.

"Dad, why do you always do this?" I complained. "It's frustrating. My friends are looking forward to meeting you. They made lunch for us."

He appeared hurt, then upset that he had disappointed me. "Sweetheart, I won't feel comfortable in a strange house. I know you want to share this with me, but I feel like a dummy sitting in a chair in the home of someone I don't know, with strangers staring at me, and I can't walk around and socialize."

I surrendered. I couldn't give him the "good life" I wanted for him. I was being too presumptuous. I should have known better. I needed to let him decide what was good for him and accept my own disappointment.

Even with my spiritual training and experiences during these past eight years, I shared with Bernice my insight of how easily I could pick up my father's traits, how I have in the past, and how lucky it was I could now acknowledge this. He always worried and rarely showed anger, instead repressing it. He stayed controlled except when we cried together. I warned her not to be afraid to confront me when I acted out those traits with her.

A few weeks after this incident, Bernice and I spent time with friends and returned home a few minutes before eleven to a scene from a sitcom, albeit heartrending. My father had become rattled while in bed when the dogs launched a barking frenzy at nine o'clock, presuming we had arrived home. Also, now that Luba was gone, the cats weren't afraid to go into his bedroom. So they had chosen to play with the toilet paper roll, dragging it into his room. He said he thought he had broken the lamp by the couch attempting to greet us at the door. Bernice easily fixed the lamp. I sat on his bed holding his hand, feeling remorseful about leaving him home alone for longer than expected. I didn't dare tell him we were late because our car had gone off the road in a sudden snow squall and needed to be towed out.

I accepted that I couldn't change my father. I also accepted that I couldn't give him the joy I'd like to see him experience and share with me. I was no longer the little girl in the orphanage seeking his love and approval. And he was no longer the father the little girl needed.

One morning he cried, sitting on his bed. I stood next to him, holding him close for a few moments. I wished I could have looked at him, seen spirit, and understood his soul's learning. I took a solitary, chilly walk on our dirt road, through the woods and field, and unearthed my goal: to look at him through my frustration and his anguish and see our mutually joined spirit.

He taught me lessons through his moroseness. They were

reminders to appreciate life, see the positive, live and love fully and passionately—to not be afraid to confront feelings and express wishes.

I found myself repeatedly saying my mantra: "This is a spiritual test; this is a spiritual test." I told Bernice it was so easy to be spiritual when you had no struggles or conflicts but not so easy when you did!

When in the past I had visited him in the city, I'd say it was my spiritual test to see if I could stay centered there. But now, *there* was *here*. The test was in my home—tolerance, patience, and acceptance.

Mandy, the dog I had found at the supermarket six months after moving here, became ill. The vet said she had cancer. After surgery, we rushed to the hospital to spend time with her, sitting on the floor petting her worn-out body. The surgery went well, but suddenly she developed breathing problems. We screamed for the vet, who tried twice to resuscitate her with a breathing tube. I finally told him to stop; it was clear she wouldn't survive. We stayed by her body for a half hour, later burying her in our pet cemetery. Our household was despondent, our spiritual test more daunting.

At breakfast one morning, I had an awkward conversation with my father about burial. "Dad, how do you feel about being buried here, near me, rather than in Long Island next to Mommy? We never go to her cemetery anymore. At least here I can visit you. It's a beautiful Jewish cemetery."

I waited for his response, unable to read his face. He stared away and declared, "That's okay. Do whatever you want to do. I'll be dead."

I finally accepted the fact that I wouldn't ever know what he honestly thought, but I knew I had a need to have his body close by, at a place to visit.

One early evening I invited some friends for dinner. As we sat around the table, Martha, a nurse, suddenly asked my father, "What happened to your hands?" I looked over at his hands and was stunned.

The skin on both palms was raw and weeping. He sheepishly said he had been walking past the woodstove when his phone rang. He went to answer it from the bag hanging on his walker and lost his balance. As he fell, his hands had hit the hot woodstove.

"Dad," I exclaimed, "I can't believe you didn't tell me when I came home from work! It's been hours!"

He said nothing. He never wanted to be a problem. Martha cleaned and wrapped his hands until he saw the doctor the next day. To our amazement, his hands healed faster than expected.

My father was a thoughtful man with no traditional schooling. He'd been a seeker of knowledge and had educated himself by reading newspapers and magazines and keeping up on world affairs. We easily discussed and argued life's issues, most always ending in agreement. We spoke about life and death looking forward. It was painful for him to review the past.

During several visits with my father over the years, he and I had discussed the importance of being self-sufficient and what it meant to us. We both agreed we didn't want to live if we couldn't be independent and savor life on our own terms. During one conversation, his eyes welled up. "I don't want to live in a nursing home like my brother Saul."

"Dad, I know. Uncle Saul's experience was terrible. I'll never let that happen to you. Remember, Saul lived alone and had no place to go, but I'm settled now in my own home, and you can live with me."

He stared at me and responded, "I'm okay with dying if I can't be independent, even if I'm not at death's door. I don't want to get like Saul, with Alzheimer's. That was so hard on you when you were made responsible for him by a court."

"Dad, you wouldn't be a burden, and you don't have Alzheimer's and I'm confident you won't get it."

Now he was living with me, gratefully without Alzheimer's but with considerable depression, as expected. I couldn't deny the burden of his care, but it was one I had accepted and one I could never refuse. I flashed back to my own fear as I watched him walk through the orphanage gate without us. I couldn't watch him walk through death's door alone.

Chapter 50
Lifeblood

Fourteen months after moving in, my father's body and strength were again failing. Somehow he had broken a rib, and then the doctor discovered a blood clot in his right lung. He decided he was ready to die, and I accepted his choice.

I resigned myself to the fact that I couldn't make him happy, but I could make him comfortable. We spoke about his decision at length. He first chose to stop eating. We discussed it with his doctor. The doctor honored his resolve but pointed out that he had a strong heart; the dying process could take a long time. I hired an aide to help us. After about six weeks, he woke up one morning and in a subdued voice asked me, "How come I'm not dead yet?"

Not knowing what to say, I bleakly shrugged and said, "I don't know."

After speaking to the doctor, he decided to stop drinking. We put a baby monitor in his room and in our room so I could hear if he called out. My sleep quickly diminished. Soon we had hospice help.

During the day I sat and chatted with him in his room. He was skin and bones. In a quiet voice, he said I had made a "good choice" with Bernice. "She's very generous and helpful. I'm sorry if I hurt her."

I held my tears and thanked him. I trusted his words were genuine and not from fear this time. I delighted in telling Bernice what he had said; she needed to hear his positive words.

While I sat with him, I wrote in my journal, recording his life with me and my deep, bleeding emotions in a way I couldn't record in my teenage diary when we returned from the orphanage to live with him. A few times he looked at the wall and told me he'd seen his parents and a deceased brother. I believed him.

I prized being his caregiver, working with the aide to change his bedding while he was in it. I was impressed by how effortless it was when we rolled him from side to side. It was much easier than dealing with his negative nature. Yet I was still his daughter. Part of me wanted him to eat, but I wouldn't force-feed him. The doctor agreed.

He abruptly decided he wanted to go to a hospital or a nursing home thinking he'd die sooner and not be a burden to me. I again explained he wasn't a burden, he couldn't decide when to die, but that God would decide. I wasn't ready for him to die; we needed more time together, for what I wasn't sure. Yet I admired his tenacity. *Can I do the same when my time comes?*

The last week of a cold and windy Maine November, he shared his emotional pain with a close friend of mine who stayed with him for two hours. To my surprise, he told her he felt God was punishing him for "putting us in an institution." My friend responded that he had been a good father for doing all he could after our mother died when Fred and I were babies, and she reminded him he visited us regularly while we were in the orphanage. This was a window into his torment.

Later in the week I sat on his bed, softly washing his face and hands, reiterating that he was a good father and recollecting the loving things he had done for us. "Dad, Fred and I loved that every birthday you called and sang to us, even after I moved to Maine. Also, remember when I was about twenty and suffered from cysts on my legs, moving up my arms? The doctors couldn't figure it out. Then on New Year's Eve you took me to the doctor who brought me into this world, and you stood by me as the doctor released the painful cysts, me crying, you crying. The doctor chuckled with assurance that I'd be fine. And I was." He smiled, but not the strong smile he once had.

My father's brother, Aaron, his only remaining sibling, called him every Saturday. My aunt and I had not let Aaron know the seriousness of his brother's condition. They had been remarkably close in Brooklyn. Finally I told him the truth, and as I did, all the emotions I thought I had held in check surged out in weighty tears and a runny nose, especially when I told him my father always loved him.

Three weeks before he died, he became more confused and anxious, keeping us up most nights. I was drained like an empty vessel. One morning, between the time one hospice volunteer left and another arrived, he devolved into an anxious state with the phone wire wrapped around his neck, attempting to call me. He finally relaxed with additional medicine. Later he described seeing "a light, first a candle, then a beautiful light." He also saw one of his deceased brothers and his parents, in a light, lending some peacefulness to his spirit.

I gently told him, "Dad, go into the light. It's okay."

He said softly, "I tried to touch it but couldn't."

I wondered if his dying was hard for him because of his negativity and fear of living, his belief that God was punishing him because in his eyes he was a "bad person."

One morning he called for help, saying, "Angels are here. I wasn't sure I wanted to go with them." I strove to talk him through going, letting go, trusting. At times he murmured, "Yes, it's time to go." He saw people, stated names. I sat on the bed by his side. He then uttered, "Stay five more minutes, then I'll go. This will be a good experience for you." The last few words were so odd, they made me question whether someone else was talking through him!

Sometimes when I sat with him, he talked incessantly, not making much sense, except for an intermittent glimmer of clarity and understanding. When I walked Maya one morning, he whispered to Bernice that I was in the light with others. Six days before his death, his medicine was changed, helping him to be less anxious and to sleep calmly.

I newly appreciated that being a family caregiver challenged one on a different level than being a hospice volunteer. It demanded the nitty-gritty of body and soul, developing a humility in the face of illness and death and unfinished business, pushing one to give so personally, and binding together the caregiver and the dying person.

The nights became the hardest. He regularly called for me, even when Bernice tiptoed downstairs at four in the morning. He spoke about wanting to go home. I asked him, "Home to where? Do you mean home to God?" He nodded his head.

He then asked, "Will I experience so much pain like here on earth?" I told him there would be no pain, that he'd be with his parents and Mommy in the beautiful light he saw.

On a December evening, the nurse informed me he was in the dying process. His body was severely mottled. I was surprised by my reaction on hearing the words "in a few days." I had thought it would be longer. Maybe it was I who needed more time.

Later he whispered "When am I going home? I want to go home soon."

That night I had a warm phone conversation with a rabbi from one of the Bangor synagogues. I had never met him, but his voice calmed me. I shared our family history, and we discussed preparations for the service.

Remarkably, the next day my father was very talkative, slowly and sometimes painfully, seeming more alive than dying. I understood this sometimes happened soon before death, being a spiritual gift to the family, allowing us to again experience the dying person in a way we had known him before. It was a better memory than the immediate pain and sadness.

But then a swift transformation struck later that night. He was again agitated, repeating in Yiddish, "Make me dead! Take me!" To my surprise I understood what he was saying. He stretched his hands up to God and called out, "I've suffered enough." I asked him to tell God, aloud, his suffering. He said, "I tried to be a good father."

I sobbed, "Dad, you *were* a good father." I repeated how hard he worked to take care of us when we left the orphanage, of the many times he gave me dollar bills signed by many famous people who had ridden in his cab, how he still loved me when he didn't like the boys I dated in high school, how he took us to Radio City Music Hall for the shows and to the beach and park on Sundays with family and neighbors. I reminded him of when he was strong and swam in the ocean at the 69th Street beach, telling him to imagine himself swimming to God.

We said prayers together, his words barely audible. I read him the prayer the rabbi had given me, which I had written down on paper as we spoke. I sat quietly in the rocking chair next to his bed, trying to meditate away his pain.

My brother arrived. He saw our father and cried, not knowing what to do. Our dad was now in a coma yet turned toward the sound of my voice.

I felt like I was sitting shiva, with friends coming over bringing food and hugs, an occasion that normally happened after death. I wasn't planning to sit shiva, which is sitting seven days at home with visitors and remembrances. Who was there to sit with? No relatives would come this far, except my brother. But here I sat before death. Not traditional, yet meaningful.

Another oddity I mused on: this Jewish man was dying in a house with Chanukah candles, a Christmas tree, and colorful lights outside. The house was warm and welcoming with the woodstove fire and white lights curling around the banister. It was a peaceful place to die.

We said prayers and read poems and letting-go meditations, many times. I regrettably considered that, in some way, my father had been dead since the time he chose not to live life fully anymore, walking through life passively. But then, by that definition, we are all dead at times when we're not living fully in the moment or attempting to. It was a matter of degree.

My household was at the point of restiveness, waiting for death, especially Fred. He barely knew Bernice. My life in Maine wasn't familiar to him. He was a city person, like our father. I looked at my brother's face with melancholy, remembering all he had lost as a child.

The animals were generally quiet. Hospice scrambled to schedule more people, expecting he would have passed by now.

It was interesting, this restlessness of ours. It was hard to just sit and especially hard to sit with death. We wanted to move on with life. The sitting was so devotedly tiring. The air was cold outside. Thankfully no snow fell. More friends arrived, sitting shiva with us.

I made my peace with my father's death. His body passed at 9:42 on a Saturday evening, serenely, with a strong heart to the last breath. We all wept, friends and family, even the hospice caregivers.

The undertakers came shortly thereafter. They respectfully took his body, enclosing him in a wine-colored body bag on a stretcher; it was surreal seeing his body leave this house, never to return, and a reminder to me that someday all of us will have our bodies go that way, no longer our own.

I learned from the rabbi that at the funeral home, ten Jewish men would wash my father's body. This was a Jewish tradition called a *tahara*, a cleansing of the body before burial. Of course my father never met these men. My stomach cramped, recognizing that if he still lived in his Jewish community of friends and relatives, this act would likely have been done by men he knew.

On Sunday we buried him in the Jewish cemetery a half hour from our home. His grave was near a stone bench under a tree. The gravestone would be a footstone, rather than the traditional upright type. The cemetery was like a park. I had not met the rabbi, other than having spoken to him on the phone, so I was pleased at how meaningful he made the service. None of our family lived in Maine, but fifteen friends joined us. After the rabbi spoke, I read a poem I had written years ago for a hospice event. My tears didn't allow me to finish reading, so the rabbi did.

Following another Jewish tradition, we all shoveled dirt into the grave, one shovel each. I thought back to when my mother died. My brother and I were considered too young to go to the funeral. Now I was shoveling dirt for my father—and my mother. After I shoveled, I looked at my mother's ring on my finger, turning it around a few times, imagining that my parents had now met one more time, to hug and smile and remember the purpose of their journey in this life.

At the end of the service, the rabbi had the attendees make a double line so family—Fred, Bernice, and I—could walk through, acknowledging the support surrounding us. After sharing lunch with everyone, we returned home exhausted.

As I rested my eyes in bed, in a state near sleep, I had a vision of my dad's face. I saw it sharply. A subtle honest smile looked at me, a smile that conveyed he was no longer shackled to his worn-out steamer trunk.

Despite all that had happened in this house I called Crumblesweat, Bernice and I had not "crumbled" under our labor of love.

Yet it dawned on me, I was again an orphan—no longer someone's child.

Chapter 51

Chambers of the Heart

I am not what happened to me.
I am what I choose to become.

—C. G. Jung

It was four in the morning. Bernice and our pet family were sleeping. I was curled up in a blanket in front of the woodstove, the fire warming the icy chill of my father's death, remembering so many losses, especially little Roberta waking up one morning and never seeing her mother again. The house was finished, as much as a house could ever be considered finished. Bernice had brought the finishing touches to the gardens just as she'd brought finishing touches to my life in Maine, and we looked forward to more growth and sharing, even with the reality of unexpected life changes.

My journey of building and improving my home took eleven years, years filled with love, loss, grit, and finally soulful self-acceptance. Home was no longer a building. Home was within. My roots in this no-longer-new place were deep, as deep as my spiritual roots. Looking around at the beauty of the home I had created, I saw a reflection of the beautiful life that was now mine. I smiled broadly, seeing my smiling face looking back at me in the window glass.

I turned the ring, my mother's ring, on my pinky finger, the metal warm to the touch. It sat next to the gold commitment ring that Bernice and I had exchanged. The promise of the ring, of my mother's legacy, had been fulfilled. I could see her smiling face in my mind. I always seem to remember smiles. When I thought about the major loves of my life, it was their glittering smiles that stood out, smiles that also laughed and opened in vulnerability. Even when a relationship ended, I still trusted the smile, the honesty.

My mother's smile wasn't wide, but it quietly glittered until she faded away at age thirty-two.

My father's smile was thoughtful, careful, a smile unsure of the future. Yet it was always honest, even when hard to understand.

My brother's smile was protective, shielding a child's pain from early loss.

Of the many friendships, relationships, and lovers in my life, I was privileged to share four smiles that intersected with each other without knowing, a connection I discovered in my later years, when life became more precious and I became more aware.

My first romantic love, my boyfriend Ernie, with whom I shared an on-again-off-again relationship for five years in New York, had a broad smile that twinkled.

Later, in Connecticut, Mary Ann, my first woman partner, together for seven loving, learning years, had a smile that lit up her face like a pixie.

One precious year with Nancy in Maine, the short-lived relationship birthing a new family for me and an eight-year spiritual search—another radiant smile I conjured up behind my closed eyes.

And then Bernice. Behind her luminous smile, I saw the blossoming of a soul connection, the physical embodiment of the promise of my mother's ring.

The human heart has four chambers. One chamber holds the family I was born into. One chamber holds the major loves in my life. One holds all the others whose paths I have crossed and who helped me become who I am, even when those paths were hard and painful. The final chamber holds my spirit, my soul, and connects and ensures that all the chambers keep pumping.

As I sat filled with a deep appreciation for the gifts of love that had been bestowed upon me throughout my life, I knew it was time to let my mother know I was okay. I took out my journal and wrote my most important "Dear Eva" letter.

Dear Eva, dear Mother,

The month of January, including New Year's Eve, was a contradiction of feelings for me. Mixed emotions. Both celebration and loss.

You died on January 27, 1951, a day that shattered my life. I no longer had a mother. "Mommy," "Mama," "Ma"—words I could no longer say or experience, representing togetherness, sharing, belonging, only used in my letters to you. I was always searching for answers, for understanding, for acceptance.

Dad always drove his cab on New Year's Eve. Was he safe? He said not to worry; there was laughter and celebration in his cab, young people hobnobbing around NYC. He got good tips. But I did worry, even though I was also hobnobbing at New Year's parties. If I arrived home before him, I couldn't sleep until I heard his key in the door. When he lived with me before his death, I couldn't sleep until I heard his snoring or steady breathing.

Dad's birthday was January 6. When we lived with him, we celebrated his birthday. Other times I called him, but I didn't have the voice to sing him "Happy Birthday" the way he did to me every year.

New Year's Eve at a dude ranch, I was seventeen. My first

weekend away from Dad. Kids were drunk. Meaningless partying. All I wanted was to be home with Dad.

New Year's Eve 1986, an alluring beginning on the dance floor with Nancy, nervously and eagerly stirring dormant feelings. It lasted a euphoric year, until her car accident in January 1987, sending me on an eight-year search for meaning and granting me the gift of an additional family.

New Year's Eve 1995, another remarkable January. I discovered Bernice, a gift from Soul. Delectable dancing, laughing, talking. Consummate love. A lasting celebration turned into a long, full, and absorbing life. My disheartening perception of January changed to gratitude. The cloak of January angst was lifted.

Dear Mother, January represented life and birth and death and all that is human—all the sadness and passion and exhilaration of living fully, allowing love fully, grieving fully, trusting in the next step—a season of life all rolled into one erratic month.

And finally, I found "home." It was not only the physical place I worked so hard to build. Home is inside me. I carry it wherever I go.

Your daughter

Acknowledgments

This book would still be in gestation but for the unfailing support and caring of so many people.

An enormous thank-you to my mentor and developmental editor, Cathleen O'Connor. In 2016 I attended a weeklong workshop she presented at the International Women's Writing Guild (IWWG) Conference. At the end of the week I asked her if she would assist me with the writing of my memoir. Without her uplifting and supportive help, this project would have surely taken an additional five years.

Deepest thanks to the friends who encouraged me through this process: Laura Engel, Mary Ann Moran, Sally Esposito, Lynnsey Carroll, Sandy Collier, Pat Ould, Kate Sherrill, and my cousin Cheryl Lauzon, some of whom have been my beta readers. I importantly include my "Home Kid" childhood friend, Carrie Weinblatt, who read my first draft and helped me remember experiences and facts regarding our orphanage life.

I also want to acknowledge my relationship with Nancy's mother, my second mother, whose love and sustenance continues to this day.

With deep appreciation I thank my stellar Maine "Brooklin Writers Group" for their honest feedback and advice over the years, specifically Cynthia Barlow, our teacher extraordinaire, and John Frawley, Willow Runningwater, and Nancy Comeau.

I joyfully acknowledge the ongoing education and inspiration from the women writers and teachers of the International Women's Writing Guild. The conferences and teaching workshops over the years have been a major source of learning, connection, and belonging. I would be greatly remiss not to mention my yearly conference roommate and friend, Sharon Larsen, with whom I shared tears, laughs, poetry, and story.

I further wish to thank the professionals at She Writes Press: publisher Brooke Warner and project manager Shannon Green for their education and support to ensure my memoir would read well and professionally; Jennifer Caven, copy editor; and Laura Matthews, proofreader, for polishing my final draft.

Last but never least, without the compassion, insight, and love of my best friend and beloved spouse, Bernice Palumbo, my memoir would not have been written. She came into my life as a "gift from soul." As I mentioned in a poem I wrote for her, she is the "grace in God's prayers; I sing your Psalms." I cherish her smiles, quick wit, and humor that she always shared with me, most often when I became frustrated or stumped. She was and is my backbone.

And during this time, I could not have stayed fit without the walks and playtime with our sweet rescue dog, Ruby.

Questions for Reading Groups

This memoir is about relationships, family, loss, spirituality, and resilience. In Roberta's story, we see the evolution of a woman who emerges undaunted and at peace with both her past and her joyful present.

1. Thinking about Roberta's childhood in an orphanage, one in which she was separated from her only sibling, how did you feel? You may not have experienced an orphanage, but at some point in life each of us becomes an orphan as we lose the parents who have loved and guided us. Did reading about the loss of her mother at such an early age and then her time in an orphanage cause you to reframe your own experiences of loss of family? Have there been times in your life when you've felt abandoned or that you didn't fit in?

2. Roberta's relationship with her father had many layers. As an adult, she understood that he did what he thought was right in placing her and her brother in the orphanage, but she also knew he had choices; he could have placed his children with other family members, for example. He didn't want to relinquish his role as a father. What might

you have done in a similar circumstance? Would you be able to forgive him for the choice he made?

3. Roberta found not only solace but also healing in a spiritual quest—but she was always interested in religion, as her story about the rabbi showed. Even as a child she was asking and wanting the answers to the "big" questions. That curiosity took her beyond the religion of her family and childhood and on an exploration of spiritual paths that helped form the life view she has today. What is the role of religion or spirituality in your own life? How has it evolved (or not) as you have aged? Do you see it, as Roberta did, as a support in dealing with the challenges you've faced in life? If not, what do you rely on and why?

4. Roberta is frank about her use of sexuality as a young woman to get attention and the things she wanted. Not having a mother to talk to about her changing body in puberty, she relied on the older girls in the orphanage. She explored with boys and her first real love, Ernie, only to find out that he was married. Gradually, she noticed a growing attraction to a woman and began her first major relationship with Mary Ann, initially hidden from family and office mates. Do you think Roberta would have had greater support from teachers and family to help her understand her own body and her desires if she were growing up today? Did it surprise you after reading about her intense relationship with Ernie that she was then attracted to a woman? What experiences can you relate to in your own life or in the lives of those you know that might be similar? Did Roberta's experience alter your perception of the way someone gets to know their true orientation?

5. Roberta grew into adulthood at a time when women were not welcome in many professions. She encountered instances of misogyny and prejudice and was told that there were limitations to what she could achieve, but something in her rebelled and refused to accept what others said. In that way she was a true feminist, leading the way for women's rights. Do you relate to Roberta's experiences of bias from men? How would you have handled a similar situation? Would she have faced the same issues today? Even with all that has changed, what do you think still needs to be done?

6. Why do you think Roberta decided to become a lawyer? She could have chosen from several professions; what is it about the law that you think spoke to her and her life experiences? Did it have a role in helping her put her early childhood experience into context? If so, in what way? What is your perception of lawyers?

7. Roberta experienced Nancy's death as particularly crushing. Yet in that loss she bonded with Nancy's bereaved parents and ended up having herself viewed as a much-loved daughter of theirs. That special relationship was a gift that came out of her love for Nancy, and it seems to have been beneficial not only for Roberta but also for Nancy's parents, who had not fully accepted their daughter's sexual orientation. Why do you think that relationship was so important for Roberta's healing? And for Nancy's parents as well? What relationships do you have in your life where someone not related to you has played a loving, mothering role? What difference has it made to you?

8. Roberta stayed friends with Ernie. She stayed friends with Mary Ann. She has an ability to grieve the loss of these relationships, even the betrayal in each, and yet not lose that loving connection of

friendship. Did that surprise you? Would you want to maintain those friendships after the romantic relationship was over?

9. Shortly after Roberta began her relationship with Bernice, she asked her father to move in so he could be cared for as his health deteriorated. Caregiving puts an enormous strain on the emotions and living situation of the caregivers. Have you been in the situation of caregiving an elderly parent? Would you have done what she did? Do you think her experience in hospice helped her accept her father's transition? Is being able to be present for others as they prepare to die something you would want to do? What do you think would be the challenges and gifts of such a role with a loved one?

10. In spite of all she experienced, Roberta emerged as a positive person. She had an innate ability to look at life in an optimistic way. Is that just because she needed rose-colored glasses to survive a difficult childhood of loss and abandonment? Or is it a fundamental part of her personality that was revealed the older she became? Did her perspective help her to have a better life than she might have achieved otherwise? What is your perspective on life? Do you consider yourself a glass-half-full or half-empty person? What experiences in your own life have contributed to your view? Is there a takeaway from Roberta's story that might alter your perspective somewhat? If so, what might that be?

About the Author

photo credit: Dana Bement Portraits

Roberta Kuriloff is a writer, author, speaker, community activist, and former attorney. She is the author of *Everything Special, Living Joy: Poems and prose to inspire*; the short story "Unearthing Home," published in the Spring 2020 issue of *Yellow Arrow Publishing Journal*; and the essay "Musings on the Word Atonement," in the anthology *Art in the Time of Unbearable Crisis: Women Writers Respond to the Call*, published June 2022. As an attorney, her legal work centered on families in emotional and financial crises. She is a founding member of an elderly services organization and two domestic violence projects, and she has also worked as a hospice patient-volunteer and bereavement workshop facilitator. In between her community work, she makes time to enjoy her passions for writing and dance. She lives in the home she built in the woods of Orland, Maine.

SELECTED TITLES FROM SHE WRITES PRESS

She Writes Press is an independent publishing company founded to serve women writers everywhere. Visit us at www.shewritespress.com.

You Can't Buy Love Like That: Growing Up Gay in the Sixties by Carol E. Anderson. $16.95, 978-1631523144

A young lesbian girl grows beyond fear to fearlessness as she comes of age in the '60s amid religious, social, and legal barriers.

Affliction: Growing Up With a Closeted Gay Dad by Laura Hall $16.95, 978-1-64742-124-3

Laura Hall was born in a small city on the San Francisco peninsula to a straight mother and a gay father who lived in the shadows. This is her tender, frank account of how her father's secret became her inheritance and, ultimately, the path to her own healing.

I'm Still Here: A Memoir by Martina Reaves. $16.95, 978-1-63152-876-7

Martina Reaves weaves the story of her early life—coming of age in the 1960s, living and works in various small towns with her hippie husband, coming out in 1980, and eventually having a son with her life partner, Tanya—with that of her 2008 tongue cancer diagnosis, after which she fights to maintain hope even as she accepts that death might come.

Life's Accessories: A Memoir (And Fashion Guide) by Rachel Levy Lesser $16.95, 978-1-63152-622-0

Rachel Levy Lesser tells the story of her life in this collection—fourteen coming-of-age essays, each one tied to a unique fashion accessory, laced with humor and introspection about a girl-turned-woman trying to figure out friendship, love, a career path, parenthood, and, most poignantly, losing her mother to cancer at a young age.

In the Game: The Highs and Lows of a Trailblazing Trial Lawyer by Peggy Garrity. $16.95, 978-1-63152-105-8

Admitted to the California State Bar in 1975—when less than 3 percent of lawyers were women—Peggy Garrity refuses to choose between family and profession, and succeeds at both beyond anything she could have imagined.